HUGH MACDONALD

Chath mi deagh chath,
Chriochnaich mi mo chuairt,
Gleidh mi an creideamh

Bonum certamen certavi,
Cursum consummavi,
Fidem servavi

I have fought the good fight,
I have run the course to its end,
I have kept the faith

Hugh MacDonald

Highlander, Jacobite and Bishop

John Watts

JOHN DONALD

To Moira, John Joseph, Pádraig,
Caoimhín, Caitlín, Fiona and Ciorsdaidh,
with love

First published in 2002 by
John Donald Publishers,
an imprint of
Birlinn Limited
West Newington House
10 Newington Road
Edinburgh
EH9 1QS

www.birlinn.co.uk

ISBN 0 85976 560 1

British Library Cataloguing-in-Publication Data
A catalogue record for this book is available from the British Library

The publisher acknowledges subsidy from

Scottish
Arts Council

towards the publication of this book

Designed and typeset by Carnegie Publishing Ltd, Lancaster
Printed and bound by Antony Rowe Ltd, Chippenham

Contents

List of Illustrations and Maps

Illustrations

Maps

Acknowledgements

The author is especially indebted to Rt Rev. Mgr Donald MacKinnon, parish priest of St Mary's, Arisaig, who very kindly read the text in draft and made valuable suggestions for its improvement.

Tearlach MacFarlane, Glenfinnan, generously shared his expertise with me, and provided an authoritative genealogy of the MacDonalds of Morar upon which Appendix I is based.

I owe a general obligation to the numerous scholars of post-Reformation Scottish Catholic Church history whose names appear in the Bibliography, and a particular debt to George Dorrian, whose thesis on Bishop Hugh was written a decade ago: our subjects were similar, though our purpose and treatment very different.

I gratefully acknowledge the support of the Society of Antiquaries of Scotland in providing a research grant to aid my travels.

I wish also to thank the Keeper of the Scottish Catholic Archives at Columba House; the staffs of the National Archives of Scotland, the National Library of Scotland, the National Museum of Scotland and the Edinburgh University Library; and the following who readily helped in various ways: Miss Christian Aikman, Hon. Sec. of the '45 Association; Pat and Tim Burgess, Grimsby; Fr Michael Hutson, St Cumin's, Morar; Mrs Margaret Fox, Archivist at Traquair House; Alasdair MacDonald, Port na Dòbhrain; Allan MacDonald, Arisaig; Ewen MacDonald, Morar; Very Rev. Canon John Angus MacDonald, Fort William; Mairead MacDonald, Kinsadel, Morar; the late Peter MacDonald, Bunacaimb; Rt Rev. Prof. Mgr Malcolm MacDonell, Antigonish, Nova Scotia; Archie MacLellan, Morar; Alistair MacLeod, Morar; Alasdair Roberts, Bracora, Morar; Deirdre Smythe, Glenfinnan; and Rt Rev. Mgr Thomas Wynne, Roy Bridge.

Lastly, a loving 'thank you' to my wife, Moira, and our children, for support and forbearance. To them this book is dedicated.

A Note on Personal and Place Names

The names of persons and places are usually given in their English forms in the text, since these will be more familiar to most readers and are also how they appear in Hugh's own correspondence and other contemporary documents cited. According to the general practice of the day he did not, and probably could not, write in Gaelic. And to have used bilingual forms throughout the book – 'Hugh MacDonald/Uisdean mac Alasdair mhic Ailein 'ic Dhùghaill', for instance – would have been cumbersome to say the least! But it is worth keeping in mind that Gaelic was the language Hugh habitually spoke when among his own people, the language that he thought in throughout his life, and that, in matters liturgical and spiritual at least, English was not even his second tongue.

Lands Spread Out Beneath the Cross

If you take the Road to the Isles almost to its end, and have reached the west coast, with the dark saw-toothed mountains of Skye already in sight, and reaching the village of Morar, beside the level-crossing, you mount the 137 steps that climb among bushes to the vantage point, and emerge breathless on the bald top of the knoll, there standing before you is a huge cross.

Beside it is a brass map set upon a stone stand, shaped like a wheel with spokes radiating out, pointing to the landmarks visible in every direction. With powerful symbolism the cross stands at the centre of a circle, with the lands spread out beneath it.

Here we are in a part of Scotland where the Christian faith is still at the centre of most people's lives; one that was in fact entirely Catholic until a hundred years ago, when the railway, that snakes in a broad 'S' bend beneath our feet, opened up the fishing port of Mallaig, and opened up Morar to the world.

This was, in Penal times, one of the fastnesses of the Old Religion, that had remained unbroken and essentially unchanged since the time of Columba. There are other places, certainly, and sites elsewhere that have survived to recall that faith. But if any one place in the West may be called the *lieu de mémoire* of the Penal Church in Scotland, it is surely this.

It was here that Hugh MacDonald's story began some three hundred years ago, and here that much of it took place. Inland, where Loch Morar bends, is the mouth of Glen Meoble, where he was born. Closer to hand lies Eilean Bàn, the island in the loch where he began his training for the priesthood, and where later he trained others. To the west, beyond the golden estuary and out across the sea is Uist, the furthest extent of his authority as bishop – so far away is it that its two highest hills seem to be separate islands on the horizon. To the north, the grey peaks of Knoydart, and to the south, hidden by Morar's own hills, Arisaig and the high round mass of Roshven in Moidart, heartlands all of the Church he served. And on the eastern horizon Gaor Bheinn above Loch Arkaig, pointing onwards to Aberchalder beside Loch Oich, where he spent his

1

last years, nearby Cullochy where he died, and Kilfinnan where his body lies.

In his lineage, upbringing and temperament – in everything he was, indeed – he epitomised a unique native religious tradition within Scotland, and for this alone his story may be thought worth telling today.

But in addition, he chose to dedicate his life to the service of that tradition as priest and bishop, at a time when this could only bring him danger, sacrifice and opprobrium. An ordinary man, called by circumstance to live an extraordinary life, he knew the path he was taking and willingly suffered much at the hands of his Church's enemies. The enmities of his day are now largely healed and forgotten, and men and women in present-day Britain rarely suffer for their beliefs. But he serves as a caveat that this was not always so, and that in many parts of the world it is still not so today. He stands as a model of loyalty to one's faith whatever the cost, and also as a reminder of the blindness that can make loyalty the victim of oppression or, equally, the pretext for oppressing others. And for this too his story merits the telling.

Just now the steam train *The Jacobite* is labouring up the stiff climb below us, punching out black smoke as it carries its tourists on towards Mallaig; the new wide road has driven a cutting through the hill and thrown a concrete bridge over the estuary; and the Cal-Mac ferry is heading out for Eigg. There are yachts moored on Loch Morar, and beside its shore stands the little dark granite church of Our Lady and St Cumin with its striking round-tower, almost at our feet beneath the cross.

What view would young Hugh MacDonald have had from this hill, three hundred years ago? Looking inland (plate 1) he would have known that all the country north of the loch, as far as his eye could see and much further, belonged to Glengarry, whose seat lay forty mountainous miles to the east. But south of the loch was his own family's land, familiar hill and glen that one day his father would fall heir to. How had they come to own it? And what kind of a world was it that he had been born into, in the very last year of the seventeenth century?

The World He Was Born Into (1699)

Dugald the chief of Clanranald fled for his life up onto the hill and there staggered, gasping for breath, into the shelter of a small hollow. But they had sighted him. And now they had him surrounded. He could expect no mercy from them, for the one who led them had murders, even fratricide, already on his hands. He knew that this man – Allan of the Knife as everyone called him – had been hired by his own kinsmen to kill him, so that they could set up his uncle Alexander as chief in his place. Now he was fending off the blows as they came from all sides, until, dazed and barely able to see, he was dispatched at last by the leader's dirk. The date of the murder was 1520, and the site of it bears the name Coire Dhùghaill (Dugald's Hollow) to this day.

In the hope of playing down the crime, one of the Clanranald historians later claimed that Dugald was killed in retribution for his own bloody tyranny while chief. Another even disputed that he was ever the rightful heir, asserting that he was in fact not the son but the nephew of Ranald, the previous chief. But the local tradition in Moidart repudiates both these claims.

With Dugald's murder Alexander duly succeeded to the estate. But the dead man had left a son and heir, Allan, whose mother, knowing his life to be in danger, had him taken away to be raised among her own people, the Camerons of Lochiel. Before the lad had reached manhood Alexander was dead and the estate had passed to his bastard son, John of Moidart. But in 1538 the true heir returned with a party of Camerons to claim his own by force. Though he failed to win back the title of Clanranald, a compromise was struck whereby John ceded to him the whole of South Morar and part of Arisaig as well as tracts of land on Eigg, Uist and Benbecula.[1] Thus Allan became the first of the MacDonalds of Morar, who, since he was Dugald's son, were thereafter in the Gaelic styled 'Mac Dhùghaill'.

The arrangement seems to have been amicable in the end, for six years later Allan was fighting for John in battle; and in future engagements, up to the Rising of 1745, the MacDonalds of Morar would always make their contribution to any force of men raised by Clanranald.

The lands ceded to Allan were retained by his descendants and confirmed by royal charter in 1610.[2] Nearly all of them were still in the family's possession in the last year of the seventeenth century, the year our story begins.

The charter of 1610 is particularly useful to us in that it names the individual farms that existed on the estate at the time. A later charter from the 1720s reveals a very similar division of the land, with several newly created farms, and in addition defines the valuation of each farm for rental purposes.[3] Between the two they afford us a good idea of the land-use of South Morar at the end of the seventeenth century (map 1).

The first thing to notice is that South Morar at that time extended further in a southerly direction than it does today, stretching as far as the Caimb river, with several farms lying within its boundaries that today carry Arisaig addresses.

We can see too that farms were established wherever there was soil that could be cultivated, usually at low level where small mountain rivers fell into the loch, or in the narrow hinterland between the hills and the sea. Some were tiny, precarious patches, mere fingerholds on the land. The two obvious exceptions were Glen Meoble, a glacial valley that penetrates deep into the hills and which supported several farms; and Cross, where the hinterland of good soil stretches further inland than elsewhere. The latter was named as the senior farm of South Morar, and valued at three times that of any other.

As the map shows, the habitations were scattered far inland to beyond the head of the loch. There was no concentration of people in any one area, no real nucleus or centre of the estate. And the same held in Glengarry's country on the north side of the loch – today's village of Morar did not exist, and the fishing port of Mallaig with its population of a thousand was then but a farm like any other. It was quite possible at this date to sustain farms in remote places far inland, and only in the nineteenth century would they begin to be abandoned and the whole centre of gravity gather towards the coast.

Though no documentary evidence survives to tell us how much of the estate was cultivated at this time, traces still visible on the landscape itself suggest that it was only a tiny fraction.[4] Between the farms lay small patches of shieling land – good grass conserved for summer grazing – and vast tracts of 'commonty', hill pasture which as the name implies was held and used in common by adjacent farms for grazing throughout the year. The grazing grounds were all too often over-stocked, and winter fodder was still unknown, so that the cattle and all the other beasts were lean and under-sized, and mortality was high among them.

The staple crops were oats and bere. With land at such a premium the former had the advantage that it produced a higher yield; but the latter

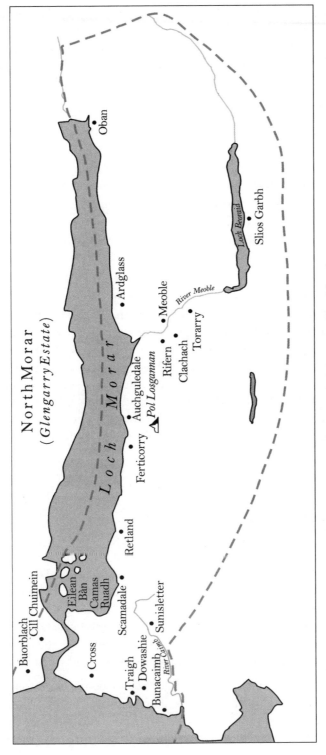

North Morar
(*Glengarry Estate*)

Oban

Ardglass

Meoble

River Meoble

Torarry

Rifern

Clachach

L o c h   M o r a r

Auchguledale
Pol Losgannan

Ferticorry

Slios Garbh

Loch Beoraid

Retland

Buorblach
Cill Chuimein

Eilean
Bàn
Camas
Ruadh

Scamadale

Cross

Traigh
Dowashie
Bunacaimb
River Caimb

Sunisletter

Map 1. The South Morar Estate of the MacDonalds of Morar (*c.*1700)

had a greater tolerance of Morar's acidic soils, and could thrive where other crops would not.[5] Wheat was out of the question in such terrain. But even for the hardy oats and bere, yields were low, for the West Highland farmers knew nothing of enclosure or drainage, and much of the land lay stagnant between the worked ridges and suffered heavy leaching.

Many of the farms were still 'farm-towns' at this time, nucleated farms leased by several tenants from a tacksman or chief tenant, who in turn paid the rental for the whole direct to MacDonald of Morar. These subsistence farmers worked the land in runrig, each holding a number of strips or patches interspersed among those of his neighbours, either by a fixed agreement or in rotation. Such a farm-town might also support one or two cotters, who were granted their house, plot of land and grazing rights in return for assistance on the tenants' holdings and services to the landlord.

The wide distribution of communities over the estate, their social make-up and the ties that bound them, even the way they worked the land, were all interrelated aspects of the clan system of the West Highlands. For the clan was traditionally based on the acquisition, defence and sharing of land; on production of food, not for an external market but to uphold a way of life; and on recognised, mutual obligations to loyalty among people bound by real or imagined ties of kinship.[6] It was a society in which the chief had traditionally offered protection and largesse, the clansman the fruits of his labour and manpower for battle; one that had always measured its wealth in men not money. It was everything that a market economy is not.

West Highland society at the close of the seventeenth century repre-sented a late phase of this tradition, in which vestiges of the old customs still touched the daily lives of the people, even if their original purpose and meaning were now almost forgotten.[7] It was still largely self-contained and self-sustaining. At the most local level, each farm-town was largely self-sufficient, being able to produce its own basic requirements and, at least as regards its tenants and cotters, having neither need nor notion of more. At a broader level, the clan itself was jealously autonomous: autonomy indeed was the very basis of its existence. And at the widest level, the whole of North-West Scotland, where the clan system mainly survived, was effectively detatched from the rest of the country by fundamental differences of race, language, custom and mentality.

Crown and Parliament had long sought to break the autonomy of the Gaelic Highlands and bring them under central control. They would finally achieve their aim through the punitive laws enacted after the Rising of 1745, but these were merely the end of a long process, the *coup de grâce* for a clan system that had been under siege and in decline for a hundred and fifty years. Recent scholarship has discredited the popular image of the Highlands as a static, medieval society, fixated in the past until suddenly shaken out of its time-warp in the aftermath of Culloden.

As far back as the end of the sixteenth century, in fact, the first anti-clan laws had been introduced. These were consolidated in the Statutes of Iona in 1609, which with subsequent legislation struck at the power and life-style of the clan chiefs, and made them responsible for their dependants' keeping the king's peace.[8]

It was no coincidence that James VI had granted the MacDonalds of Morar their charter in the very year after the Statutes of Iona, for the document was in part an instrument of control. In confirming their right to the estate it also, implicitly, imposed upon them the obligations and restrictions enacted in the statutes; and by setting down their right '*pro perpetuo*' it forestalled any possible expansion of land and power by their neighbours.

The laws, and increasing intercourse with the Lowlands through trade, had already gone a long way towards eroding the old clan ways by the time Hugh MacDonald was born.[9] The last great clan battle was fought at Mulroy in 1688, and though feuds, sustained by acts of arson and the theft and maiming of cattle, would continue well into the eighteenth century, disputes were now more and more being resolved by recourse to law rather than the sword.

Some chiefs and their tacksmen were already very willing to involve themselves in commercial enterprise, and for them the old farm-towns were an obstacle to progress. So long as crops were sown and cattle grazed promiscuously and without enclosure, yields must remain low, disease would be easily spread, and selective breeding impossible. They wanted change, and it was with a view to change that radical new laws were enacted concerning runrig and common grazing in 1695, just four years before Hugh MacDonald's birth.[10] We have no data for South Morar, but we know that in nearby Arisaig and Moidart, where conditions were comparable, some of the old farm-towns had already been taken over by the tacksmen, who were working them no longer for subsistence but for the market, with their one-time tenants now their labourers.[11]

Far more than a mere change of agricultural methods was involved in the move from farm-town to enclosed farm. A whole mode of life was at stake. For the old way was based on beliefs at the heart of the old clan system – paternalism, co-operation and solidarity; the new upon competitiveness, individualism and profit.

A new commercial nation was beginning to emerge – on which road the founding of the Bank of Scotland in 1695 was both a real and a symbolic milestone – and it was a road that some leading men of the

West Highlands were keen to tread. The chiefs were on the way to becoming landlords.

But their ambitions were not to be realised overnight. Reluctance on the part of the tenant farmers and of a number of the lairds themselves, the endurance of old personal clan ties and sentiments, the intractable terrain, the sheer magnitude of the task, all conspired against rapid change. A form of social hysteresis obtained, and it would be some decades yet before the laws of 1695 made any noticeable mark upon the landscape of Morar.

The Government's bid to emasculate the clans had particular point in the case of the Clanranalds and their related families, whose loyalty to the Catholic Church and the House of Stuart posed a special threat to the Crown and the Protestant succession.

It was only ten years since they had brought out their people at Killiecrankie, where Hugh's father himself had fought. William III's accession and his victory at the Boyne were still fresh in the memory, and for many his right to the throne remained in dispute and unresolved: just three years previously an assassination attempt had been hatched against him, and plans for a Rising to topple him by force continued to simmer. In 1699 there was every urgency for His Majesty's Government to deal with the Jacobite clans.

The Catholicism of these clans was in the Government's eyes merely another side of the same coin. After the near-annihilation of the Catholic Church at the Scottish Reformation perhaps only 25,000 Catholics remained in the whole country at the end of the seventeenth century, out of a total population of around one million, and in many places they had disappeared entirely.[12] At least ninety per cent of those who had survived were confined to a quite narrow swathe of country that ran from the north-east coast through Lochaber to the Outer Isles; one or two tiny pockets hung on in the south; elsewhere, both north and south of this band, there were virtually none.[13]

The lands of MacDonald of Morar lay at the centre of the greatest concentration of Catholicism in the whole country, an area stretching from Loch Shiel to Loch Hourn, where the Faith had remained unchanged for more than a thousand years. The local Kirk synod reckoned that within this area comprising Moidart, Arisaig, North and South Morar and Knoydart, all but five of an adult population of several thousand were Catholic.[14]

That these unlettered people had a profound and devout belief we know from the witness of the priests who laboured among them. They were, one tells us, 'as firm in their Faith as rocks ... their simple piety recalling the lives of the primitive Christians'.[15] But the state of their

Church was parlous. The Scottish Mission had been established for less than half a century, and remained under the authority of the Congregation *De Propaganda Fide* in Rome. Its first bishop, Thomas Nicolson, merely held the title of 'vicar apostolic', that is, Propaganda's representative.[16] He had only been appointed in 1694, and had begun his episcopate in prison. He had not yet visited the West Highlands or laid down rules for his priests.

The latter were far too few in number to meet the people's needs, and it was in the hope of producing more that a small seminary was opened in Glenlivet in the very year of Hugh MacDonald's birth.[17] The dearth was greatest in the Highlands. There was almost no recent tradition of Highland youths training for the priesthood,[18] and the Lowland clergy were of no use there without Gaelic. It had been necessary to fill the gap with priests from Ireland, whose Gaelic was close enough to the Highland to be intelligible,[19] but this solution had never been wholly satisfactory. Yet without these men the Faith in the West would have withered on the branch.

It is almost impossible today to appreciate the extent and vehemence of anti-Catholic sentiment in Scotland at this time. The language of Knox and the *Book of Discipline* of 1560 was still being invoked,[20] and its repetition over nearly a century-and-a-half had succeeded in creating a national *idée fixe*, according to which Catholicism was an evil to be extirpated, its leader the Man-of-Sin, its beliefs superstition and its Mass idolatry. From such darkness and thraldom the Reformers had rescued the Scottish people – so ran the general belief – and it remained their God-given duty to free those few who still lived in delusion in pockets of the country like Morar 'where the Reformation never obtained'.

The Catholic leaders for their part saw it as their own task to hold onto those followers they had, and wherever possible win back others lost to heresy to the jeopardy of their immortal souls. For both sides the issue was a matter of (spiritual) life and death.

The Catholics had suffered bitterly in the decade following William III's accession to the throne. In the first year of his reign he had issued a proclamation restricting their movement, and he followed this in 1698 with an edict that reaffirmed all previous legislation and enjoined law officers to search out and arrest all Catholic priests on sight.[21]

Nine garrisons were sent to the Highlands for this purpose, and the priests avoided capture only by hiding up in the mountains and ministering to their people by night. If they ventured out by daylight they were forced to adopt disguise. Intelligence from the garrisons reported that 'they frequently change their names and habits, and except the tyme of their idolatrous service [the Mass] they goe ordinarily in highland habit and

armour, soe that strangers cannot easily distinguish them from the countrey people'. Though they each received a quota from Rome, the report
added, their main income came from 'the heads of those popish Clans
particularly Glengarrie old and young, Captain of Clanronald, Bara,
Moror, Beinbecola, exacting from their people liberal maintainances'.[22]

It was only through this financial support from the Catholic gentlemen,
and through their hospitality and protection, that the priests were able
to survive. As the report makes clear, MacDonald of Morar was among
those who helped them. He maintained an aged priest on Eilean Bàn, who
served as chaplain to the family and pastor to the local community,
and gave hospitality to priests visiting his estate on the mainland and the
islands whenever they needed it.[23] It would be hard to overstate the importance of his support, and that of lairds like him, in ensuring the survival
of the Faith at this time of trial.

These man-made hardships must have seemed as nothing, however,
compared to the great affliction that hung over the West Highlands and
indeed much of Scotland at this time. The country was in the grip of
famine, the worst in living memory. The Hunger of the 1690s has been
called the last of the great medieval famines in Scotland: great in its
mortality, medieval in that it struck a nation that had as yet no state
machinery to respond to natural disaster.[24] Eye-witnesses speak of corpses
lying at the roadside, and infants dying at the empty breast. In some
inland areas of the North-East death may have carried off as many as
two-thirds of the people,[25] and though few records survive for the West
Highlands, the position there may have been little better.

By 1699 the west coast had in fact been hungry for five years already,
following the first harvest failure of 1693. The '96 and '98 crops had been
the worst. In the case of the latter the harvest was still not gathered by
the New Year in some parts; when it was finally cut the snow was still
on it, and it produced bread that was said to have an unnatural sweet
taste.[26] Not surprisingly, as many were dying from famine-related diseases
– typhoid and dysentery – as from hunger itself.

The main victims, as ever, were the tenants and cotters. The dearth of
grain left them with nothing either to eat or to sow, the scarcity of meal
drove prices to an all-time high, while the high mortality of beef cattle
deprived many of their only means of income or of paying their rent.
Great numbers, in fact, did not pay. The Highland tradition of 'rests' –
postponement of rent in cases of hardship – was never more invoked than
now. The best of the landlords, remembering the old clan obligations and
solidarity, permitted rests or wrote off debts altogether, and bore the
burden along with their people.

For the Jacobites and Catholics in the West the seasons of hunger were

'William's ill years', further proof that his reign was a root cause of the country's woes, and a sure sign from Providence that the House of Stuart must be restored.[27]

The year 1699 saw, with 1697, the height of the suffering. It would prove to be the lash of the famine's tail, for the healthy harvest that autumn, and for several seasons thereafter, would gradually restore normality to the people of Morar and their neighbours.[28]

At this date the laird of Morar was Allan, the great-great grandson of his namesake who had first received the estate from Clanranald after the murder of his father. He himself had three younger brothers, Alexander, Ronald and Lachlan, and a sister Mary, the youngest of the family. He was in his mid-thirties at this time, and already had a son, Donald, and a daughter by his first marriage. Sometime in the mid-1690s he had entered a second marriage with a daughter of Clanranald, by whom he would in time have a second family of four girls.

The exact date of Allan's death is not known, but it could not have been earlier than 1723, since he was signatory to a deposition of the estate at this date;[29] nor later than 1726, since he is referred to as the *quondam* laird in a document of that year.[30] Nor do we know the date of the death of his son Donald, except that he predeceased his father, so that at Allan's death leadership of the family passed to his own next oldest brother, Alexander.

Alexander himself also married twice. To his first wife were born two boys and a girl – Allan Ruadh, Alexander, and Mary. But about 1697 he remarried. His new wife Mary was a daughter of MacDonald of Kinloch-moidart, and by her he had two more sons, Hugh and John, and a daughter Catherine.

It is the elder son, Hugh, who is the subject of the present story. He was born, by his own account, on 2 February 1699.[31] No documentary record of his birth survives, but since his father was always known as 'Alexander of Meoble' we may take it that he was born in Glen Meoble, and raised there with his brother and sister and the children of his father's first marriage. Appendix I traces his genealogy and that of his closer relatives, and in doing so points up how closely the MacDonalds of Morar and the other major families in the West were inter-related, and often sought to strengthen these ties by marriage.

Hugh MacDonald is habitually referred to today as 'the son of the Laird of Morar', but the description is somewhat misleading. He was not born the son of a laird. At the time of his birth his uncle Allan was laird, and was alive and well; Allan's son Donald may also have been living, and there was every prospect of more male children to follow from his second marriage. Hugh's father was simply the tacksman of Meoble. There was no thought of his succeeding to the estate, and it would be more than twenty years before he did so, by which time Hugh would be far away from Morar and embarked on a career of his own. Nor even then was it conceivable that Hugh himself, as the third son, would ever inherit: had this ever been remotely likely, his life might have followed a quite different path.

His formative years were thus spent as a younger son of the tacksman of one of the chief farms of South Morar. This was the world he was born into. And from it he would inherit the fundamental values that have been adumbrated in this chapter – a personal loyalty and obligation to kindness, deeply held political convictions, a resolute faith expecting and prepared to suffer, an abhorrence of heresy, and an implicit sense of Providence. These, carried into manhood, profoundly shaped the man he would become – the Highlander, Jacobite, and bishop.

Notes

1. The present account based on that in MacDonald, C. (1889; Edinburgh, 1996 edn), pp. 30ff.
2. Copy of charter of James VI, 15.3.1610 (in Latin), extracted 1769, Clanranald Papers, GD 201/5/1, NAS. The charter does not in fact mention the lands granted in Uist and Benbecula.
3. Copy of charter of George I, 25.4.1726, before Council of Session 16.11.1721, GD 201/5/24, NAS. The valuation is made in 'pennylands', an assessment of a farm's capacity to sustain crops and livestock, based not only on its actual acreage but also on the quality of the land.
4. An eighteenth-century survey of a nearby estate in Knoydart reveals that only 80 of its 13,000 acres were then under the spade – survey of the forfeited Barrisdale Estate; statistics cited in Devine T. M., chap. 14 of Devine T. M. and Young J. R. (1999), p. 228.
5. See Fenton A. (1976), p. 167; and Whyte I. (1995), p. 137.
6. The interaction of these aspects has been fully and persuasively analysed in Dodgshon R. A., in Houston R. and Whyte I. D. (eds) (1989), and Dodgshon R. A. (1998).
7. To take but one example, the payment of rent in kind rather than cash – still a common practice at this date – was a vestige of the ancient *cuid oidhche*, the clansman's obligation to give hospitality to the chief and his retinue.
8. Text of the statutes in Masson D. (ed.) (1889), pp. 26ff. Among other things the statutes outlawed sorning and feuding, and set limits on the size of the chiefs' retinue and the extent of their table. Further legislation of 1616 required that they reside in one place rather than living as wanderers off the labours of their dependants, and held them responsible for those dependants keeping the peace and observing the law.
9. Some of these changes had certainly reached Morar, which was, for example,

very probably importing grain from the Clyde by this date – cf. Whyte I. (1979), pp. 229f. and fig. 19. Though Morar is 'the end of the road' today, in the days when bulk goods were more readily carried by sea than road its proximity to the coast made it in fact less isolated from outside contact than some places further inland.

10. 'Act anent Lands lying Run-rig' and 'Act concerning the Dividing of Commonties', Acta Parliamentorum Gulielmi, 1695, *APS*, vol. ix, pp. 421 and 462 respectively.

11. Dodgshon R. A. (1998), pp. 128 and 137.

12. A census conducted by the Kirk some forty years after this date found no Catholics at all in 934 of its 964 parishes – 'A State of Popery in Scotland containing an Hint of the Reasons of it's continuance there, Places where, and proposing some Remedies for removing these Evils', n.d. (but *c.* 1737), CH 1/5/119, p. 5, NAS. In 1699 the number in which Catholics were to be found would have been, if anything, even less. See also Darragh J. (1953 J).

13. For a more detailed account, with map, see Watts J. (1999), pp. 4ff. The Catholic districts did not form a continuous 'swathe' from the North-East to the Isles. Even after the growth of numbers in some inland parts of the Highlands, notably BraeLochaber and Badenoch in the 1720s, there remained gaps. The two greatest concentrations were in the West on the lands of Clanranald, MacNeil and Glengarry, and on the Gordon lands of the North-East. This was reflected in the perception of the missionary priests of the day, who habitually referred to the Highland areas in general as 'the West', and the Aberdeenshire-Banffshire districts as 'the North'.

14. 'A Representation of the most deplorable State of Severall Paroches in the Highlands both in the Western Isles and Continent within the Bounds of the Synod of Argyle in which Places the Reformation never Obtained', 1703, in *Miscellany of the Maitland Club*, vol. III, part ii (1843), pp. 424ff. The same source reckoned that all but *c.* 17 of the 1,500+ adults on Uist and Barra were Catholic.

15. Itinerary of Alexander Leslie, 1677–78, original in Latin; English version SM 2/9/1, p. 7, SCA.

16. In 1727 the Mission would be divided into two vicariates, Lowland and Highland (cf. p. 57f.); and exactly one hundred years later (1827) reorganised into three Districts, Northern, Eastern and Western. Not until 1878, with the restoration of the hierarchy, would Scotland cease to be a Mission under Propaganda. The *Sacra Congregatio de Propaganda Fide* (hereafter referred to as 'Propaganda') had been founded by Pope Gregory XV in 1622 to regulate ecclesiastical affairs in the 'mission territories' where no hierarchy existed. Such territories included both the newly discovered parts of the world where no hierarchies had yet been established, and those now Protestant countries of Europe in which they had been discontinued after the Reformation.

17. Set up in Glenlivet by Thomas Innes. Cf. T. Innes to Lewis Innes, 15.7.1699 and 15.10.1699, BL, SCA. It closed in 1701.

18. Report of Alexander Leslie to Propaganda, 4.3.1681, original in Latin;

English version SM 2/9/3, SCA. Also, Report of Alexander Winster to Propaganda, Propaganda Archives Scotia Scritt. rifer. 1, summarised in Bellesheim A. (1890), vol. IV, pp. 116ff.; Winster attributed the lack of vocations from the Highlands clans to the opposition of parents.

19. In the year of Hugh MacDonald's birth eight of the ten priests serving in the Highlands were Irish – Report of John Irvin on the State of the Church in Scotland, 5.9.1698; English version in Bellesheim A. (1890), appendix VII. Irvin was procurator of the Scottish Mission in Paris.

20. Numerous contemporary tracts and pamphlets could be cited, of which the *Noveltie of Poperie*, published by Rev. W. Guild, DD, in 1656 may serve as an example. Dr Guild describes the Catholic Church as 'mother of harlots and abominations of the earth ... mistress of witchcrafts, whose skirts the Lord hath discovered upon her face, and will more and more shew the nations her nakedness', etc.

21. 'Proclamation for the Confinement of Popish Recusants within Five Miles of their respective Dwellings', 17.9.1690, GD 103/2/237, NAS. The edict of 1698 was aimed mainly at priests; from the beginning of his reign, in fact, William had protected the Catholic laity from the severe persecution they had suffered during the Revolution of 1688–89 – cf. Thomas Nicolson to Superior General of Society of Jesus, 26.1.1691, in Forbes Leith W. (1909), vol. II, pp. 155ff.

22. Intelligence Report from Garrison at present-day Fort William, n.d. but *c*. 1702, CH 1/2/29/569, NAS.

23. 'Representation' etc. of Synod of Argyll, 1703, loc. cit.

24. It is worth remembering that it was only two generations since Scotland's last recorded bubonic plague.

25. Cf. the tradition of 50% mortality in Grange, Banffshire, in Whyte I. (1979), p. 249, citing OSA, ix, p. 557; and Thomas Innes to Lewis Innes, 27.3.99, BL, SCA, claiming 2/3+ dead in Upper Glenlivet between 1697–99.

26. Flinn M. (1977), espec. pp. 169ff, and appendix A (mortality indices by regions).

27. Cf. Devine T. (1999), p. 35.

28. See also Smout T. C. 'Famine Relief in Scotland', chap. 2 of Cullen L. M. and Smout T. C. (1977), espec. pp. 22–25.

29. 'Extract Deposition of Corroboration By the Laird of Morror To the Laird of Moydart', Edinburgh, 6.2.1723, GD 201/5/11, NAS.

30. 'Copia Carta Adjud Allani MackDonald Terrarum de Slismain', George I, 5.4.1726, (in Latin), GD 201/5/24, NAS.

31. HMD to George Hay, 29.10.1767, BL, SCA.

2

Boyhood at Meoble
(1699–1711)

One of Hugh's very first memories in life was of the soldiers coming. It was the vivid red coats and the buttons that stuck in his mind, so unlike the dun woven plaids of his own people. He could not understand a word they said, for they spoke in English, but he had been warned that they were enemies and were there to catch the priest.

He was already quite familiar with priests, because they sometimes stayed at his home. All the ones he had seen were Irishmen, and indeed the little boy perhaps believed that a sprinkling of strange words and an Irish *blas* were actual requirements of the calling. One of them, Mr Antony Mongan, had baptised him. Another, old Mr James Cahassy, lived in a little house on Eilean Bàn, the 'White Island' in Loch Morar, and was dying of consumption.

Hugh's parents had told him of the visit of Bishop Nicolson in the first year of the new century, which was – the old people said – the first sight that Morar had had of a bishop in over a hundred years.[1] He had arrived from Glengarry's country the week before midsummer, and stayed on the island with Mr Cahassy. Having no Gaelic himself he had enlisted Mr Mongan to translate for him, and when he left for the Outer Isles he took him as his interpreter. At every stopping place he conferred the sacrament of confirmation on great numbers of people, for without a bishop until this time even the oldest had never been confirmed. At Morar he would certainly have met the MacDonalds of Meoble and their children, including fifteen-month-old Hugh, and he perhaps took the toddler up in his arms and blessed him.

Later that summer he had called all the priests to Eilean Bàn for a meeting that was to be a milestone in the rebuilding of the Church in the Highlands. He gave each of them a fixed 'Station', where before they had moved from place to place as they saw fit, and presented to them his new Statutes, which would form the basis of church practice and discipline for the next eighty years.[2] Finally, he appointed two pro-vicars, Mr Robert Munro for the Mainland, and Mr Mongan for the Isles, to oversee and support their fellow priests and report regularly back to him.[3]

But as the bishop was seeking to build, the State was seeking to tear down. In the very year of his visitation a new law 'for preventing the grouth of Popery' was passed in Edinburgh,[4] which outlawed Mass attendance on pain of deportation (or death on the second offence), deprived Catholics of all rights of inheritance, and required their children to be taken away from home and brought up as Protestants. In short, it treated Catholics as non-citizens, almost non-persons. It was in fact merely the latest in a series of acts, the first of which dated from the Reformation Parliament of 1560 itself, aimed at wiping Catholicism off the map of Scotland. Throughout the seventeenth century successive governments had been fine-tuning the existing laws to make them more effective, reissuing and amplifying them no less than twenty times.[5]

If the Act of 1700 had been enforced to the letter the Old Faith would certainly have been annihilated. But its authors intended it rather as a threat, and a power available *in extremis*. And the threat seems to have had some temporary effect, particularly among the propertied class who had most to lose. Conversions dried up, and a few people apostatised. 'There is still some of the Commonalty coming in to the Church,' one correspondent reported to Rome the following year, 'but Worldly interest keep of [off] the Great folks, and I am much affrayd the strict laws anent Inheritances will pervert more.'[6] In the remote West apostasy was not an issue meantime. But the act was to remain on the statute book for nearly a century, and in time (as we shall see) 'worldly interest' would indeed finally draw many of the leading families there away from the church of their ancestors.

There had been garrisons stationed in the West Highlands since the year before Hugh's birth. It was the habit of the troops when away from base to impose themselves on the reluctant hospitality of the local gentlemen, and it is more than likely that some of them were billeted from time to time at Bunacaimb, Cross and Meoble itself. The Act of 1700 had strengthened their hand. It gave them greater authority, and also the incentive of 500 merks rewards for information leading to conviction. The promise of reward also encouraged other informers, through whom the military built up their intelligence networks. In time they were able to gather detailed information on the whereabouts of all the priests in the area.

In June 1701 they succeeded in capturing Mr Mongan. He was escorted to Edinburgh by the local garrison commander, who was hoping to pick up the reward of 500 merks personally.[7] There he was imprisoned, tried, and banished in accordance with the act, on pain of death should he ever return.[8] His treatment alarmed the rest of the clergy, particularly his fellow countrymen in the West Highlands, to the point that several made open threats to quit the Mission. Their reaction only confirmed Bishop Nicolson in his conviction that Irish priests were a liability to be avoided if possible.[9] Yet he could not do without them.

The garrison also held intelligence on Mr Cahassy and laid plans for his arrest. They knew that he was supported by Hugh's uncle Allan MacDonald of Morar, and that he stayed on Eilean Bàn, where he kept his boat. 'There appears noe way soe feazible for catching of him,' their commander reported, 'as for a pairty to be in wait upon the next adjacent land in order to command the boat whensoever she comes to shore and soe they cannot possibly miss him.'[10] But they missed him every time. They lacked numbers on the ground, and – on roads unfit for route marches – their means of communication were snail-paced compared with those of the local people.

These events, important though they were for Hugh's own future career, would hardly have touched him at the time. He was now four years old, and Glen Meoble seemed to him a safe and self-contained world, encircled and protected on all sides by the mountains (map 1 and plate 2). His home lay on the east side of the river, a mile from its mouth. Looking downstream he could not see the loch, but he could see over it, and through the gap of Tarbert in North Morar, on to the grey mountains of Knoydart.[11] If he turned to look upstream the land was strangely flat, and fertile as far as the Slatey burn; this was the infield of his father's farm, with dug patches here and there, and wet land by the river where the cattle roamed. Two miles beyond, the hills closed in, but this was not the valley-head that it seemed to be, for the river took a right-angled turn to the east, out of view, and the glen continued for six more miles into the high mountains. Much of this narrow upper glen was filled by the waters of Loch Beoraid, from whose banks the hills rose sharply to north and south.[12]

This was by far the largest of the glens of South Morar, and of the waters that fed into the loch this was the one real 'river'. It did not tumble; it meandered on the valley bottom. In places it was twenty metres wide, and on its every bend was a shingle strand. It had its own islands, and one large 'winter island' which the boys could easily reach except in the season of spate. It was the one river to which salmon came in numbers to spawn. It was full of trout too, and below Hugh's house, close to where the Abhainn Chlachaich joined it, there was a fine pool for guddling. Beyond it was Clachach farm, and further again the rigs and the black cattle of Rifern on the shoulder of the hill.

Three-quarters of a mile upstream the scattered huts of Torarry stood out on the slope of a low hill. Until recent times this had been shieling land belonging to the farm, and close enough for the milk to be brought home daily.[13] But when Hugh's father was a boy the family had begun to use shielings higher in the hills, where the women and children stayed

all summer, and Torarry had been turned into a farm.[14] Below it the
Meoble river ran through a narrow channel, and here its banks were
rocky, the strata jutting upwards in jagged slivers, bleached white on dry
summer days. It was from here that Hugh's people quarried their grave-
stones, when they buried their dead on the flat spit of land down on the
shore of Loch Morar; they used upright slivers for adults, and smaller
flat stones for the infants.

The path that passed Hugh's house ran to the very head of the glen,
but where it took the right-angled turn a second path branched off,
heading south over into the valley of the Ailort river. This was at the
time the main inland through-route in South Morar, linking it with North
Morar and Knoydart to the north, Arisaig and Moidart to the south, and
via Moidart with Loch Eil in the east. Today, because of the road and
the rail, we think of the coast as the only possible route through Morar,
but in the days before wheeled transport the Glen Meoble road was the
easiest and most direct. What is now an unfrequented track would then
have been quite a thoroughfare, and the sight of travellers no cause for
alarm or wonder to young Hugh.

Some of those travellers used to call at the house; a few even stayed
there. It stood one storey high under a heather thatch, with walls of turf
set upon a course of stones. It was built upon a framework of *ceangail*
or 'couples', set some eight feet apart, and was long and narrow, since
houses of this style could only be extended lengthwise. Hugh's father had
extended it when he began his second family, by throwing up two or
three more couples on the end. Except in size it was barely distinguishable
from the tenants' houses scattered in the farm-town nearby.[15] At the far
end of it, and merely an extension of it, was the byre.

As soon as the 1700 Act became law the synod of Argyll, within whose
bounds South Morar lay, had drawn up a petition to the justiciary of the
county, urging them to implement it with all severity.[16] The following
year they persuaded the commander of the garrison to harass the priests
of the west coast and the master of the little Catholic school at Arisaig,
in the hope of driving them out.[17] They also selected several of their own
ministers and catechists to visit the Catholic districts, to evangelise the
people and at the same time gather information for the courts. But this
was a thankless and dangerous task, and most of those whom the synod
volunteered for it contrived to find excuses to evade it.[18]

Nor was the Kirk satisfied that the magistrates themselves were using
the powers at their disposal, and its General Assembly sent a number of
'Addresses' and 'Informations' to the Scottish parliament complaining
of their alleged lack of relish for the task. In March 1704 it was rewarded
with a proclamation issued by the queen, ordering all officers of the law

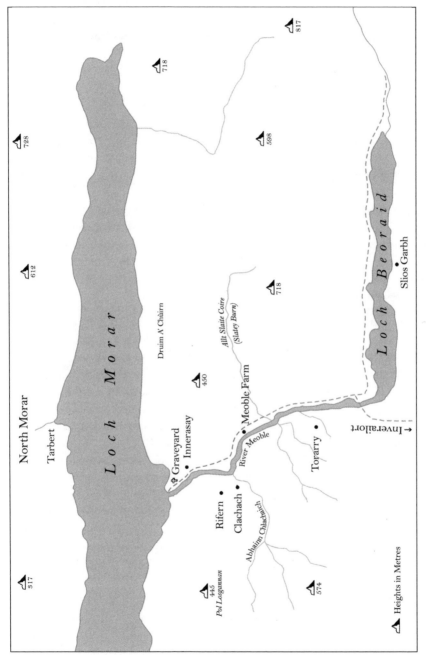

Map 2. Glen Meoble and Loch Beoraid (*c.* 1700)

North Morar

Tarbert

L o c h   M o r a r

Druim A' Chùirn

Graveyard
Innerasay

Meoble Farm

River Meoble

Rifern
Clachach

Torarry

Abhainn Chiachaich

Pol Losgannan

← Inverailort

Allt Sluite Coire
(Slatey Burn)

L o c h   B e o r a i d

Slios Garbh

Heights in Metres

817

728

718

612

718

598

450

574

445

517

to put the act of 1700 'to exact and diligent execution' or be themselves 'punished as malversers', and instructing every parish minister to compile lists of known or suspected Catholic families.[19] The list drawn up for South Morar provides valuable information concerning the local community, but also presents us with an enigma in regard to Hugh's own family (see appendix V).

The proclamation prompted a flurry of anti-Catholic activity in the West Highlands. The priests all took to the hills again. Mr Cahassy, desperately ill though he was, fled from Eilean Bàn, and by the time he ventured back in the summer he was quite broken and only weeks from death. Three of the Irish Franciscans finally carried out their threat and quit the Mission, leaving Uist and Barra with no priest at all.[20] Finally, at the very end of the year, Mr Robert Munro was seized by the military in Glen Garry. He had already been twice banished from the country, each time under pain of death if he should return, and had twice slipped back and resumed his work. When the soldiers took him this time they found him lying exhausted in a barn, too sick even to walk, so they threw him over a horse like a sack and brought him to their headquarters at Invergarry Castle. There he was locked up, with neither straw to lie on nor water to drink. Within two days he was dead.[21]

When Hugh was eight years old James Gordon, the newly consecrated coadjutor bishop of the Scottish Mission, made his first episcopal visit to the West.[22] He brought with him George Douglas, a Ross man recently ordained deacon, as interpreter.[23] The precipitous path from Glen Garry over into Knoydart, where they were often reduced to crawling on all fours, came as a rude shock to him. But he was determined to set an example by travelling on foot, sleeping on straw and heather, and eating the same whey and barley bread as everyone else.

The party reached Eilean Bàn on 23 June, and after an overnight stay there sailed for Arisaig, and thence to the Isles. A month later they were back, lodging one night at the home of Hugh's uncle Ronald at Cross, and a second at Beoraid in North Morar, where they baptised a thousand people. On 22 July they recrossed the loch to Glen Meoble. Here their programme was to be the same as at every stopping place – arrive in the evening; stay overnight; the next morning celebrate Mass, baptise and confirm; in the afternoon move on.

Hugh would have been among the crowd that pulled the boat ashore beside the little cemetery, surrounded the visitors and swept them up to his house. There we may imagine him hovering in the background as his mother and his half-sister Mary served them their supper. Then he and the rest of the children would be sent off to stay in some of the tenants' houses, so that the bishop and his friends might sleep in some comfort that night.

In the morning families from every farm in South Morar gathered on the flat land between the rigs of green corn for Mass. There was a garrison stationed in Moidart at this time, and because of it Bishop Gordon had been unable to enter that country.[24] Now some of the Moidart people, hearing that he was at Meoble, had made the long trek to be there. Before the Mass Mr Douglas preached the sermon in Gaelic, and led the people in reciting the Litany of the Saints.[25] After it the bishop himself spoke briefly, his words interpreted by Mr Douglas, and then administered the sacrament of Confirmation to seventy-nine people.

Hugh was not among those who stepped forward for Communion, since according to the practice of the day the Sacrament could only be received on reaching one's mid-teens. But in most other respects he was already very much a part of the religious life of the community. He was considered old enough to attend Mass every Sunday (if a priest was available to celebrate) and on the thirteen designated Holy Days 'of Obligation' in the year. He was also expected to obey the rule of abstinence from meat on Fridays, on Ember-days (the vigils of the major feasts) and the forty days of Lent, sixty-three days in the year in all. And a few years from now, when he attained the age of twelve, he would be obliged to fast on all these days also. He played his part in family devotions, the rosary and the rich Gaelic tradition of prayers of praise and supplication for every occasion of the day.[26]

After lunch the bishop's party returned to their boat, with a swarm of young and old around them, and rowed to Tarbert, whence they took the difficult path along Loch Nevis-side, and then another boat across the Kyles into Knoydart.

There three days later George Douglas was ordained to the priesthood at the house of MacDonell of Scottas. It was the first ordination in the Highlands for a century and a half, and the bishop must have been torn between celebrating the event as it deserved, and keeping it private and as hidden as possible from the ears of the military. Hugh's father and uncle Allan would certainly have attended, as leading gentlemen of the area, and it would be good to think that young Hugh may have travelled with them, especially as in later years Mr Douglas was to be his first mentor when he himself was a newly ordained priest.

Bishop Gordon spent only two more days in Knoydart, and then headed east. He had now been journeying for eight weeks with barely a break, and he was badly run down. But he continued his punishing daily routine, trying to shake off a worsening fever, never sparing himself, until reaching Lochaber he was near to death and at last forced to rest. This was to be the pattern of his episcopate for the next forty years – dedication to the edge of endurance.[27]

The journey was a watershed for him. Until now he had only known *of* the Catholic Highlands and Islands; now he had felt their texture with his own hands. His understanding of the Scottish Mission would never be the same again.

He estimated that some 2,200 persons had been baptised or reconciled to the Church during the visitation. But he had seen the chronic shortage of clergy, and knew that further progress would be impossible without more priests. 'We have now very few capable laborers, and extream difficulty to get our own customers well serv'd by 'em,' he reported.[28] He had also seen their low morale, and a lack of discipline even among the hand-picked administrators, whom he had found 'allmost all so opinionate, there is hard guiding of them separately, much more to make them all agree, and not fall into jarrs.'[29] The obvious long-term solution would be to select and train his own priests locally, monitoring them from a young age and instilling in them the qualities needed for the Spartan life of the Mission, something not possible in the comfort and intellectual atmosphere of the Scots Colleges abroad. This had long been his conviction,[30] and his experience on the road only served to confirm it.

He was actually offered a substantial sum of money to set up a small seminary at this time by Lewis Innes, the principal of the Scots College Paris, but had to turn it down for want of a suitable priest to run it.[31] The best he could do meantime – and it was very much second best – was to place two students in one of the Catholic schools in the West, and get them additional tutoring by the local priest. There were several such schools to choose from. The one at Arisaig, which had been wrecked by the military six years before, had now reopened in another house close by.[32] The old school on Barra had also been re-established following his visit there, and a new one had now been opened at Cross,[33] with the sons of the laird and tacksmen of Morar as pupils. Almost certainly Hugh himself was now attending this school with one or two of his brothers, for he was just of an age to do so. If so, he may well have met Bishop Gordon's two protégés there, and found himself rubbing shoulders with young men who were serious about the priestly life.

By now he was taking a share in the farm work whenever he was at home. His father had a light Highland plough,[34] the only one in the glen since his was the only land flat enough to take it, and in February or March Hugh's task was to lead the horse, while the man behind guided the plough one-handed. In the same season he watched the tenants of Torarry and Rifern using the *cas chrom* (the 'bent foot' hand-plough) on their hillside rigs, working backwards up the slope so slowly that in half a day they scarcely seemed to have moved. In the spring he took his place in the line of men sowing the oats or bere, moving in echelon formation and flinging the seed broadcast from a 'bag' made out of a sheet pinned at the shoulder.

Summer was the season of the peats and the droving. They had been exporting cattle from the West for a hundred years at least, but in the last generation the trade had expanded beyond recognition, and some landowners were now organising droves not only to the Lowland trysts but even as far south as East Anglia.[35] Meoble was the main assembly point for cattle from the farms of South Morar, where Hugh's father was one of the organisers. Every year young Hugh would watch as up to fifty beasts set off in line along the south shore of the loch towards Oban farm and the mountain passes.

At the autumn reaping he and his young brother John were always given the last sheaf of the field, to fashion into the figure of a *caileach* (old woman) which was hung above the door. There was a drying kiln at the farm, and a 'horizontal' mill worked off the burn, but the tenants still often dried their corn by burning it over a chaff fire, and ground it with the hand quern. Once the grain and meal were stored it was time to manure the land for next year. The beasts were let to roam freely upon it, and to their dung was added turf pared off the land, or pulled off the roofs if this was the year for re-thatching.

Down at Cross farm there was shell sand and seaweed close to hand for fertiliser, and with it Hugh's uncle Ronald could get a yield of bere three or four times greater than was possible at Meoble. But it was a massive task – perhaps a hundred creels of seaweed for every acre to be sown. All the relatives were called in to help, Hugh and his brothers among them, and the whole enterprise was turned into a social event lasting several days.

It was in 1707 that the bitterly contested union of the Scottish and English parliaments was finally effected. Ironically, union would actually benefit the Catholics of Scotland in the long run, by giving them access to men of influence in London, and by mollifying the bigotry of the Scottish Establishment through contact with the less parochial issues of the South. But at the time it served to give Scottish Jacobitism a new lease of life, and a new, focused aim – the restoration not alone of the House of Stuart but of the nation state itself.[36]

Hugh could not fail to be aware of these happenings, and to grasp something of their meaning. He would hear the constant discussions, and see the military at close hand. His family and neighbours 'lived' the effects of their Jacobitism almost daily, just as they 'lived' the effects of their suspect faith, and he had grown up with these two great issues of his life since ever he could remember. He was already a Jacobite, just as he was a Catholic, in his bones.

In this year and the following spring Morar was alive with rumours of a new Jacobite attempt, all the word being of an imminent landing with French support somewhere on the west coast. It is now known that several priests of the Scottish Mission, including Bishop Nicolson himself, were implicated in the plans.[37] Aware of the planned landing and the involvement of leading Catholics, the Government issued an order for the arrest of James and his supporters on entry into the kingdom, and at the same time instructed that the arms and houses of Catholics be seized, and that restrictions be placed on their movements.[38]

Harassment continued through 1709. In June Bishop Gordon managed to make a second visit to the West Highlands,[39] but his plans for opening more schools there had to be shelved meantime, and he even had to accept the closure of the short-lived school at Cross. On his return he was summoned to appear in court, but knowing that several laymen had already suffered banishment and the loss of their entire property for harbouring priests that year, he prudently failed to appear, and was declared fugitate.[40]

This same year saw the founding of the Society in Scotland for Propagating Christian Knowledge. Its main purpose was to promote the Protestant faith and combat Catholicism by funding new schools in the north and west, particularly in areas where no parish schools existed.[41] Its first school opened on remote St Kilda before the year was out, and with major funding and prudent housekeeping it eventually established more than 320, including several in the Catholic heartlands of the west.[42] The eighteenth-century historian of the Catholic Church, Rev. John Thomson, writing seventy years on when the achievements of the society had become clear, judged its founding in 1709 to be 'one of the severest trials the Mission had ever met with, and the most alarming in its effects'.[43] For the bishops it brought home again the absolute necessity of holding onto their Catholic schools and extending them if possible, and in particular of setting up a seminary, however small and basic, for training their own priests in Scotland.

In the autumn of 1710 Bishop Gordon paid a third visit to the west. Bishop Nicolson had given him charge of the Church's affairs in the Highlands and Islands, at his own request, and he planned to stay long enough to get to know the clergy, familiarise himself with the culture, and learn at least something of the language.[44] In the end he stayed seven months, through the Highland winter and into the spring. He made Eilean Bàn his base,[45] and must have paid several visits to Meoble, where he was already known to the family. We can picture Hugh showing him around the farm in the snow and again at ploughing time, and teaching him the Gaelic names of the animals and crops and the changing features of the landscape.

If his visitation three years before had given him a first memorable taste of the Highlands, his sojourn now afforded him a slower, deeper draught. And he found that he took naturally to the life, the people, even the climate, as he explained with some warmth to the Scots agent in Rome:

> Some people may wonder at my being able to stay so long in our montanous countrys (that seem so uneasy to others) with abundance of comfort ... my health was never better than in the hills last winter, & I never had more comfort every way than amongst them, & was so farr from wearying of them, that I rather Long to shut myself up for ever within them. I do not question but I could do greater service there than anywhere else (tho 'tis very litle I can do in any place) & if it were the will of Exch. [Exchange, i.e., Propaganda] I should confine my self so long as I live among our hills, & consecrate my days to serve the poor people that live in them.[46]

It had long been accepted, even in far-off Rome, that the Highland Church had its own unique needs and required its own solutions. Historically, linguistically and spiritually it had far more in common with Ireland than with the Scottish Lowlands. For part of the previous century it had effectively been run from Co. Antrim, and for a time had actually been placed under the authority of the Archbishop of Armagh. In the 1630s Propaganda had seriously considered re-establishing the ancient See of the Isles, but no action was taken and the matter had been shelved.[47]

James Gordon was in effect resurrecting this idea. He had in mind a separate vicariate for the Gaelic Highlands and Islands, with its own resident bishop enjoying the autonomy and authority of a vicar apostolic answerable directly to Rome. And ideally he would be that bishop. To free himself for the task would require the appointment of a new coadjutor for Bishop Nicolson in the Lowlands, and he particularly asked the Scots agent to put this proposal to the Cardinals of Propaganda.

In the event, a number of priests of the Mission opposed the plan on the grounds that it would be divisive and urged the agent not to pursue it in Rome, with the result that it was shelved meantime. But the concept of a bishop for the Highlands had taken shape, and it would remain in the mind of Bishop Gordon, to be brought out again at the opportune time. His Highland sojourn of 1710 to 1711 was to prove, in fact, a critical moment in the development of the Church, and – eventually – in the life of Hugh MacDonald.

Notes

1. The present account based on Bishop Nicolson's Report to Propaganda, 1700 (in Latin), SM 3/1, SCA.
2. 'Statuta Missionis', 1700 (in Latin), SM 3/2/1, SCA. A good summary also in Bellesheim A. (1890), vol. IV, pp. 168ff. Crucially, the new arrangements

also gave the bishop authority over the regular clergy and the Jesuits, enabling him to deploy them within an overall national strategy for the first time. It has been assumed that assigning priests to fixed stations was an unqualified boon to the Mission. But, granted the undoubted benefits, it probably had one damaging result: the priests were no longer able to reach outlying areas or areas with small Catholic minorities, which until now had at least had occasional visits from them. The point, which was made by Canon Duncan MacLean fifty years ago (MacLean D. 1952 J), seems to have been ignored by historians since. In some of these places the Faith gradually died out as a result. Thus areas such as Harris and Kintyre that still sustained small Catholic populations in the late seventeenth century – cf. Report of Alexander Leslie to Propaganda, 1681 (in Latin), English version SM 2/9/3, SCA – had ceased to do so two generations later.

3. Thomas Innes to William Leslie, 13.10.1701, BL, SCA. In effect, Antony Mongan had charge over his fellow Irish priests, most of whom were working in the Islands, and Robert Munro had charge of his fellow Scots on the mainland.

4. 'Act for preventing the grouth of Popery', Acta Parliamentorum Gulielmi, 1700, *APS*, vol. x, pp. 215ff.

5. MacInnes A. I. (1989 J), which includes details of the legislation, with *APS* references.

6. Thomas Innes to Cardinal Protector, 13.10.1701, BL, SCA.

7. Thomson J. 'Some Account of the State of Religion in Scotland' etc. (*c.* 1780), Th/10, SCA; relevant excerpt also in Forbes Leith W. (ed.) (1909), vol. II, p. 185. The commissioners of the treasury procrastinated regarding the reward, and eventually money was collected for the commander by Kirk ministers.

8. He went to France, where he took up a comfortable charge near to Chartres, but he pined for 'the hills and rocks of Moydeart and Arasaig and their poverty': Antony Mongan to Thomas Innes, 12.7.1703, BL, SCA.

9. Re threats – Thomas Innes to William Stuart, 13.10.1703, BL, SCA; re Bishop Nicolson's reluctance to accept Irish priests – see e.g., Walter Innes to Lewis Innes, 25.5.1699, BL, SCA, instructing that no more were to be taken on.

10. Intelligence Report, n.d. but *c.* 1702, CH 1/2/29/569, NAS.

11. Tarbert: from the Gaelic *tairbeart*, 'an isthmus'. It formed a low lying through-route between the hills.

12. The name of the loch-side farm, *Slios garbh* ('wild slope') aptly describes the landscape here.

13. Its origin indicated by its name 'Torarry': from the Gaelic *tor araidh* ('shieling summit').

14. Torarry does not appear in the 1610 charter, being then a shieling, but it appears in its own right, i.e., as a farm, in the 1726 document. It cannot be proved that the change took place towards the end of the seventeenth century, but this was a common occurrence at that date in the West Highlands, in an attempt to cater for a growing tenant population: cf. Whyte I. (1995), chap. 14. In all, eight ruins of habitations may still be seen on the hill.

15. Bishop Nicolson stated that all the houses he saw in the West Highlands, apart from those of the chiefs and very highest gentlemen, were of this type – Bishop Nicolson, report to Propaganda, 1700 (in Latin), SM 3/1, SCA. And visitors to the Highlands even after this date remarked how little the tacksmen's houses differed from those of their tenants: cf. Burt E. (1754; 1974 edn), p. 193. For good accounts of the various local styles of vernacular building at this date, see Fenton A. and Walker B. (1981), and Dunbar J. (1966), passim.

16. Synod of Argyll minutes of meetings, Petition, 17.10.1700, CH 2/557/7, NAS.

17. Synod of Argyll minutes of meetings, October 1701, CH 2/557/4, NAS, p. 21. The schoolmaster was George Panton – see Thomas Innes to William Leslie, 13.10.1701, BL, SCA. He had previously run the school on the Isle of Canna – see Thomas Innes to Lewis Innes, 9.8.1698, BL, SCA.

18. Cf. Ferguson W. 'The Problems of the Established Church in the West Highlands and Islands in the Eighteenth Century' (1969–71 J), p. 19. Ferguson also shows how relatively weak the Kirk itself was in many parts of the Highlands outside Argyll at this time, only a dozen years after the Revolution Settlement, with many of the old pre-Settlement ministers still in post, a shortage of Gaelic-speaking clergy, poor, and indifferently supported by the local heritors.

19. 'Proclamation for Apprehending Seminary-Priests, Jesuits, and other Trafficking Papists', 17.3.1704, RH 14/550, NAS. The proclamation's wording makes it clear that it was issued in direct reponse to pressure from the General Assembly. The requirement that the lists be presented to the Privy Council within three months proved hopelessly unrealistic, and, as we can see from the lists sent in (*Miscellany of Maitland Club*, vol. ii, part iii, 1843), the ministers' responses were patchy. A second proclamation was issued a year later, imposing the responsibility for compiling the lists on the local chiefs and landlords – 'Proclamation Anent Papists', 9.2.1705, RH 14/550, NAS.

20. They were Frs McFie, O'Hagan and O'Shiel. Re their leaving and the impossibility of filling their places – Thomas and Lewis Innes to James Gordon, 16.11.1704, BL, SCA.

21. Based on Thomson J. op. cit., espec. p. 402; part of Thomson's account is printed in Forbes Leith W. op. cit., p. 218. Invergarry Castle, the ancestral seat of MacDonell of Glengarry, had been occupied by Government troops since the '89.

22. The present account based on Bishop Gordon's Journal, Latin and English versions, SM 3/9/3 and 4 respectively, SCA.

23. George Douglas was ordained deacon at the Scots College Paris in 1706. Since then he had been staying with Bishop Gordon in Banffshire. He was also known as Dalgleish.

24. He had been obliged to go to the point of Ardnish, the part of Arisaig closest to Moidart, to where many of the Moidart people came by boat. The place is still known as Port na h-Aifrinne, 'the harbour of the Mass'.

25. It seems to have been the general practice at the time to preach before rather than during Mass, perhaps in order to minimise the time that the priest

would be vested and thus liable to arrest. The practice was maintained even on occasions such as this when the celebrant was among friends and in no danger whatever.

26. Re seventeenth- and eighteenth-century Catholic worship, see Dilworth M., chap. 8 of Forrester D. and Murray D. (eds) (1984). Re the rosary, see McRoberts D. (1972 J), pp. 81ff. Re family devotions, see the example from Deeside in the last decade of the seventeenth century in Anderson W. J. (1967 J), pp. 151ff. Some of the Gaelic 'occasional' prayers are used to this day, especially in the Isles; many others have been preserved in Carmichael A. (ed.) (from 1900), 6 vols.

27. He would make twenty such pastoral journeys in all.

28. Bishop Gordon to Lewis Innes, 12.10.1707, BL, SCA. Those whom the bishop 'reconciled' to the Church were persons who had either given up the practice of their faith (often for want of a priest visiting their neighbourhood), or who had been attending Protestant worship (again often for the same reason) without actually giving up their own faith.

29. Bishop Gordon to Thomas Innes, 20.11.1707, BL, SCA.

30. James Gordon 'Narratio' to the cardinals of Propaganda, 1703 (in Latin), SM 3/8, SCA, espec. sections 25–28.

31. Bishop Gordon to Thomas Innes, 20.11.1707, BL, SCA. Lewis Innes supported the Mission with great generosity over several decades. His wealth derived in part from a pension from James III (as a member of his court in exile). Bishop Gordon judged James Carnegy of the Edinburgh station to be the one man in Scotland capable of running the proposed seminary, but he could not spare him from his duties in the capital (see also note 35 infra.)

32. Bishop Nicolson to Propaganda, 1.11.1706, BL, SCA, referring to three schools, two of which had previously been destroyed by the military. The local tradition is that the Arisaig schools were at Carnach and Morroch. These two farms, still in existence, are about a mile apart and quite close to Glen House, one of Clanranald's residences, near to the present village of Arisaig.

33. It is probable but not certain that the school was at Cross, and that the teacher was Alexander Paterson – cf. Clapperton W. (1870; transcript, Wilson G., 1901), p. 1707. Re the school at Barra, Bishop Gordon to Lewis Innes, 12.10.1707, BL, SCA.

34. The most detailed (and illustrated) account of Highland agricultural equipment is in Dwelly E. (1901–10), passim alphabetically; the present account also based on Fenton A. (1976), Fenton A. (1962–63 J), and Grant I. F. (1961; 1995 edn), chap. 5.

35. Haldane A. R. B. (1952; 1973 edn), passim; Whyte I. (1979), pp. 235ff. The expansion was due to the opening up of the English market, especially through the reduction of cross-border duties and the Irish Cattle Act of 1666 which had effectively killed off competition from Ireland. Some West Highland drovers took their cattle all the way to East Anglia, where they were fattened for the English market; others passed them on to English drovers in the Lowlands or at the Border. Cf. Whyte I. (1970), p. 70.

36. Cf. e.g. MacInnes I. A. 'Scottish Jacobitism: in Search of a Movement', chap. 5 of Devine T. M. and Young J. R. (1999), p. 74.

37. Gibson J. S. (1998) – re Carnegy, pp. 43, 47, 62 and 89; re Bishop Nicolson, p. 59. And see Carnegy's correspondence with Hooke in Macray W. D. (ed.) (1870), vol. i, pp. 3034ff. It may have been because of Mr Carnegy's ongoing involvement that it had been impossible to release him to run the proposed seminary (cf. note 31 supra.)

38. 'By the Queen a Proclamation', 1708 (no more detailed date), RH 14/569, NAS.

39. Bishop Gordon to Fr Tamburini, General of the Society of Jesus, 3.6.1710, in Forbes Leith W. op. cit., pp. 256f.

40. Letter Robert Fordyce SJ to Fr Tamburini, 17.12.1709, in Forbes Leith W. op. cit., pp. 254f.

41. Combating Catholicism was one of the explicit aims of its Constitution, as were instilling loyalty to the Crown and replacing Gaelic by English as the spoken language of the Highlands.

42. For a detailed contemporary account, covering the period of the present biography, see Belsches A. (1774), copies GD 95/11/1 and GD 95/14/19, NAS. The first SSPCK school in a Catholic area was opened to serve Eigg and Canna in 1728 – see Register 1710–61 enclosed with SSPCK Records, GD 95/9/1, NAS.

43. Thomson J. 'Some Account of the State of Religion' etc., in Forbes Leith W. op. cit., p. 265.

44. Bishop Gordon was forty-five at this date, Bishop Nicolson about twenty years his senior, and far less able to trek through the harsh terrain of the West Highlands or cross the Minch to the Islands.

45. Bishop Gordon to Thomas Innes, 17.10.1713, BL, SCA, where he writes, in reference to Eilean Bàn, of going back to 'where I was three years ago.'

46. Bishop Gordon to William Stuart, 19.6.1711, BL, SCA.

47. The difference between the Highland and Lowland Church had been highlighted in successive reports to Propaganda, including those of Prefect William Ballentine in 1660 – (in Latin), copy SM 2/3, SCA, also printed with English translation in Anderson W. J. (ed.) (1957 J); and Alexander Leslie twenty-one years later – English version SM 2/9/3, SCA. Re the running of the Franciscan Mission from Bonamargy, Co. Antrim, from 1626–47 cf. Giblin C. (1964), passim; re Propaganda's consideration of the plan of re-establishing the See of the Isles, and the proposal in 1637 that Patrick Hagerty OFM be nominated bishop, see MacLean D. (1952 J), p. 8; according to the early eighteenth-century historian of the Mission, Thomas Innes, Ranald MacDonald had been proposed for nomination in 1634 – cf. Anderson W. J. (1956 J), p. 119, and Hay M. V. (1929), appendix V, p. 249. Re the Hebrides being placed under the jurisdiction of the archbishop of Armagh from 1669, see Moran P. F. (1861), pp. 172ff., and Giblin C. (1974–75 J).

3

Eilean Bàn and the '15 (1712–16)

Bishop Gordon returned to the West in the spring of 1712. He was anxious to pursue his idea for a seminary there, using the money previously donated by Lewis Innes,[1] and as soon as he arrived he met the priests of the area to discuss his plans with them. He also spoke with Allan MacDonald of Morar, since the site he had in mind, Eilean Bàn, though closer to Glengarry's land on the north side of the loch, was in fact a part of the South Morar estate.[2] Whether the laird demanded a rental for it we do not know, but the talks must have been productive, for on his return home the bishop reported to the Paris principal that he had made arrangements for setting up the seminary, and asked him to send his nephew George Innes back to Scotland as soon as possible to run it.[3]

During the visit he also made a point of meeting and befriending the gentlemen's sons of the area, and discussing the priestly life with those who seemed interested and suitable. There was no recent tradition of West Highland youths choosing the priesthood – most aspired to follow in the footsteps of the fighting men of the clan – and he knew that if he was to catch their imagination he must do so early, before they turned their thoughts elsewhere. Hugh MacDonald struck him as one of the most promising of those he met.

George Innes arrived in Scotland that October, but Bishop Gordon's hopes of sending him to the West at once were dashed when he saw his wretched state of health.[4] The young man suffered from both asthma and the ague, and spent the whole winter convalescing at his parents' home. The bishop returned to Eilean Bàn the following April, and was now even thinking of setting up and running the seminary himself, if he could find no-one else.[5] Meantime he took the opportunity to renew his contacts with the boys whom he had met the previous year. By now it was a quite natural thing for the MacDonalds of Meoble to have him as their guest. His visits had become an accepted part of their family life, and he was keeping Hugh – though the boy did not know it – like a Meoble salmon, on a long line.

His visit passed without anything definite achieved, however, and he spent a frustrating autumn in Edinburgh anxious to return. 'If I could get that length,' he wrote to Paris, 'I would strive still to be doing something in it one way or other & not lose time; for my life is passing off, & 'twill be long ere any fruits can be expected thence, however diligent we be.'[6] But his work kept him in the capital all winter, and it was not until the following March (1714) that he was able to get back to the West. He left instructions that George Innes should follow as soon as his health allowed.[7]

He waited until after the busy Easter season before opening the seminary, and then only stayed long enough to see the house furnished and supplied with a rudimentary stock of books, before continuing his itinerary to the Outer Isles.[8] On his return he gathered the three or four boys he had selected, including Hugh, and moved in with them for a few weeks in order to prepare them and establish a regimen and a basic curriculum ready for Mr Innes' arrival. Since Hugh was now fifteen, it is likely that his preparation included reception of the sacraments of Eucharist and Confirmation, and that his first Holy Communion was received on the island from his bishop's hands.

Bishop Gordon would have preferred to stay until George Innes arrived, but he had pressing work elsewhere, and as soon as he received word that he was definitely coming he himself set out for the South. There was a gap of a month or more between his departure and the young man's arrival,[9] during which the boys were lodged in the gentlemen's houses in Morar, Hugh himself staying at his own home, perhaps with a fellow student. When Mr Innes reached Morar in July he gathered them together, and he and they were taken by boat and left on the island's tiny sandy beach, close beside the house that was to be their home.

We can well imagine the apprehension as well as the excitement in Hugh's mind as he stood there on the strand. He was only five minutes from the shore, and only a short step from Meoble: were it not for the other islands in the loch he could actually have seen the entrance to his glen. He was not cutting adrift from home entirely; not like one of the other boys who had come across the Minch.[10] But it was still a step into the unknown. How long might he be staying here? Perhaps five years, with a further four or five at Paris or Rome. Or, if he were to complete his whole training here, he could be staying ten. The priesthood offered a tacksman's son no hope of worldly gain, but on the contrary every prospect of poverty, sacrifice, and a fugitive's life outside the Law. What then had brought him to Eilean Bàn? Only his own devout nature, nurtured since birth in a devout family and community, fired by the lives of Mr Munro, Mr Cahassy and the rest, and won over by the discreet prompting and example of Bishop Gordon, could have given him the discernment and the courage to answer his vocation.

The dense, barely penetrable growth of timber that covers Eilean Bàn today is the result of planting in the nineteenth century. In 1714 the island was largely bare of trees, and used for grazing. The house they were to live in had been Mr Cahassy's until his death ten years before, and had been occupied only occasionally since then. It must have been a building of one or at most two rooms, built of turf upon a course of stones, with a roof of turf underlay and heather thatch, much like those at Meoble. Remains of the course of stones, as well as a garden wall of earth and stones, may still be traced today among the membresia, moss and self-seeded birch that cover this corner of the island.[11]

In time seven students were enrolled, and the community soon outgrew the house. They saved space wherever they could – clearing the beds away during the day to create their classroom, for instance – but given the master's need for privacy, and the routines of cooking, dining, prayer and religious services, they found a house of three rooms their very minimum requirement. So there must have been some early building.[12]

George Innes was thirty-one, and had spent his whole adult life in the urbane, intellectual world of the Scots College Paris. He was a devout young priest and a scholar. But he was useless with his hands, too otherworldly to deal in practical affairs, so inept in money matters that he could not be trusted to look after them alone, and inclined to be easily rattled.[13] By no means the ideal man, in short, to build and take sole charge of an enterprise in which he must be master, spiritual director, housekeeper, and guardian of the purse. On the other hand, it would have been hard to find one more apt for giving boys leadership in the two most important aspects of their training – piety and learning. Thankfully also, the all too common problem for incomers, the upsetting effect of the West Highland climate on their health, seems not to have touched him, and he was able to settle well and quickly to his task.[14]

The bishops' original intention was for the seminary to prepare some of the boys for the Scots colleges, and to give others their entire training up to ordination.[15] Apart from the two oldest none had more than a rudimentary education before they arrived. They would therefore have started at or near the beginning of a Latin course planned to last five years, similar to that taught in all grammar schools in Scotland at this time, but with certain additions – Scripture, spiritual writings, lives of the saints – appropriate to their calling. The intention was that those transferring to the colleges would do so at the end of this course, while those staying on would progress to a further five years of philosophy and theology similar to that taught in the colleges. But events would overtake these plans, and during Eilean Bàn's brief existence most of the boys probably never got beyond the first half of the Latin course.

Paris must have provided the blueprint for almost every aspect of Eilean Bàn. Both Bishop Gordon and George Innes had been educated there, and the latter remained very much under the influence of his uncle Thomas, the prefect of studies at Paris, in regard to matters educational. But the bishops were determined that the new seminary would avoid what they saw as the over-theoretical learning of the Scots colleges abroad – mere 'intellectual trifling', Bishop Nicolson called it [16] – which they believed offered a quite unrealistic preparation for the rigours of the Scottish Mission. Its purpose, as Bishop Gordon saw it, was to teach 'true, solid & zealous piety, ... the knowledge of things not nice, sublime and speculative, but practical, popular and edifying, ... and [also] the skill of Western language'. [17] With George Innes in charge he knew he could count on the first. As to the second, he urged the young master, to whom the practical did not come as second nature, to adapt the Paris courses and make them more relevant. Regrettably, 'the skill of Western language' was not a possibility in the present circumstances: Mr Innes had little or no Gaelic, so that the languages, inside and outside the classroom, would of necessity be confined to English and Latin. [18]

Following the timetable of Paris, Hugh and his classmates were roused from their beds at 5 a.m., and began their studies at about 5.45, with Mass shortly after 7.00, breakfast at 8.00, lessons thereafter until lunch and again (after some recreation) until mid-afternoon, supper at about 7.00, and bed at 9.00 or 9.15. [19] Such a routine fitted well with a self-contained community like Eilean Bàn, where the students lived as well as learned. And it seemed natural enough to Scottish boys, for an early start and long working hours were normal practice in the burgh schools at this time, where it was quite usual for pupils to begin lessons at 6 a.m. and to endure up to ten hours at the desk. [20]

The seminary was wholly dependent upon others for its provisions. The boys were not allowed off the island – the site had after all been chosen precisely to shield them from the outside world – so George Innes either made the journey to 'the Mainland' himself for their weekly supplies, or arranged to have them ferried across from Camus Ruadh, the nearest point on the South Morar estate.

In its hours, its Spartan comforts, its set-apartness, Eilean Bàn was consciously placing itself in the centuries-old monastic tradition, and we may guess that it even adopted certain particular practices of the monasteries. The monks' Great Silence between evening recreation and morning breakfast, for example, and silence at the main meal of the day, would have been especially appropriate in a seminary, and were already the practice in the Scots colleges abroad. But it was perhaps not so much the quasi-monastic regimen as the strict limit on freedom set by the island itself, and by the primitive buildings, that was the boys' chief penance. The latter must have taxed them and their anxious master to the limit on the many days of rain that Morar enjoys. And when the skies were cloudless blue, though there was swimming in the loch and space enough on the island to race and stretch their legs, the world beyond the water must have looked even greener and freer to their young eyes.

Shortly after he returned from the West in summer 1714 Bishop Gordon had been in touch with the Inneses at the Scots College Paris, expressing to them in coded but unambiguous language his hopes for an early rising.[21] A year later, almost to the day, the Jacobite standard was raised on the Braes of Mar.

The majority of the 12,000 men eventually mustered to march behind it hailed from the Grampian Highlands and the North-East. Almost none mustered from the Outer Isles, while those from the Western Highlands were drawn mainly from the lands of Clanranald and Glengarry.

Alasdair Dubh MacDonell of Glengarry, who had carried King James' standard at Killiecrankie in the '89, and who because of it had seen his six-storied Invergarry Castle occupied by Government troops ever since, called up 500 men as soon as he heard that the Rising was on, and within the month recaptured his ancestral home.

Allan MacDonald of Clanranald, another veteran of the '89, hurried from his Uist home at Ormaclate to Caisteal Tioram, the 'Dry Castle' on a little spit of land in the mouth of Loch Moidart that was his mainland stronghold. There he gathered 400 of his men and sent them ahead to join Mar's forces in the East. He himself stayed back a day. Perhaps he knew that the cause was in the hands of an incompetent, and was likely to fail. If so, Caisteal Tioram would be taken, and his lands and people could expect no mercy. Rather than risk such an outcome he gave secret orders to one of his tacksmen to torch the castle as soon as he was away. Then climbing up into the hill he headed east, turning to look one last time upon his 500-year-old home, and his lands stretching as far as the western horizon. Before he reached Glenfinnan the castle was in flames.[22]

On 13 November, at Sheriffmuir, the Clanranalds took their customary place on the right flank, with the Glengarries close by. Allan Clanranald had his men in formation, and had moved his horse into the van to lead the charge, when he suddenly fell, hit by a ball in the chest. Those about him could see that he was dying. The flank hesitated, and seemed likely to break, when Alasdair Dubh galloped to the front, and shouting to the Clanranalds and his own men, 'Revenge today, mourning tomorrow!' himself led the charge. The left flank of the enemy broke, turned and scattered. Allan was carried dying from the field.

With superior numbers to the tune of four to one and his enemy's left flank broken, Mar could and should have moved in to clinch the victory. But he disengaged, leaving the battle indecisive, the moral victory Argyll's, and the tide of the war turning against him.

By January his army was in retreat, and before the end of the month he and James had taken ship at Montrose and abandoned their followers to their own devices. Most escaped into the Highlands, where two weeks later they dispersed and made their best way home.

The Clanranald men, their chief and their cause both lost, reached Moidart to find the charred remains of his castle. Many headed for Uist, from where some of the officers took ship to France.[23] The Glengarry men could not appear freely in their own land, which that spring was plundered by the troops of Colonel Clayton, who shot the cattle, stole horses, mistreated both women and children, and finally in August put Invergarry Castle to the torch.

In the persecution that followed the Catholic clergy were prime targets. Several of Bishop Gordon's relatives were arrested and, as he himself reported to Paris, a similar fate befell Bishop Nicolson despite his age and infirmity.[24] Most of the priests, he added, were being 'constantly threaten'd, & often sought for', and had been driven into the hills, where some had suffered irreparable damage to their health. Several were threatening to quit the Mission. A few were doing extraordinary work against all odds, but generally, as he phrased it in the usual coded language, 'times were very hard for any kind of trade or business'.

The Catholics of the West were especially hard hit, that summer and for some years thereafter. With the death of Allan Clanranald at Sheriffmuir they had lost one acknowledged as 'the most gallant and generous young gentleman among the clans',[25] who – in the view of Bishop Nicolson – had done more than any other man to ensure the Church's survival in the Highlands and Islands.[26] The estate passed to his unmarried brother Ranald, who soon after escaped to Paris, where he would remain until his death in 1725. Alasdair Dubh of Glengarry would live for only five more years, and on his death in 1721 would be succeeded by his son John, a mere shadow of his father and more noted for indolence and insobriety than action. The real and the psychological effects of the death of the one chief and the eclipse of the other, and the spectre of their burned castles, could hardly have been greater. It must have seemed that the leadership and protection the Church had long enjoyed in the lands of Clanranald and Glengarry were all but swept away.

They were now a no-go area for bishops and clergy. 'I can't get to West,' Bishop Gordon reported on 1 June, 'thou Long extreamly; that country is allmost desperate & will probably do something very odd; & my friends can hardly have access to me or I to them, the ways are so unsafe.'[27] George Innes was entrenched on Eilean Bàn, unable to do much 'for the stirr of folks about him', but the seminary was still being 'kept in some manner, at least some of the prentices together'. Several of the boys had been sent away for their own safety. Hugh, being the nearest to home, was probably one of those still hanging on. But its survival could only be a matter of time.

In December George, first duke of Gordon, died and was succeeded by his son Alexander. The family, Catholics for generations, were the most powerful in the north-east of Scotland. The new heir, whose mother was a staunch Jacobite but whose Episcopalian wife Henrietta Mordaunt was an equally convinced Whig, had fought for James at Sheriffmuir, but after it had distanced himself from the cause and opened his castle to government troops. By these means, though he suffered a brief spell in prison, he contrived to retain the family title and estate.[28]

The Catholic tenants on the extensive Gordon lands in Banffshire and Lochaber had long enjoyed the protection of the first duke, and now seemed set to receive even more effective support from the second, who was a man of redoubtable ability, character and mettle. Indeed, his influence would carry beyond the borders of his estate and, with the weakening of leadership in the West meantime, he would become the mainstay of Catholicism in Scotland. For a dozen years, until his death in 1728, the Gordon lands of the North-East would replace the Western Highlands as the nerve centre of the Church.[29]

With Eilean Bàn's situation parlous – unprotected and too close to the sea to be safe from surprise attack – it was to the Gordon lands that the bishop now turned for somewhere to relocate it. And he found what he was looking for at the furthest, remotest end of the duke's estate, high in the hills of Banffshire.

Close to the head of the Braes of Glenlivet there was a small turf house, tucked in a hollow of the land. It had been built only that summer by John Gordon, the priest of Glenlivet, who had been an active supporter of the Jacobite cause in the Rising, and had now moved up from the lower end of the glen to get away from his Hanoverian neighbours. It was the very last house in the Braes, lying at the foot of a shieling known as the *Tom* or Hill of Scalan from which it took its name, and hard against the bank of the Crombie burn that issued from the great black heathery hills close by (plate 3).[30]

On Gordon land, at the extreme end of the Catholic Braes, approachable only by hill tracks or by a path across a treacherous moss that required local knowledge to traverse, this Bishop Gordon decided would be as safe a place as any for the seminary. He at once consulted with John Gordon and persuaded him to move out and take up the station at Mortlach down in the Banffshire Lowlands. He then got word to George Innes to gather the boys and bring all who were willing to come, with whatever sacred and household goods they could carry, and as soon as possible, since early October would be the very latest they could safely travel.

Their route from Morar lay over the mountains into Glen Pean, then beside Loch Arkaig, across the open breadths of the Great Glen, along Glen Spean in the shadow of the Nevis range, over Badenoch into wide green Stath Spey, through Abernethy to Strath Avon, and thence up Glen Conglas and over the last hill. It was a journey of a week or more even if led by one accustomed to hard travel, and George Innes was scarcely that. For Hugh, everything on the road was a new experience. As they moved east the crags and tumbling burns of his own mountains gave way to great rounded hills and broad rivers. And here and there at the roadside they passed dead or dying animals, unmistakable signs of the cattle plague that was to strike the Highlands that autumn.

They arrived at last, towards the middle of September, with peats already stacked beside the house, the dark cattle of nearby Tomnalienan farm among the junipers on the Hill of Scalan, and further downstream the corn yellow and soon to be cut.[31] For Hugh, as he stood beneath the lintel and looked about him, the overwhelming feeling was of an *inland* place. There was no cry of gull or oystercatcher, no scent of the sea just over the hill. Like the other boys he was determined to settle to his new life at Scalan and make a success of it, but the homesickness must have been like an ache in him, and the feeling would stay with him all the days he lived there.

Notes

1. Bishop Gordon to Lewis Innes, 15.4.1712, BL, SCA.
2. Eilean Bàn is not specifically referred to in rental documents, but MacDonald of Morar is described as 'the proprietor of it' at the time of his meeting there in 1746 – *The Scots Magazine*, appendix for year 1747, p. 614. The coastal farms of Buorblach and Cill Chuimein in North Morar also belonged to the South Morar estate (see Map 1).
3. Bishop Gordon to Lewis Innes, 23.7.1712, BL.
4. Bishop Gordon to Lewis Innes, 9.10.1712, BL.
5. Bishop Gordon to Lewis Innes, 23.3.1713, BL.
6. Bishop Gordon to Thomas Innes, 17.10.1713, BL.
7. Bishop Gordon to Thomas Innes, 16.3.1714, BL, written on the day he set out.
8. J. Thomson 'An Account of the State of Religion' etc. (*c.* 1780), Th/10, SCA, based on contemporary correspondence, states that he took in the Isles that spring.
9. Bishop Gordon to Thomas Innes, 13.8.1714, BL, written at Drummond Castle: 'nevew Geo: did not come when Fife [himself] was there, but went after I came South.'

10. Allan MacDonald, son of the tacksman of Stoneybridge, South Uist, was two years his senior.

11. These remains were easier to see when Dom Odo Blundell visited the site early in the twentieth century – Blundell O. (vol. ii, 1917), p. 94; and when Fr Antony Ross sketched it more than forty years ago. It is most unlikely that the garden dates from this time: very probably it was laid out when the seminary was reopened in the 1730s – cf. pp. 77f. infra.

12. Of the seven students only three names have come down to us – Allan MacDonald, John MacLachlan, and Hugh himself. No documents and virtually no correspondence have survived concerning Eilean Bàn, in fact, and my description of the seminary is of necessity largely conjectural, based on comparable contemporary practice in the schools of Scotland and the Scots colleges abroad, and knowledge of the local topography.

13. This at least was Bishop Gordon's opinion – cf. '[He] is so timorous and helpless in these hard times ... not having much discretionem spirituum ... he understands so litle oeconomy, that another must be with him to help him' – Bishop Gordon to Lewis Innes, 25.3.1718, BL; 'His chief fault is to be easily discourag'd especially in temp^{ls} [temporal matters], in which he is one of the most shiftless & least skillfull you know' – Bishop Gordon to Thomas Innes, 10.1.1727, BL.

14. 'Nevew Geo: is doing well, so I am inform'd from thence' – Bishop Gordon to Thomas Innes, 12.10.1714 (a fragment), BL; re upset to health being a very common problem for incomers, see e.g. Austin MacDonald to Propaganda, 10.9.1771, in Blundell O. (vol. ii, 1917), p. 136.

15. James Gordon 'Narratio' to Propaganda, 1703, SM 3/8 (in Latin), SCA, especially section 26, makes it clear that giving the boys their entire training in Scotland was the preferred option if possible.

16. Bishop Nicolson 'Report to Propaganda', 1697 (in Latin), English translation in Bellesheim A. (1890), vol. IV, appendix VI. William Ballentine the Prefect Apostolic had made much the same criticism to Propaganda some forty years before – *Report*, c. 1660, in Anderson W. J. (ed.) (1957 J), p. 114.

17. Bishop Gordon to William Stuart, Scots agent in Rome, 8.12.1713, BL.

18. It was common practice in the Scottish Grammar Schools at this date to use Latin as the actual medium of communication. At Aberdeen G. S. censors ensured that it was the language of the playground as well as the classroom – Scotland J. (1969), vol. I, pp. 57ff; the pupils of Dumfries G. S. were expected to speak Latin in school and outside it! – Grant J. (1876), pp. 161ff.

19. 'Statuta Collegii Scotorum Parisiensis' (in Latin), CA 10/2, SCA, cap. vii Regula Generales, section 5 'Ordo diurnus diebus legibilibus sive non feriatis', and Section 6 'Ordo diurnus diebus feriatis sive non legibilibus'.

20. For example, the hours at the High School of Edinburgh in the seventeenth century were 6.00–9.00, 10.00–12.00, 1.30–6.00 – Ross W. C. A. (1934; 1949 edn), p. 45.

21. Bishop Gordon to Thomas Innes, 7.9.1714, BL.

22. The present account based on MacDonald C. (1889), pp. 92f, itself based on local and family traditions. The place where Allan Clanranald reputedly

stopped to look back is still known as *Aite Suidhe Mhic 'ic Ailein*, 'the sitting place of the son of the son of Allan'.

23. Tayler A. and H. (1936), p. 229.
24. Bishop Gordon to Thomas Innes, 1.6.1716, BL. One of the bishop's immediate family, George Gordon of Glastirim, was among the Banffshire lairds who surrendered at Banff in March 1716. They were held under slack house arrest, from which they made an easy escape.
25. MacDonald C. op. cit., pp. 94f.
26. Bishop Nicolson 'Report to Propaganda', 1700, loc. cit.
27. Bishop Gordon to Thomas Innes, 1.6.1716, BL.
28. Tayler A. and H. op. cit., pp. 204 ff. At his trial he was described as a 'trimmer'. He was imprisoned at Edinburgh from March to early November 1716.
29. This would also be the view of the Church's enemies – see further pp. 56 and 65 infra.
30. John Gordon moved up to the Braes about Easter 1716, and sheltered for several months in a barn or shieling hut on the south-west side of the Hill of Scalan until receiving permission from the landlord, Grant of Tomnavoulin, to build his house – cf. Bishop J. Geddes 'A Brief Historical Account of the Seminary at Scalan', 1777, CS 1/3, para 5, SCA.
31. The exact date is not known, but a letter from Bishop Gordon to the Scots agent in Rome written towards the end of October suggests that the new seminary was open and established by this date – Bishop Gordon to William Stuart, 22.10.1716, BL.

4

The Scalan Years (1716–25)

Everything about Hugh's new home was different, strange. Where his own glen in the West lay almost at sea level, this was a broad upland saucer where the corn was slower to yellow, and where just a few hundred yards from his door the hills rose abruptly to the watershed. Here the rivers ran north not west, the Crombie burn into the Livet, the Livet into the Spey, and the broad Spey into the coastal Lowlands and the sea. Gaelic was the language of the local farms, but it was almost as strange to his ears as that of the Irish priests at home, for this was its most easterly redoubt in Scotland, and beyond this nearest wall of hills the everyday language was English.[1] Compared with the crags of Morar, where eagles soared, this landscape was upland rather than Highland. Looking north, across the almost treeless Braes, beyond the smoke of scattered farm-towns, it seemed to him that the distant peak of Ben Rinnes, standing upright like a grey set-square upon a blueprint, was the one undoubted mountain in this landscape of hills. In the last days of summer, when he first arrived, it was a world of green and blue and purple; but within a month, and through the long winter, it would turn into a land of grey and dun and black.

Only the house itself seemed much the same as he was used to at home. Two-roomed, built of turf upon a latticework of withies, and thatched with heather, it strikingly resembled the tenants' houses at Meoble.[2] Attached to it was a finger of land of some seventeen acres extending almost to the top of the Hill of Scalan, which the new seminary rented for the purpose of growing bere and oats and grazing a few cattle. Within a few months they would also acquire ten acres of good flat land facing the house across the Crombie burn, which was ideal for grazing cattle and horses, and to which they gave the name 'The Park'. In time they would enclose both areas within a single head-dyke, since it was the bishop's intention that Scalan should be a working farm as well as a seminary, in order that it could be made as self-supporting as possible.

This, however, was in the future. For though the new seminary was in fact to survive for eighty-three years, and become an irreplaceable cornerstone for the recovery of the Catholic faith in Scotland, there was nothing in its first few months to suggest that this would be so. Bishop

40

Gordon at this time saw it merely as a brief *pied-à-terre* for Eilean Bàn, rather than as something likely to last.

George Innes moved out before the winter, almost as soon as the boys had settled in, complaining that his health could not take the Scalan climate, and the bishop was obliged to replace him by the young priest, Alexander Smith.[3] The new man made no favourable first impression when he arrived. He had no presence at all. He was diminutive, so noticeably so that his fellow priests, when writing coded letters, often referred to him by the alias 'Mr Short'. His face was darkened and disfigured with scrofula, and his voice was weak and piping. He was as incompetent in financial matters as his predecessor, a failing exacerbated in his case by his generosity to a fault with his own and the Mission's money.

But in fact he turned out to be an admirable replacement. For, again not unlike George Innes, he was also a man of disarming piety, and a scholar, and when he warmed to his theme a highly gifted teacher. As one colleague expressed it, 'Had he a better coram vobis and utterance to his knowlidge, he would have appeared a great man, but the want of this made him ever seem litle to the most part of people.'[4] But Bishop Gordon knew his worth,[5] and the students themselves soon learned to look beyond appearances to the real man.

The following summer the bishop made his most ambitious journey yet, visiting places where the people had not seen a priest for years. He discovered them reduced to misery in the backlash that had followed the '15, and he gave whatever material and spiritual succour he could. 'I went there furnish'd with all I could scrap together,' he told the Scots agent, '& yet I was forc'd to borrow severall times, & return'd with hardly a farthing in my pocket.'[6]

His journey gave him fresh evidence of the shortage of priests in the West Highlands, and of their human frailties. While hardship had brought out the heroic in some of his team, it had exposed the worst in others. Scalan was his long-term hope, for providing the kind of home-produced priests he needed, trained 'with such mortification as might fitt them not to weary of the toyls to be undergone in the West', and though he was now penniless and in debt he was determined not to let it fold.[7]

At the end of the year he was forced to release Mr Smith to the Scots College Paris. He had no-one remotely comparable to replace him, and was obliged to draft George Innes again, despite that man's shortcomings and his continuing refusal to live in.[8]

A further problem was the small student roll, which made it virtually impossible to run the preparatory course for those intending transfer to the colleges, as well as the longer course for those completing their entire training at Scalan. Only two boys were following the latter – George J. Gordon of Fochabers and Hugh himself – a situation that was neither economic nor intellectually stimulating. The attempt to make Scalan serve two purposes was already causing strain, and Bishop Gordon even toyed with the thought of opening a separate seminary for the transferees. But the Mission's purse would not run to such a solution. Hugh and George J. Gordon had to make do with half the master's attention, and spark off each other as best they could.

Over the next year or two routines of 'best practice' were developed at Scalan, based on the ideals and aims of the Mission, the experience of seminaries elsewhere, and the realities of life in the Braes. Though these were not codified until the summer of 1722, when Bishop Gordon himself drew them together into a set of *Rules*, most of them must have been in place *de facto* by about 1718.

The priority was to train the boys in piety and learning, but of the two the first was considered 'infinitely more valuable' than the second, which indeed without it was to the bishop's way of thinking 'but a sword in a madmans hand'.[9] From these two principles all the seminary's regulations and practices followed.

To foster piety time was set aside for prayer, not only every morning and evening but before meals and when beginning study. Meditation, memorising passages of the Bible, and 'some pious lecture' were made daily routines. Meals were taken in silence, with one boy reading to the rest from the scriptures or an edifying book, while on Sundays and holy days everyone was expected to join in the Divine Office. The boys confessed fortnightly and received Holy Communion at least once a month.[10] In the name of piety, in fact, Scalan was made almost as truly an island as Eilean Bàn itself, for Hugh and his fellows were under orders to converse as little as possible with strangers, servants and tradesmen, never to enter the kitchen, and to 'shun the company of women entirely'.[11]

As regards learning, the core curriculum for junior students remained the Latin Grammatica. The method of study was to memorise a passage from one of the Roman authors by heart each morning, and then to spend the rest of the day subjecting it to analysis, picking out grammatical points and new vocabulary. Other subjects – Church History, French (in preparation for Paris), Geography, History, 'Chronology', 'Critick', and Gaelic (in preparation for a future Highland posting) – were fitted in whenever time allowed: these were considered 'easier studys' and something of a 'diversion', because they did not involve rote learning and were taught through the medium of English.

At a time when life in the grammar schools of Scotland was one of authoritarian rule and almost unrelieved drudgery, the attitude to study at Scalan was notably caring, and built upon concepts of individual need and *mens sana in corpore sano* that seem remarkably modern, but in fact hark back to the traditions of Jesuit education and the balanced monastic day. As the *Rules* specified:

> Let the dayly time of their studys be proportion'd to what their health can bear; & let them never be dull'd by keeping them too Long close; but let them seek leave, when they want it, to go out a litle even out of time of recreation ... All must be left to the prudent management of the Master ... according to every one's age, state of health & genius.[12]

Bishop Geddes, who was educated at the Scots College Rome and who as master at Scalan in the 1760s had the experience of applying the *Rules*, remarked on their similarity to those of his own *alma mater* and the other Scots colleges; and there is no doubt that Scalan imitated them in both letter and spirit, as far as was practicable in a small turf house in the Scottish uplands.[13]

By 1720 Hugh and George J. Gordon had completed the Grammatica and were now in their first year of philosophy. From the evidence of his later correspondence, some of which was written in Latin, Hugh had mastered the language well and had a particular facility for elegant prose.[14] It is therefore quite likely that he had already by this date made a start on the rudiments of Greek, since the *Rules* allowed for students of proven competence in Latin to learn 'some litle of the Greek, & likewise of Rhetorick'. And since they also recommended 'somewhat of the Hebrew' for those seniors who like Hugh had 'a genius for tongues', he may have acquired the basics of that language also in his final years.

The boy who before coming to Scalan had never strayed a dozen miles from Meoble had already learned a great deal in his new home, from the masters, his fellow students, and the visitors who occasionally called. He still saw Bishop Gordon from time to time. The bishop had from the outset expressed his intention of living in at the college whenever his work allowed, and now as vicar apostolic of the Mission tried to include at least one annual visit in his crowded calendar.[15] In the summer of 1720 he stayed longer than usual, for he was worn out and his doctors had advised him to use his visit to rest and convalesce on the fresh air and goats' milk of the Braes.[16] During those weeks he spent as much time as possible with Hugh and George J. Gordon, the other senior student.

That summer another staff member arrived at the seminary. Archibald Anderson had spent ten years training for the priesthood in Paris, and had already been ordained a deacon when he was struck by a brain fever that left him disabled for life. Bishop Gordon had recalled him to Scotland, but did not dare promote him to the priesthood because the fever had impaired his self-control and left him prone to fits of anger in which he would come out with every kind of oath and obscenity. He brought him to Scalan to keep him out of the public eye. Mr Anderson settled well to his new home, strange choice though he was for a teacher of boys.[17] He too must have had an influence upon Hugh, if only to extend his by now quite fluent English in some new and unexpected directions.

From the evidence of two Church of Scotland reports from this date we know that George Innes was now living in at Scalan.[18] From these documents, also, it is clear that despite all precautions Scalan's existence was perfectly well known to its enemies, and that any hope it had of safety lay in keeping a low profile rather than in a pretence of real secrecy.

Living in the closed world of the seminary Hugh would perhaps barely have heard of the abortive Jacobite attempt on the West coast in 1720, that had ended in tragic farce on the heights above Glen Shiel.[19] But he must have heard from his own family of the event that was the main talking point in South Morar the following year, his uncle Allan's sale of Meoble as a wadset to MacDonald of Kinlochmoidart. The news reminded him that the same man had taken over Sliosmean and Sliosgarbh further up Glen Meoble in similar circumstances in 1704 when he was a young child. Now his own home had gone the same way.[20]

That his uncle had resorted to wadsetting Meoble – pawning it in plain English – must have alerted Hugh to the family's financial embarrassment. The following year the extent of that embarrassment was to emerge, when the laird was forced to sell most of the remaining part of his estate in Morar, and his holdings on Eigg, South Uist and Benbecula, to MacDonald of Clanranald for 13,000 merks (about £722 sterling), to clear his debt with him.[21]

In May 1722 George Innes moved out of Scalan to become chaplain at the family home at Balnacraig. His leaving was acrimonious, and against the express wish of Bishop Gordon.[22] Once again the students had to get used to a new master, and they found the man sent to them, John Alexander Grant, deeply pious but even more nervous and fussy than his predecessor. From Scalan's first days they had never enjoyed the continuity in teaching that they might have expected; nor had the seminary itself been given the continuity of leadership necessary to get it firmly established.

This might have been acceptable at the beginning, when it was not expected to be more than a temporary home. But now, six years on, it was obviously going to be a permanent fixture. Considerable building work had already been put into it.[23] A report presented to the General Assembly of the Church of Scotland at this time speaks of 'a fashionable house ... lately built ... for the better accommodation of this College', words that imply that the present house was not the original of 1716, but either a completely new building or at least a recent major extension. The Report also refers to 'suitable office houses' [outhouses] and 'a large garden and great Park for graseing well fenced about', evidence that the farm was now well established with barn and byre, that the community were growing their own vegetables and herbs, and that the major work of enclosing the ten-acre park was now complete. Such a substantial outlay of money and labour would only have been sanctioned by Bishop Gordon if he had already decided that Scalan had a long-term future.

Hugh and George J. Gordon had by now completed their philosophy course, and had made a start on theology. It was now time for them to receive the four minor orders of porter, reader, exorcist and acolyte, one step before the sub-diaconate on the road to the priesthood. Bishop Gordon arranged to make a prolonged stay at Scalan over the winter in order to supervise their preparation personally.[24] His stay also gave him the chance to judge the new master at first hand. He was not convinced that Mr Grant was the right man for Scalan, knowing that his piety tended to the scrupulous, and his scruples to indecision.

Mr Grant was glad of his company and support, but only felt the more at a loss after he left. He was brought to near-panic by the thought of his responsibility for the minds and souls of his students.[25] He had a horror of the desolate landscape of Upper Banffshire, and pined for the warmth and culture of Paris. He was the victim of a dilemma not unknown to the devout priest, torn between the call to service and the pull of the interior spiritual life. It can hardly be supposed that one so diffident, vacillating and overwrought could give the kind of authoritative leadership the students looked for. Though Hugh could admire his sensitivity and obvious goodness, what he himself most needed, at this stage of his preparation, was the example of an uncomplicated man of action.

Bishop Gordon returned to Scalan in June, in order to administer the subdiaconate to Hugh and George J. Gordon, and also to visit the people of Glenlivet and Strathavon. He spent three weeks there, to prepare them thoroughly, before setting out on another episcopal visitation to the West.

Uppermost in his mind on the journey was the new law passed in Parliament earlier that year, and its likely implications for Catholics. This act required all citizens to abjure the rights of the Stuart line, but in the case of Catholics it also included a clause requiring abjuration of their faith. It was a quite cynical and opportunist use of law, which, he warned Rome, revealed the Government's 'deadly hatred' of the Church and its determination to 'wipe out the Catholic Religion at one stroke'.[26]

As he made his way across the country, large numbers were converted or reconciled to the Church at his every stopping place, often where there had been few Catholics or none before. He reported particular success in Glenmoriston, around Keppoch, and elsewhere in Lochaber.

This was in fact the time of a drive by the Church into 'new' areas. In the Braes of Lochaber, where there were only known to be four practising Catholic families hitherto, some 400 persons had recently been baptised by the Irish priest Peter MacDonald,[27] and more again by Iain Mór MacDonald, who had succeeded him in 1721. It was no coincidence that most of the area was owned by the duke of Gordon, or by the family of MacDonald of Keppoch, long a closet Catholic and to whom Iain Mór was related by blood.[28] Nor had these priests confined their work to the immediate neighbourhood: Iain Mór was making converts far into Badenoch, while Peter MacDonald had made successful inroads into episcopalian Glencoe.[29]

In the West, also, there was a thrust outwards from the traditional Catholic heartlands. Colin Campbell, a convert of the family of Lochnell, was now working in Moidart, from where he could reach the Protestant Campbell country across the Shiel river, including his own family's lands in Ardnamurchan, where in time he converted his two brothers and a number of their tenants.[30]

These encroachments did not go unnoticed by the Church of Scotland, and indeed figured as a main *leitmotif* of its meetings at this time. A string of memorials and representations warned that priests were 'trafficking' with ever more freedom, and were actually being abetted by some of the local magistrates. Their usual tactic was to disappear when summoned to court: they simply 'suffered themselves to be fugitat', the reports noted ruefully, 'and then there is no more of the matter, but a new Information next year, and so on'.[31] As a result, the Catholics on the estates of sympathetic landlords were growing bolder by the day. In the Gordon country of Lochaber and the North-East they were brazenly flouting their immunity, 'and spared not openly to say that the Government knew better things [than to] disturb them, Yea that they dare not do it'. In the neighbourhood of Scalan priests were going about their work quite openly, despite being under sentence of banishment.[32]

Since the local Kirk saw little prospect of help from the law, some extreme elements now decided to take the law into their own hands. Scalan was one of their first targets. Throughout the summer and autumn of 1723 they subjected the master and boys to almost daily harassment, in the hope of finally driving them out. According to Bishop Gordon's account, they even 'bought with money certain lost men, ready for any crimes', to do the work for them. For a while the seminary was virtually a fortress. Never had Hugh and his companions been more vulnerable, for their remoteness – normally their best hope of safety – only left them the more unprotected against the malice of the hired thugs. That they survived was due not least to the Christian goodwill of several of the Protestant gentlemen of Glenlivet.[33] These local men of influence must have known full well that Scalan was harming no-one and that its business was spiritual, not political, and they had come to respect the piety and idealism of those who quietly went about their business there.

But the situation remained parlous. The Kirk had continued its opposition to the Catholics of the North-East through official channels, and before the end of the year won an order from Whitehall for the arrest of all priests in the area and the suppression of Scalan itself.[34] The order was not carried out at once, but it seemed only a matter of time before it would be.

Following its 'Act for more effectual disarming the Highlands' of 1724 the Government sent one of the army's most senior officers, General George Wade, to assess the situation there and report back with proposals for a strategy of 'pacification'. Wade produced his report in December.[35] He recommended an enhanced and permanent military presence in the disaffected areas, greater mobility of the army, and total disarmament of the clans. The previous attempt at disarming in 1716, he pointed out, had been so ill-executed that the enemies of the Crown had actually emerged better armed than before. Accompanying his proposals he presented a list of the 'disaffected' clans (with the numbers they could muster in the field) and, significantly, a second list identifying the Catholic clans.

Even before his report was presented he made a start at putting its recommendations into effect, strengthening the troop presence, improving barracks and transportation, and overseeing a new and more thorough-going surrender of arms. On his orders all the Jacobite clans of the West, Lochaber, the Great Glen, Glenmoriston and Strathglass handed in weapons at the barracks at Fort William and Killiechumen on 15 September.[36] Every significant Highland Catholic district on the mainland was included within the net.

The Kirk was well aware that its own lack of manpower in many parts of the Highlands was leaving the way clear for Catholicism to expand there. Numerous committee and synod reports to the General Assembly at this time pointed out the shortage of suitable Gaelic-speaking ministers, and the impossible task that confronted even the best of them in trying to cover their huge Highland parishes, and warned of the need for restructuring and more effective ministry.

This soul-searching and new will to put its own house in better order in fact marked the beginning of a period of more positive, effective action by the Kirk at local level in the Highlands. One of the first signs of this was the decision taken by the synod of Argyll in 1724 to divide its

over-large area into two, creating a new, separate synod of Glenelg to
cover its northern districts, and at the same time streamlining a number
of its presbyteries on the west coast and the Isles. This and other initiatives
were explicitly taken 'to contain the popish threat',[37] by improving the
Kirk's effectiveness in those areas that it traditionally considered its own.

This was a time, in short, when Parliament, the Church of Scotland
and the military were all taking active steps to strengthen their position
in the Highlands. The effects of their actions were already beginning to
be felt and would become even more apparent in the second half of the
decade. Their cumulative effect would be to stem the Catholic recovery
of new areas and bring its period of expansion virtually to an end.[38] Hugh
MacDonald was due to be ordained within a year. It was his misfortune
that their endeavours would coincide with the beginning of his priestly
ministry.

In September 1724 John Alexander Grant left Scalan to take charge of
the Aberdeen station made vacant by the death of its resident priest. To
provide temporary cover at Scalan Bishop Gordon drafted in the thirty-
year-old John Tyrie. If the seminary's masters to date had had their
shortcomings, by and large these had been in regard to administration.
But in Mr Tyrie's case they concerned more deep-seated matters of
character, matters that were to emerge more clearly a decade later, as we
shall see, when they would tax the authority of Hugh MacDonald to the
limit, and cause great damage and scandal to the Mission.

Fortunately, Mr Grant returned within six months. When he arrived
he found Hugh suffering from severe pains in his arms and legs. A
phlebotomist was brought in, who bled each limb in turn over a period
of several days, and succeeded in easing the pain.[39] Even in youth Hugh's
health was delicate, and illness was to dog him throughout his life.

It was a remarkable crop of students under the one roof in the little
seminary at this time. There was Hugh himself, the senior at twenty-six
and one day to be bishop of the Highlands. Then George J. Gordon, a
future master at Scalan. Then the nineteen-year-old James Grant from
the Catholic enclave of the Enzie in Lower Banffshire, the younger brother
of the present master. In time he would be consecrated bishop for the
Lowlands, and eventually succeed to the position of vicar apostolic. Then
Peter Grant, just seventeen, a local boy from Blairfindy and a native Gaelic
speaker, who like James hailed from a poor family who could not even
afford to contribute towards his 'viatic' (travelling espenses) to Rome.
Within two years of his ordination he would be appointed Scots Agent
in Rome, where he would fight the Mission's corner in that highly
influential, 'political' post to great effect over forty-seven years.

In May Bishop Gordon returned to Scalan. Hugh and George J. Gordon were due to be ordained priests that autumn, while Peter and James Grant would be leaving for the Scots College Rome at about the same time, and he wished to leave instructions for the master as to their preparation. He himself planned to spend the summer in the West Highlands, and then return in order to give them their final preparation personally.

He arrived back at Scalan in mid-July and for the next two months used the seminary as his base, spending as much time as he was able there but also paying flying visits to a number of the local Catholic communities.[40] Hugh and George J. Gordon had both told the master of their wish to be posted to the Highlands once they were ordained, and he had already suggested to the bishop that one of them might usefully work in Morar, where the two priests were in bad health and barely able to move about their difficult station.[41] The obvious person to assist them was Hugh, and this was the arrangement agreed between bishop and ordinand that August.

The day fixed for their ordination was 18 September, Ember Saturday,[42] nine years almost to the day since Hugh had first come to Scalan. It has not come down to us what kind of day it was. Gathered in the cramped main room of the thatched house were the bishop, the master, fellow students, and perhaps the servants and one or two priests from the North-East. The ordination Mass was rich in symbolism: the candle of light; the two ordinands lying prone in cruciform to signify their imitation of Christ in self-giving; the stole crossed over their breast, symbolising the 'Yoke of the Lord'; the anointing of the hands that would henceforth confer the sacraments; the chasuble, representing the 'Robe of Innocence', unfolded and placed upon their shoulders. And once ordained the two young men continued the Mass, their first, joining their bishop in concelebration.

For Bishop Gordon it was a day of immense significance. Here at last were two 'heather priests', priests, that is, who had received their entire training in Scotland, as he had always envisaged. They were the first since before the Reformation, and the first fruits of Scalan. It was appropriate that they had been ordained there, since their ordination was the strongest, most tangible vindication of the seminary, in which he had invested so much vision, energy and hope. Appropriate, too, that one was a MacDonald from the West and the other a Gordon from the North-East: they seemed to stand as representatives of the two areas of Scotland and the two families that, more than any others, had held the line for the Catholic faith.

Notes

1. Withers C. W. J. (1984), chap. 4, and espec. p. 56, fig. 9, '*Gaidhealtachd in 1705*'.
2. Bishop Geddes' description of it as being built 'almost entirely of turf'

identifies it as a cruck house, probably built upon a course of stones –
Geddes, Bishop J. 'A Brief Historical Account of the Seminary at Scalan',
1777, CS 1/3, para 8, SCA. Though straw was used extensively for thatching
in the eastern Highlands, heather (which was preferred as being far more
durable) was probably the material used at Scalan, being plentiful and close
to hand in the neighbourhood.

3. Bishop Gordon to Thomas Innes, 1.12.1716, BL, SCA. It was the bishop's
original intention to support the inexperienced new master by staying as
often as possible at Scalan himself.

4. James Carnegy to Thomas Innes, 5.6.1718, BL.

5. Bishop Gordon to Lewis Innes, 25.3.1718, BL, describing Mr Smith as
'more fitt to educate boys than all that are of trade here, put them all
together'.

6. Bishop Gordon to William Stuart, 16.10.1717, BL.

7. Ibid. 'I keep the Sem^y still on foot but with great difficulty and charges.'

8. Bishop Gordon to Thomas Innes, 25.3.1718, BL.

9. Bishop Gordon *Rules*, June 1722, CS 1/2, SCA., para. 10. A version with
slightly different spelling and punctuation published by Anderson W. J. (1963
J), appendix I.

10. Ibid., paras. 11, 12–14, 23, 26–7.

11. Ibid., paras. 1–4.

12. Ibid., paras. 15, 18 and 30.

13. Geddes, Bishop J. op. cit., para. 10. The rules of constant supervision,
authority through exhortation and example, and considering individual
needs in matters academic and spiritual, all closely resemble those of the
Scots College Paris – cf. 'Statuta Collegii Scotorum Parisiensis', 1707 (in
Latin), CA 1/10/2, cap. iv.

14. Even in his English letters he at times used an attractive Latinate mode of
thought and turn of phrase – cf. appendix IV.

15. '& J. Fife [himself] seems resolv'd to reside with them as much as possible',
Bishop Gordon to Thomas Innes, 1.12.1716, BL. He had become vicar
apostolic on the death of Thomas Nicolson in October 1718.

16. John Wallace to Thomas Innes, 7.6.1720, and Robert Gordon to same,
15.6.1720, BL.

17. Re Archibald Anderson, see Anderson W. J. (1963 J), appendix IV.

18. 'Memorial', MS 3430, f. 234, NLS, and 'Additional Memorial Concerning
the growth of Popery', n.d. but 1720, MS 68, f. 31, NLS. The latter, which
repeats and extends the first, states that 'Scala' is 'under the inspection of
one father Innes who Still [i.e. constantly] resides there'. Also John Wallace
to Thomas Innes, 7.6.1720, BL.

19. Cf. Dickson W. K. (1895).

20. Allan Ruadh MacDonald of Morar to John MacDonald, Edinburgh,
29.7.1730, MS 68, f. 107, NLS, refers to the wadsetting of 'Sloismein &
Sloisgarve att Lochborad' to Kinlochmoidart on 5.5.1704 by his uncle Allan,
and the wadsetting of Meoble in 1721.

21. 'Extract Deposition of Corroboration be the Laird of Morror to the Laird

of Moydart', Edinburgh 6.2.1723, according to their agreement of 30.7.1722, Clanranald Papers, GD 201/5/11, NAS.

22. George Innes to Thomas Innes, 29.1.1723, BL. Bishop Gordon responded by stopping his Mission quota.

23. 'Representation by the Committee of the Commission of the General Assembly of the Church of Scotland Anent the Growth of Popery in the North', 1722, MS 3430, ff. 239f, NLS.

24. Bishop Gordon to ?, 17.10.1722, BL.

25. John A. Grant to Bishop Gordon, 8.1.1723, BL: 'I litle understood the weight of that burden I went to take on, nor the sanctity & functions belonging to it, q^{ch} when I came to see something into conturbata sunt omnia ossa mea', etc.

26. Bishop Gordon, Report to Propaganda, October 1723 (in Latin), copy BL, 2/249/7. A translation of the original is printed in Bellesheim A. (1890), vol. iv, appendix X. 'An Act to oblige all Persons, being Papists, in that part of Great Britain called Scotland ... refusing or neglecting to take the Oaths ... to Register their Names and Real Estates', etc., 1723, 9 Geo. I c. 24. Most previous legislation had outlawed the *practice* of Catholicism (attendance at/celebration of Mass, etc.), but this had often been hard to prove unless on the word of spies or apostates. The real damage of the new act was that it put the onus on the Catholics themselves, either to prove their innocence (by forswearing their faith) or admit their guilt (by failing to do so).

27. 'A Representation of the Circumstances of severall parishes in the Bounds of the Synod of Argyle where popery is prevailing', August 1720, MS 3430 f. 228, NAS.

28. When Keppoch declared himself a Catholic in 1728, he admitted that he had been one 'in judgment' since the beginning of the century – letter of James Gilchrist, 4.4.1729, reporting presbytery meeting in Kilmonivaig parish, General Assembly Papers, CH 1/2/59, p. 83v., which also noted the 'great advantages' to Iain Mór MacDonald of being a blood relation of Keppoch.

29. Re Iain Mór in Badenoch – 'Memorial concerning Popery', 1726, in Royal Bounty Records 1725–30, CH 1/5/51, p. 75, NAS; re Peter MacDonald in Glencoe, MS 3430, f. 228, NAS, supra.

30. 'The Register of the Proceedings of the Provincial Synod of Argyle' (from 1708), entry for 14.8.1723, CH 2/557/5, p. 319, NAS, reports Bishop Gordon's visit, and states that Colin Campbell has been 'settled' in Moidart under the alias 'Paul Alexander'. Re the conversion of his brothers and tenants – Royal Bounty Records, 1725–30, meetings of 14.3.1729 and 27.3.1729, CH 1/5/51, pp. 424 and 430 respectively, NAS.

31. 'Memorial concerning the growth of popery in diverse places in the north and Islands of Scotland, causes thereof and Some Remedies humbly proposed', General Assembly, 1718, MS 3430, f. 220, NLS; 'A Representation', etc., August 1720, MS 3430, f. 228, NLS, supra; 'Memorial Concerning the Growth of Popery', etc., 1720, MS 3430, f. 234, NLS; 'Representation by the Committee of the Commission of the General Assembly of the Church of Scotland', April 1722, MS 3430, f. 239, NLS.

32. Synod of Moray, Record of Meetings, 29.4.1724, CH 2/271/VI, pp. 211f., NAS.

33. Bishop Gordon to Propaganda, October 1723 (in Latin), BL 2/249/7. Also, George Innes to Thomas Innes, 31.7.1724, BL.

34. Order of Council, Whitehall, 30.11.1723, MS 205, f. 13, NLS. The order made explicitly in response to a Representation by the Church of Scotland. Re latter, see synod of Moray, Record of Meetings, 29.10.1724, CH 2/271,VI, p. 223, NAS.

35. 'An Act for more effectual disarming the Highlands in that part of Great Britain called Scotland; and for the better securing the peace and Quiet of that Part of the Kingdom', etc., 11 Geo I, c. XXVI, 1724. Wade, General George – 'Report Relating to the Highlands', Mitchell Papers, Brit. Mus., copy RH 2/5/12, pp. 1–14, NAS.

36. Wade, General George 'Report &c relating to the Highlands', 31.1. 1725, RH 2/5/12, pp. 18ff., NAS. Killiechumen (*Cill Chuimein*) was later renamed 'Fort Augustus'.

37. Minutes of the Synod of Glenelg, CH 2/568/1, NAS, in Ferguson W. (1969–71 J), p. 22, which also includes details of re-alligned presbyteries, and later restructuring elsewhere in the West Highlands.

38. Several of the Kirk documents were transcribed by Wilby in his article 'The "Encreasce of Popery" in the Highlands 1717–1747' (1966 J). But in fact only two of the documents (both from 1747 and reflecting the particular circumstances after the '45) are post-1720. The title of his valuable article is thus somewhat misleading since it might be taken to suggest an expansion of Catholicism between *c.* 1725 and 1747 which did not in fact occur.

39. John A. Grant to Bishop Gordon, 16.3.1725, BL.

40. Thomson J. 'Some Account of the State of Religion in Scotland from 1688 to 1787' etc., Th/10, SCA, entry for 1725; relevant excerpt also in Forbes Leith W. (1905), vol. II, pp. 302ff.

41. John A. Grant to Bishop Gordon, 16.3.1725, BL.

42. James Carnegy to Thomas Innes, 8.10.1725, BL.

5

The First Heather Priest
(1725–30)

Hugh did not leave Scalan immediately. Bishop Gordon had arranged to stay on at the seminary for several weeks,[1] and it made sense for his two new priests to use the opportunity to benefit from his last minute advice.

The bishop had a particular reason for staying on. He wanted to observe the master at close hand, and to discuss a matter of importance with him. Ever since his sojourn in the Highlands in 1710–11 he had harboured the idea of a separate Highland vicariate with its own bishop. Circumstance had dictated that he himself would not be that bishop, as he had originally hoped, but the concept had never left him. Now his own advancing age and another exhausting Highland visitation had brought it to the fore again. Furthermore, a new threat to the Mission had given it a fresh urgency. That very spring King George had granted the Church of Scotland an annual bounty of £1,000 for the conversion of the Highlands,[2] income that promised to make its missionary activity far more effective than before, and the work of the Catholic Church far harder.

Bishop Gordon had been active in promoting the case for a Highland vicar apostolic with Propaganda since the beginning of the year, and had earmarked John Alexander Grant for the post.[3] He had also contacted the Inneses at the Scots College Paris, whose influence with James III was crucial to the outcome, particularly recommending Mr Grant as 'the most accomplish'd laborer' in the whole Mission.[4] His prolonged stay at the seminary now gave him the chance to be certain, and also to discuss the matter with the master and win him over to accepting the mitre, should it be offered, something that required time and all his powers of persuasion, given Mr Grant's humility and almost neurotic self-deprecation.

Meantime Hugh was glad of a few weeks more of the bishop's company and wisdom. The college had been his only home for nine years, the place where he had learned so much, changed so much, and come to manhood. His arrival in 1716 had been a step into the unknown and the unfamiliar and, desperately homesick, he had at first doubted whether he would even stay the course. Now he was to take a new step, but a much greater one, since this was the beginning of his real work, and it would carry responsibility for thousands of souls. And again it would be a step into the unknown. He was going home, true, but not to what he had been. His place in the West would not be his old, assured place as a tacksman's son. As a priest he would in one way be at the heart of his people – accepted, looked to, totally one of them. And yet by his office he must always be somewhat apart. What would his role be, and how would he adapt to it? For all his careful preparation he would only really know when he arrived.

He set out in October in the company of Antony Kelly, an Irish Recollect friar newly recruited to the Mission, who because of his Gaelic was also being posted to the West.[5] Their destination was Arisaig. The area, with South Morar, was under the care of Mr Peter Fraser, assisted by George Douglas, the man who had been Bishop Gordon's interpreter during his first visit to the West in 1707. Though neither was old, ill health had rendered them inactive. Mr Fraser, who had been sent to the West Highlands against his will and had not really settled there, was losing a battle against alcoholism, while Mr Douglas had been suffering from palsy for years and was now barely able to celebrate the Mass.

Mr Douglas received the new arrivals and fixed up temporary accommodation for them close to his own home, while they made arrangements in their new stations. At the beginning of February he sent the bishop news that they had left Arisaig: 'M[r] Antony and Hugh have separatd. Antony for the Iles, and Hugh for Moidart and sometimes among his friends. he does extreamly well, and gathers a good deal of courage, and keeps full congreg. so that within a year heil be capable fore any parish; in the meantime heil be with us now and then.'[6]

His words suggest that Hugh had already been in Moidart for some time, and our most likely guess is that he had taken up his new post at the beginning of the Advent season.[7] What is meant by his being 'sometimes among his friends' is not clear. The phrase may refer to his mother's brothers, Donald and Ronald of Kinlochmoidart,[8] but perhaps more likely it refers to his relatives and neighbours in South Morar itself. Certainly we learn elsewhere in the letter that he was still visiting Mr Douglas at Keppoch, a part of Arisaig that actually belonged to the MacDonalds of Morar. The older man, who remained an invaluable mentor, was apparently hoping that his young protégé would eventually be sent to take his own place there, and was hinting as much when suggesting that he would soon be ready for any parish. His own strength was now utterly failed, he reminded the bishop, and he begged to be granted the retirement 'design'd long ago'. But this the bishop could not do.

Hugh turned to George Douglas when he needed to know the solution to ecclesial problems peculiar to the West: arrangements for the annual blessing and distribution of the Holy Oils, for example, or how to acquire

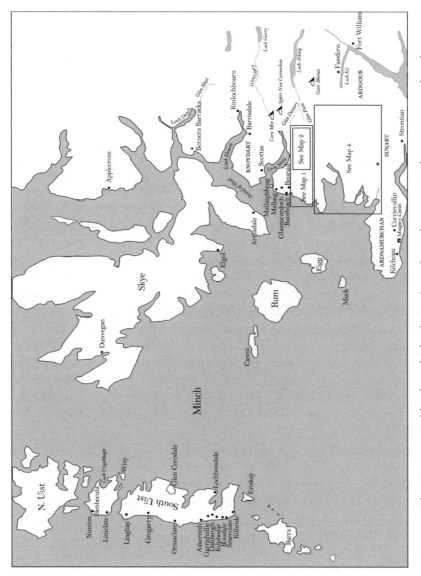

Map 3. The Western Highlands and Islands (in the eighteenth century): places mentioned in the text

sufficient Communion hosts, since wheaten flour was not to be had outside
the Lowlands.[9] At the same time he was acquainting himself with his
station, travelling the length of Moidart by horse and foot, from the
charred carcass of Caisteal Tioram and the eerie flatlands of Loch Shielside
to green Eilean Fhianain, a graveyard for a thousand years; penetrating
the inner recesses of upper Glen Moidart and Glen Forslan deep among
the Roshven hills; journeying from the eastern farms that faced Ardgour
and Sunart and could only be reached by boat, to sheltered Loch Ailort
and Smirisary open to the western sea.

On his visits home that spring he learned that his ageing father was
intending to hand over the family lands to his half-brother Allan Ruadh.
The matter had been agreed five years before, and the charter of infeftment
was now being drawn up in London. On 26 April it was signed.[10] Hugh
heard the news with mixed feelings. Knowing Allan's weak character and
his openness to influence by others, he must have had some apprehension
as to the estate remaining long intact and in the family's hands.

The committee appointed to administer the king's bounty had been
meeting regularly since May 1725. They had decided very early on that
the Catholic districts were to be the prime focus for their work, and that
most of the money at their disposal should be spent on sending ministers
and catechists to undertake special evangelisation there.[11]

In the first year they seconded fifty-one persons to work in these areas,
with very mixed success.[12] There was a natural reluctance to undertake
what was a thankless task, and it was later admitted that several of those
appointed, including two ministers and a catechist assigned to South
Morar, Arisaig and Moidart, had failed to appear. Others sent to the
same area could not persuade anyone to attend their meetings. The
minister seconded to Canna had met with a similar response, and was
forced to conclude that missionary work in the Catholic districts was
wasted effort.[13]

Despite these setbacks the committee's first annual meeting upheld the
original decision 'that those Places where Popery prevails most should be
first taken into consideration'.[14] These were to include the traditional
heartlands of the West, and the 'new' areas of growth in Lochaber,
Badenoch and the other Gordon lands of the North-East that lay within
the synod of Moray. The duke of Gordon's estates were in fact now
identified as the hub of Catholic activity in Scotland, the centre of the
Church's 'Intelligence, Counsel, Direction, Encouragment and Example',
and the one part of the country where it was still growing.[15]

The Royal Bounty Committee quite rightly saw the landowners as a
crucial factor in the battle for souls, and winning their support as a key
to its own success. As the Committee's *Memorial* pointed out, the tenants

of Rum had recently changed their religion through the influence of their Protestant landlord, MacLean of Coll, and it was to be hoped that his 'zeal' might be an example for others to follow.[16] They recommended particularly that approaches be made to Protestant landlords of Catholic areas such as Glengarry, and also to Catholic chiefs like MacNeil of Barra, who were thought to be vacillating, to gain their support if not their actual allegiance. They placed a special hope in the Protestant MacKenzie of Devlin, who had recently acquired the estate of Clanranald forfeited to the Crown after the '15, and who they thought could be a key player in the winning of the Catholic West.[17]

What the *Memorial* blandly called MacLean of Coll's 'zeal' had in fact been an act of naked persecution. Using the near-absolute power he enjoyed on his own lands and his virtual immunity from the law, he had personally driven his tenants out of the Catholic chapel and into the Kirk with his gold-topped cane.[18] It is quite clear from the Committee's private records that they fully approved of such measures, and of using whatever force might be necessary against the Catholic menace. Even their public statements recommended the stationing of troops to cover Morar, Arisaig, Moidart and the Islands, the use of the military to expel the priests from these districts, and the settling of 'collonies' of Protestants there.[19]

Thus it was in a climate of intimidation that Hugh embarked upon his priestly life. Six months later when Bishop Gordon made a visitation to the West he took a great risk even attempting the journey. One of his priests had already been arrested and imprisoned,[20] and the ministers were pressing the garrisons to round up more and claim the 500 merks reward under the 1700 Act. 'The more good the priests have done, the greater is there danger,' it was reported to Rome.[21] Fit and energetic as he was, Hugh must have been a prime target.

On his return home the bishop wrote to James III, urging him to use his influence in Rome for the creation of a Highland vicariate, and to recommend John Alexander Grant as his choice to be its bishop: 'Nothing can be resolved on this affaire till your will be known,' he told him.[22] He also wrote again to Propaganda on the same subject. The Highland Church needed the presence of a bishop for survival, he argued, and never more so than at this time of ruthless persecution. In the past his own visits had partly met the need, but now age and indisposition rendered him unfit for the task. Appointing a resident bishop was the only possible solution – one unanimously supported by his priests, the Highland gentlemen, and King James himself – and he begged the Cardinals to agree to it.[23]

That autumn he waited impatiently and in some agitation for their reply. ''Tis hardly possible', he told his friends in Paris, 'at a distance to believe how necessary & advantagious to trade a phys^n [physician – i.e., bishop] in West is; M. Fife [himself] is so much persuaded of it that he can get no rest till that affair come to an happy conclusion.'[24]

James contacted the pope personally in October, adding his weight to the case,[25] and it was shortly after his letter arrived that Propaganda finally gave its permission in principle. Word was not long reaching Bishop Gordon, for his chosen man was dispatched to Rome and already in the city before the end of November, several weeks before the formal publication of Propaganda's approval.

It was not until the following July that the pope officially ratified Mr Grant's appointment,[26] and in the interval the bishop-designate had been seized by new doubts. After much persuasion he finally appeared to accept the office and set off from Rome, supposedly bound for Scotland. But he apparently fell ill before taking ship. Whether he ever intended to return home, and exactly what became of him afterwards, are not known and perhaps never will be. Towards the end of the year he was in the seaport of Genoa, whence he wrote to the Scots agent explaining that he could not accept the mitre since he did not believe he enjoyed the unanimous support of his fellow priests either at home or abroad.[27] This was the last word anyone ever heard of him.

The whole question of a Highland vicariate had been discredited, and had to be put on hold meantime. But Rome still recognised the principle, and as an interim measure agreed to the appointment of a pro-vicar for the Highlands. The young priest Colin Campbell was chosen for the post, on account of his 'widsom, piety and learning'.[28]

One of Bishop Gordon's main arguments in favour of Mr Grant when originally proposing his name to Propaganda was the fact that as a student in Rome he had presented, *magna cum laude*, a public thesis in support of the constitution *Unigenitus Dei Filius* of Pope Clement XI. This papal bull of 1713 had finally condemned as heretical the Jansenist movement that had divided the Catholic Church in parts of Western Europe for the previous seventy years. The movement took its name from the Dutch bishop Cornelius Jansen, whose *Augustinus* was its original inspiration. Its main tenets, drawn from a particular interpretation of St Augustine's doctrine of grace, emphasised the corruptness of human nature and the assertion that Christ died not for all but for an elect predestined to salvation. Its caricature as 'Calvinism, with the Mass' was not without point. Its adherents, who were noted for their deep piety and infrequent, carefully prepared reception of the Eucharist, included eminent men and women both lay and religious. Up to the time of Clement's intervention they had considered themselves a tendency within the Church, despite opposition from the mainstream and in particular from the Society of

Jesus. The effect of *Unigenitus* had been to polarise them, drawing some back into the bosom of the Church, and hardening the position of the rest, who were now denied the sacraments.[29]

The controversy did not reach the Scottish Mission in any serious way until the beginning of the eighteenth century, when accusations of Jansenism were made against a number of secular priests by Jesuits working in Scotland.[30] The publication of *Unigenitus* had naturally brought the issue to the fore again, and questions had been asked in Rome at the time concerning the orthodoxy of the Scottish clergy, particularly in view of the powerful influence upon the Mission of the Scots College Paris, whose staff were suspected of espousing Jansenism. Bishop Gordon's assurance that all his priests were perfectly willing to subscribe to the constitution, and that he himself would vigilantly uphold it,[31] had seemed to answer the Vatican's concerns.

But suspicion had not died among the Jesuits in Scotland itself, or among some Scots in the Benedictine monasteries abroad.[32] In 1727, while on a visit to Italy, the monk of Ratisbon, Fr Hamilton OSB, went out of his way to poison the names of certain of the Scottish clergy, tarring Bishop Gordon himself as a Jansenist.[33] Further accusations followed at home and abroad. The controversy and bitterness that they inflamed were to dominate and divide the Scottish Mission for the better part of twenty years.

The following summer Bishop Gordon made another episcopal visitation to the West. He was anxious to move forward on the appointment of a Highland bishop, and called a meeting of senior Highland priests on Eilean Bàn to discuss the question of possible candidates.[34] Hugh was invited to attend, though he hardly qualified as a senior. His half-brother Allan Ruadh was the local landlord, and the bishop understood the significance of 'family' in the West Highlands. Those present unanimously agreed that John Alexander Grant remained their choice, if he was still living and could be found and persuaded.

On 20 November Alexander, second duke of Gordon died. Although the seriousness of his condition was known, his death came so suddenly that he had no chance to make his Confession or receive Extreme Unction, nor to give instructions concerning his children. Thus it happened that, despite an agreement that the sons would be raised as Catholics – and Cosmo his heir actually served at his Requiem – within two days their mother had made arrangements to have them educated in her own Episcopalian faith.[35]

The news was not long in reaching Rome and there is some evidence that the Papal Nuncio in Paris, at Propaganda's behest, may actually have discussed with James Carnegy of the Scottish Mission the possibility of the boys being abducted and smuggled over to France.[36] Rumours of a planned kidnapping, implicating Bishop Gordon himself, were circulating in Edinburgh, and the bishop was arrested and briefly imprisoned before being released through the influence of the duchess.[37] It was now becoming clear that his early hopes of the boys returning to the Church had been misplaced, and before the year was out he regretfully advised Mr Carnegy 'to think no more of recovering that family' since 'humainly speaking it was impossible'.[38]

Though the tenants and gentlemen of the Gordon estates suffered no real hardship by the change, they would never again enjoy the active promotion of their interests that they had received hitherto. Alexander's death was a body-blow for the Church in the North-East, and indeed for the whole Scottish Mission: the greatest stroke in its seventy-five years' existence.[39]

By now Bishop Gordon had all but dismissed the possibility that Mr Grant might yet be found and persuaded to take the mitre, and recognised that he would need to look elsewhere. 'I fear, thô he be alive, that he has quite forgot us,' he confided to Lewis Innes, 'in case we have lost him entirely; I don't see we can pitch on another to be phys[n] but Colin [Colin Campbell], who is extreamly agreeable both to labor[s] & custom[s] [clergy and laity]; but that affair, tho it were of the greatest importance some thing were done in't to purpose, can't be soon finish'd, even on this side.'[40]

From his words it is clear that Colin Campbell did not have his unhesitating support, even if he thought him the best alternative, and that he believed deeper enquiry was needed before a recommendation could be made to Rome. The Mission could not afford a second embarrassment.

In Campbell's favour was his previous selection as pro-vicar and the authority that this had already given him over the Highland clergy, as well as his successful missionary work over the past five years in the Protestant countries of Ardnamurchan, Sunart and Mull.[41] Against him was his inexperience, as a priest of only seven years' standing. And the fact that he was a convert and from one of the most prominent families of Argyll, though of undoubted propaganda value, made him a less than ideal candidate, and perhaps even suspect, in the eyes of some.

The bishop had, in fact, a poor field to choose from. He had never enjoyed a strong team in the Highlands,[42] and in 1729 the situation was as difficult as it had ever been. Several of his priests, including George Douglas and Angus MacLachlan, could be eliminated on grounds of health. Others, as he explained to Paris, disqualified themselves by their conduct: the Benedictine Gregor MacGregor had proved himself 'a very dangerous factious (& as farr as we can know very vicious) man'; Iain Mòr MacDonald was 'very haughty & untractable, being both extreamly headstrong & rash & imprudent'; Peter Fraser was still abusing himself with alcohol; and Alexander Paterson, working in the Highlands against his will, had 'shewn himself very humoursome & self conceited, interested & imprudent'.[43] Neil MacFie, though only two years a priest, was already showing signs of the proclivity to drink that would eventually lead to the withdrawal of his priestly faculties.

Morale was low among all his priests. They had never been poorer. Propaganda's annual allowance to the Mission, which was supposed to cover their quotas, had not been changed in eighty years, though the number among whom it was to be divided had now more than trebled. The situation was reaching crisis point.[44]

Bishop Gordon made enquiries in Rome as to the possibility of recruiting more priests from abroad, to reduce the crippling workload in the Highlands. He welcomed the news that two Dominicans based in France would be willing to join the team, but in view of previous disappointments involving the religious orders, and the troublemakers already among his own priests, he insisted on their being thoroughly vetted before he would accept them.[45]

One of them, Fr Ryan, arrived that summer.[46] But far from easing the situation, his arrival was made the occasion of a new round of dissent, such was the fractious state of the Mission. When he was sent to replace Gregor MacGregor in BraeLochaber, the word was put about that he was there to spy on his fellow priests and compile a secret dossier detailing evidence of Jansenism among them.[47] Before the year was out the suspicions, recriminations and rumours had escalated, at times to an hysterical and ridiculous level.[48] Bishop Gordon must have viewed the prospect of handing the Highlands over to another with some relief.

Such was the hardship and poverty of the Mission, the persecution from without and dissension within, as Hugh entered his fifth year as a priest. His had been a steep learning curve, and his far from tranquil apprenticeship could now be said to be over.

He had already left the Moidart station by this date and was now serving Arisaig and South Morar. He had a house at Drimmindarroch, just above the tangle and the high tide of broad Loch nan Uamh. It was a year since the last meeting of the senior clergy, and Bishop Gordon was anxious to hear from them in order to gauge their support for Colin Campbell. He now discovered that the young priest was not at all so agreeable either to his fellow priests or to the gentlemen of the West as he had supposed. He had tasted authority in the post of pro-vicar, and perhaps they already saw signs of the ruthless ambition in his character that would later so damage the Mission. When the bishop asked Hugh his opinion of him he found him non-committal, preferring to reserve judgment on him until there was firmer proof of his suitability.[49]

Another year passed without progress. With Propaganda pressing him for a nomination Bishop Gordon again canvassed the views of his priests in the West. Hugh's letter of reply, the earliest from his pen that has come down to us, was again cautious.[50] He felt no more able to give a firm judgment of Mr Campbell than before. He pointed out that most of his fellow priests and all the local gentlemen were entirely against the nomination, but left it to them to give their reasons. 'For my part,' he added, 'tho I have a great deal of respect for him and would prefer him to any oy'r Churchman yet I cannot deny what everybody sees that he is too much taken up with temporal affairs which are necessary perhaps in regaird of his Brothers yet will not excuse him in the Eyes of the people to forsaik his parish so very much.'

He therefore recommended postponing the election, if Rome would allow it. It was clearly the general opinion in the West that Mr Campbell was spending too much time and money visiting family and friends in Ardnamurchan. Reading between the lines, Hugh obviously did not think him suitable either, though he did not say this directly in his letter: with Highland tact he preferred to write 'sixpence' to his bishop and leave him to read 'a shilling' for himself.

The responses Bishop Gordon received from his priests must have convinced him to look beyond Colin Campbell. And further enquiries among them and the leading Highland laity for alternative suggestions that spring, he discovered, kept throwing up one name ahead of any other – that of Hugh MacDonald. By the time he and Bishop Wallace wrote their annual joint letter to Rome in July they were satisfied that Hugh was the man they wanted, and were able to give their reasons:

> Since Alexander J. Grant has either died, or with excessive humility rejects the burden of a bishop's office, we are obliged to bring to the notice of your Eminences another name we believe suitable for the holy office. It is Mr Hugh MacDonald, a son of one of the noblest branches of the family of MacDonalds, whose numbers and influence are great among the faithful of the Highlands. He is distinguished for zeal and piety even more than for his lineage, and is also known for his prudence and humility. He received his entire education in our seminary, concentrating on those branches of learning most useful for the confuting of heretics and the solid instruction of Catholics in faith and piety. He is persona grata to the priests working in the Highlands and to the most distinguished and prudent of the laity, with whom we have shared our proposal in confidence.[51]

It was the standing of Hugh's family in the Catholic Highlands, his personal qualities, and his general acceptability, that argued so strongly for him. And in addition, his home training stood in his favour, for the down-to-earth education of Eilean Bàn and Scalan was thought far more useful than the more theoretical and speculative courses of the Scots

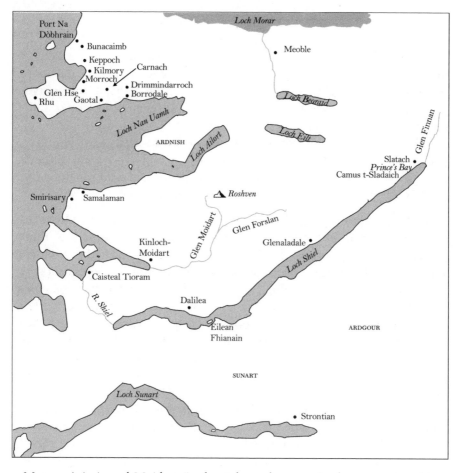

Map 4. Arisaig and Moidart (in the eighteenth century): places mentioned in the text

colleges for one who was to guide his flock and protect them against heresy. (The leader's role in 'confuting heretics' was particularly important for a small and embattled Church that lacked the educational advantages and resources enjoyed by its adversaries).[52]

Barely ordained when the original choice of Mr Grant had been made, Hugh had never come into consideration until now. But once in the reckoning, his 'goodness of fit' must have quickly become obvious.

The wording of the bishops' letter should probably not be taken to imply that they considered him a second best choice. If they did indeed harbour such thoughts, they were misplaced. The diffident and nervous Mr Grant would have been a disastrous appointment, and would almost certainly have abandoned the post, swamped by intransigent priests and unpalatable decisions. Hugh himself, blessed with greater advantages of person and circumstance, would only barely and with great difficulty survive. By Mr Grant's disappearance Providence had held the door open until Hugh was just old enough to be a credible choice.

After King James had added the weight of his support for Hugh in a personal letter to the pope that autumn,[53] the nomination was finally presented and approved at a meeting of Propaganda the following January,[54] and confirmed by a Bull of Consecration on 12 February (1731). The latter formally named Hugh as Bishop of Diana *in partibus infidelium*, according to the custom of the day whereby in Mission countries without their own hierarchy any newly appointed bishop was made titular head of an ancient, discontinued see elsewhere in the world. In this case the chosen see was *Diana Veteranorum* in the province of Constantine in Numidia, the present-day Tagou Zainah in Tunisia, once a part of the old North African Church long since lost to Islam.[55]

Though no-one on the Scottish Mission had heard of this obscure see, and strenuous enquiry failed to locate it, it provided the name by which Hugh would be known henceforth among his fellow clergy. At a time of secret correspondence and the habitual use of aliases, 'Mr Diana' gave them a useful (though scarcely undecipherable) cryptonym to camouflage their future bishop's identity.[56]

Notes

1. James Carnegy to Thomas Innes, 8.10.1725, BL, SCA.
2. £1,000, with the likelihood of its being renewed annually. The Church of Scotland set up a Committee 'for Reformation of the Highlands and Islands of Scotland, and for Management of the King's Bounty for that End', answerable to the General Assembly, in 1725.
3. Bishop Gordon to Propaganda, 20.1.1726, BL, in which he makes reference to previous correspondence on the same issue.

4. Bishop Gordon to Thomas Innes, 8.9.1725, BL.
5. James Carnegy to Thomas Innes, 8.10.1725, BL: 'M‘Donald who is to go west with Mʳ Kelly.' The Recollects were a reformed branch of the Observant Friars Minor (Franciscans).
6. George Douglas to Bishop Gordon, 2.2.1726, BL, written from Arisaig.
7. Such a date is also suggested by the fact that Antony Kelly would not have hazarded the Minch in January, nor travelled during the Christmas season.
8. Dorrian G. (1990 Th), p. 50.
9. See also p. 142 infra; and p. 177, where Bishop John MacDonald faced the same problem regarding Communion hosts. Re the Holy Oils, these were required for baptisms and confirmations, and had to be blessed by a bishop. Before the appointment of Thomas Nicolson in 1694 they had to be brought into Scotland from elsewhere. At this date Mission priests had claimed that they had been unable to baptise, having received no oils for five years. According to the report of a meeting held on Speyside in 1687, given to Propaganda by Cardinal Howard, the Scottish Mission apparently acquired its oils from London at this date – Propaganda Archives Acta, 1687 (in Italian), cited in Bellesheim A. (1890), vol. IV, p. 133 n.
10. 'Copia Carta Adjud Allani MackDonald Terrarum de Slismain', etc., 5.4.1726, signed at St James's, 25.4.1726, Clanranald Papers, GD 201/5/24, NAS.
11. Royal Bounty Records 1725–30, meetings of 18.5.1725 and 25.8.1725, CH 1/5/51, pp. 9f. and 32 repectively, NAS.
12. Report of the Royal Bounty Subcommittee to the General Assembly, 10.5.1726, CH 1/5/51, p. 71. The team comprised 12 ministers, 21 preachers and 18 catechists. Outlay on their salaries was £893 16s., the balance of the £1,000 being used to cover expenses.
13. Re Morar, Arisaig and Moidart – R. B. Records, meeting of 1.6.1726, CH 1/5/51, p. 93; Re Canna – meeting of 31.3.1726, CH 1/5/51, p. 54.
14. 'Memorial Concerning Popery', May 1726, CH 1/5/51, pp. 73ff.; quotation from p. 80.
15. Ibid., pp. 73f. Among its evidence the Memorial noted the continued existence of Scalan and the ordination of George J. Gordon and Hugh there the previous year.
16. Ibid., p. 79.
17. Re Glengarry – ibid., p. 79; re Clanranald estate – ibid., p. 75; re MacNeil of Barra – R. B. Records, meeting of 1.6.1726, pp. 101 and 137, with a high powered group including the moderator of the General Assembly and the lord president detailed to make the contact.
18. It was from this act that Presbyterianism became familiarly known in the Catholic Highlands and Islands as *Creidimh A'chall Bhuidhe* ('the faith of the golden stick') – cf. report of Rev. J. Walker – MacKay M. (ed.) (1980), p. 197.
19. Meeting of 1.6.1726, CH 1/5/51, pp. 94f. And R. B. Committee report to the General Assembly, 28.4.1727, CH 1/5/51, p. 187.
20. James Carnegy to Thomas Innes, 19.12.1726, BL. The priest was William Shand of Strathavon. Mr Shand was 'many months in an abominable prison

with thieves and whores, in summer devoured with rats and vermin, and winter killed with cold in a large room without a fire, but eight large winddows without either glass or boards'.

21. Thomas Innes to William Stuart, 15.7.1726, BL. The following autumn troops forced the closure of the seminary at Scalan. The community took refuge for several weeks in safe houses nearby, and only after the personal intervention of the duke were they able to return and resume a far from normal existence: cf. Bishop Gordon to Thomas Innes, 6.12.1726, BL.

22. Bishop Gordon to 'M. Arthur' [James III], 15.8.1726, BL.

23. Bishops Gordon and Wallace, report to Propaganda, 13.8.1726 (in Latin), Propaganda Archives, translated extract in Bellesheim A. (1890), vol. IV, appendix XI.

24. Bishop Gordon to Thomas and Lewis Innes, 10.9.1726, BL.

25. James III to Pope Benedict XIII, 6.11.1726 (in Latin), BL. James argued the case for a Highland bishop on the grounds of the need for a Gaelic speaker and Bishop Gordon's advancing age. He recommended Mr Grant for his 'piety, zeal, learning and obedience to the Apostolical Constitutions', as having Gaelic, and as an alumnus of the Scots College Rome. He also sent a letter on the same subject to the Scots Agent, penned on his behalf in Latin by the agent to the English Mission, Sir David Nairne – Nairne to William Stuart, 6.11.1726, BL.

26. Propaganda Archives, 17.12.1726 and 27.7.1727, *Acta*, vol. 96ff., cited in Bellesheim op. cit., vol. IV, p. 187. According to Paul McPherson, who had his information from first-hand witnesses, the delay was due to a dispute between James and the pope, caused by the latter's nominating a new cardinal protector for the Scottish Mission without consulting James according to normal protocol – McPherson P. *History of the Scots College Rome*, in Anderson W. J. (ed.) (1961 J), p. 124.

27. Alexander J. Grant to William Stuart, 7.12.1727, BL.

28. Letter of appointment of Colin Campbell (in Latin), SM 3/13/9, SCA. There was a precedent for the post, for Mr Mongan had been given a similar task in 1700. But the area to be covered was now much larger, since it included all the Gaelic-speaking areas other than those of the eastern Highlands.

29. The *Augustinus* of Cornelius Jansen, a commentary on the works of St Augustine of Hippo, was published shortly after his death in 1638. Jansen actually lived and died a loyal member of the Church, and it was not his work that was specifically condemned by the bull *Unigenitus Dei Filius* but the *Réflexions Morales sur le Nouveau Testament* of Quesnel. Perhaps the most famous supporter of Jansenism was the French mathematician and philosopher Blaise Pascal. Those who accepted the bull became known as the 'acceptants', while those who could not do so were known as the 'appellants' since they had appealed to a general council of the Church over the pope. The controversy was already on the wane in continental Europe by the 1740s.

30. Robert Strachan, James Carnegy and Alexander Drummond to Bishop Nicolson, 12.8.1702, BL, complaining that they had been 'branded with the

abominable name of Jansenists', along with other priests now dead and 'severals yet alive'. They had held back from raising the matter for some time, hoping it would subside, but had been forced to write when it became public and threatened to give scandal to the Catholic laity and to Protestants.

31. Bishop Gordon to William Stuart, Scots agent in Rome, 27.1.1719, BL.

32. Re the damage done in Rome, especially by the rector of the Madrid college, Fr Alexander Ferguson SJ, and the allegations against James Carnegy among others, see McPherson P. *History of the Scots College Rome*, in Anderson W. J. (ed.) (1961 J), pp. 120ff.

33. Neil MacFie, from Bologna, to William Stuart, 16.4.1727, BL. MacFie also alleged that Fr Hamilton planned to bring a team of Benedictines to Scotland, to work independently of episcopal authority, to rectify the damage being done by the secular missionary priests.

34. Thomson J. 'Some Account of the State of Religion etc', Th/10, SCA, entry for 1728; also printed in Forbes Leith W. (1905), p. 310.

35. Bishop Gordon to Lewis Innes, 25.2.1729, BL, giving details of the circumstances of the duke's death and of his widow's subsequent action.

36. Anson P. (1970), p. 125.

37. Bishop Gordon to Lewis Innes, 25.2.1729, BL, in which he describes the accusation as a 'groundless fancy'. Apparently he had been released shortly before the date of the letter.

38. James Carnegy to William Stuart, 6.12.1729, BL, relaying a letter from Bishop Gordon. The bishop remained on good terms with the duchess, who promised to treat the Catholics on the estate fairly and to protect them against harassment. In general she honoured her word, as did the future dukes of Gordon.

39. Thomson J. op. cit., in Forbes Leith W. (1905), p. 312.

40. Bishop Gordon to Lewis Innes, 25.2.1729, BL.

41. His successes had prompted the local Kirk synod to appeal to his brother Lochnell, General Wade, and even the duke of Argyll himself, to halt his 'encroachments' and the 'dangerous growth of Popery' in those districts – letter to Lochnell, at August 1728 meeting; letter to General Wade requesting a garrison, at ditto; memorial to the duke of Argyll, at August 1729 meeting: Register of the Proceedings of the Synod of Argyle (from 7.8.1728), CH 2/557/6, pp. 11 and 22 respectively, NAS.

42. At times of particular hardship it was usually the discipline of the Mission that was the loser. Thus Bishop Gordon had criticised his priests' lack of discipline in the difficult times at the beginning of the century – Bishop Gordon to Lewis Innes, 12.10.1707, BL, and to Thomas Innes, 20.11.1707, BL. And ten years later, during the persecution following the '15, he had again admitted that some of his team 'please me not at all' – Bishop Gordon to William Stuart, 16.10.1717, BL.

43. Bishop Gordon to Thomas Innes, 6.11.1729, BL.

44. This year Bishop Gordon instructed the Scots agent in Rome to present a memorial to Propaganda reminding them of this fact – Thomson J. op. cit., entry for 1729, also in Forbes Leith W. (1905), p. 314.

45. Bishop Gordon to Lewis Innes, 25.2.1729, BL.
46. Probably in June – James Carnegy to William Stuart, 18.7.1729, BL. At about the same time James Leslie, a newly ordained secular priest, also arrived.
47. James Carnegy to William Stuart, 5.7.1729, BL.
48. It was even alleged that Fr Hudson SJ claimed that the Jansenists permitted women to celebrate the Mass and hear confession, and that when a fellow priest doubted the claim he was himself branded a Jansenist – James Carnegy to William Stuart, 6.12.1729, BL.
49. We know this from HMD to Bishop Gordon, 2.4.1730, BL, writing concerning the opinion he had offered the previous year.
50. HMD to Bishop Gordon, 2.4.1730, BL.
51. Bishops Gordon and Wallace to the Cardinals of Propaganda, 4.7.1730, BL (in Latin); a translation also printed in Bellesheim A. (1890), vol. IV, appendix XII. Though the bishops refer to him as Alexander J. Grant, his true name was John Alexander.
52. A recurring theme in the correspondence of the leaders of the Mission (both secular and regular) through the seventeenth and eighteenth century was the need for clergy able to hold their own in disputation with the well-versed and informed ministers of the Kirk.
53. James III to Pope Clement XII, 17.9.1730, cited in Bellesheim A. op. cit., vol. IV, p. 189.
54. Meeting of Propaganda, 15.1.1731, Propaganda archives, cited in Bellesheim A., loc. cit.
55. Their foremost scholar, the antiquarian Thomas Innes, failed to identify it correctly, wrongly concluding Dianensis to be a mis-spelling of Tyanensis, a city of Cappodocia. See Clapperton W. (MS *c.* 1870; transcribed Wilson G., 1901), p. 2120.
56. For HMD's use of various aliases, including 'Dian', at different times, see appendix III.

6

The Westerns' Young Doctor
(1731–32)

As soon as word came back of the Vatican's approval of his nomination, Hugh contacted the Scots College Paris to make arrangements for an extended visit there. Receiving his entire education in Scotland had brought certain advantages, as Bishop Gordon had argued when first recommending him to Rome.[1] In particular, he had not been infected either with a taste for luxury or with Jansenist errors. But it had also left him entirely ignorant of the Church beyond the Scottish Mission, and if he was to become an effective leader it was essential that he broaden his horizons.

The Scots College Paris seemed the obvious place to complete his education. He had acquired something of the French language at Scalan. In the city he would experience the full range of the Church's liturgy, while the college itself offered an ideal retreat for his spiritual preparation. Its two most senior staff, Lewis and Thomas Innes,[2] knew more than anyone alive about the background and history of the Scottish Mission, its relationship with Rome, and the politics of the Scottish Church in Europe. They were the hub of communication, knowledge and influence, and what they could not tell him would not be worth his knowing.[3] Bishop Gordon was on far closer terms with them, and trusted them far more as mentors, than the Jesuit superiors of the Scots College Rome. Hugh meantime was apparently unaware of their reputation for Jansenism, and of the possibility of his coming under suspicion by association with them.

He sailed for France in February, probably landing at Le Havre and travelling by carriage up the Seine Valley via Rouen.[4] The sea voyage, the early flourishing of the Paris spring, the ambient spirit of the great city, all were new and wonderful to him. But it was perhaps only when he stood before the double doors of the College on the Rue des Fossés-Saint-Victor, gazing up at its frontage of white dressed stone five storeys high[5] (plate 4), that he began to understand what it meant to be in a Catholic country, and to see the Church in an entirely new perspective.

Once inside, his eye was drawn to the staircase of carved wood that dominated the entrance hall and gave access to the library and chapel on the first floor. In the former he discovered a splendid collection of books, based on the bequest of Archbishop Beaton's own sixteenth-century library with many additions, and an outstanding archive that included unique and priceless manuscripts of the House of Stuart. The chapel was as large as a public church, incomparably larger than any Catholic building at home. It was not its barrel ceiling or plasterwork that took the eye, but the great altar screen with its life-sized painting of St Andrew crucified.

Hugh was given a room in the visitors' quarters on the second floor, along the corridor from the staff wing and immediately under the study-bedrooms of the students on the floor above. He very quickly fell into the routine of the college, for the hours of rising, praying, dining and retiring were those that had mapped his life for eleven years at Eilean Bàn and Scalan. The 5 a.m. bell was no hardship to him. The imposed division of the day, with prayers at 5.30, Mass at 7.00, lunch with its silence and edifying reading, supper at 7.00 followed by Vespers, and candles out at 9.15, this was no novelty but an old remembered habit, a welcome discipline and a safeguard against loneliness.

Every weekday he would hear the students setting out for their classes at the Sorbonne, returning for lunch, and departing again. Their absence gave him ample time for his own studies, and for long discussions with Lewis and Thomas Innes either in the house or strolling about town. The river was but a few streets away, the university no further. Thomas took a scholar's delight in introducing him to the incunabula and other rare volumes of the library, and to the charters and manuscripts that he himself had catalogued over the years with a scholar's devotion and now guarded with a scholar's jealous eye. He showed him correspondence going back a hundred years that afforded a vivid insight into the Mission's workings, politics and personnel, and provided a model for the particular style of address required by Rome. He also had him read James Gordon's *Narratio* to Propaganda of 1703, it being, he considered, 'the best account of Trade and fittest to give a true Notion of it, that hath ever been done'.[6]

If Thomas Innes was Hugh's mentor in matters scholarly and diplomatic, Lewis was his guide in things political and temporal. Now close to eighty, he had a unique wealth of experience to offer his young guest. A man of genuine charm and great generosity of heart and purse to the Mission for more than half a century, he had long been intimately associated with the Jacobite court in exile and a trusted confidant of James III. His word probably carried more weight than that of any other Scottish priest.

Knowing that the new bishop would need hard cash to undertake his duties effectively, he contacted William Stuart, the Scots agent, urging him to 'lay asside his usuall modesty' and argue the case stoutly in Rome.[7] At the same time he himself drew Hugh's needs to the attention of his own friends in Paris. In May he found a pious acquaintance willing to support him, and was able to put into his hand 600 livres in Louis d'Or.[8]

During the day Hugh also saw a great deal of George Innes, his own first teacher who had come to the college as director of studies in 1728. And in the evening he would seek out the two Highland students, William Farquharson of Strathavon and James Campbell, the younger brother of Colin, simply for the chance to converse in his own language. James had followed his brother into the Church, and had arrived at the college about eight months before Hugh. The two men soon struck up a close friendship, and, with the Innes' approval, Hugh arranged for James to accompany him back to Scotland and continue studies for the priesthood under his guidance there.[9] They also fixed up a short holiday in the Seine Valley together in the summer, to see something of France before their return home in August.

While the Inneses had Hugh in Paris they pressed upon him the necessity of opening a seminary in the West Highlands as soon as possible.[10] Only thus, they argued, could the problem of priests be solved, while the Scots colleges would also benefit by receiving only students already part-trained and proven.[11] Too many Highland boys had 'failed' abroad because they had been sent out too young. Ideally, of course, they should receive their entire training at home, as Hugh had done, since Paris always left them prey to the temptations of luxury and the worldly influence of the university.

There was in fact an even more serious argument for opening a Highland seminary at this time. With the college under suspicion of Jansenist heresy, the archbishop of Paris had recently instructed that the ordination of its students to the level of subdeacon and above should be conditional upon their signing an acceptance of the constitution *Unigenitus*. The staff considered this an unwarranted imposition, and were bypassing it by sending them for ordination to the Jansenist Bishop Bossuet at Troyes, thirty leagues from the capital.[12] But, as Lewis Innes warned Bishop Gordon, 'sending prentices in this manner to other physicians [bishops] can not be continued without being discover'd, & the discovery of it might ruin this shop, which is but too much suspected allready'.[13]

With the very future of the college in jeopardy the case for an independent Highland seminary seemed unanswerable, and Hugh, who had grasped something of the college's current problems during his seven months' stay there, easily saw the sense in it. He agreed to make it a priority upon his return to Scotland, on Lewis Innes's promise of financial support from Paris.[14]

It was his intention to purchase a bishop's pectoral cross and ring before his departure, since he knew that these could not be had in Scotland. There was an ecclesiastical jewellers' shop quite close to the college, from where he bought the ring, but for some reason he put off buying the cross

and then forgot it entirely until he was on the point of departing. He had
left his packing until the eleventh hour, the coach was about to leave,
and his money was at the bottom of his trunk. Rather than risk missing
the coach he decided to leave the cross, in the hope of purchasing one
on the journey, in Rouen or perhaps London.[15] But his brief stops there
gave him no opportunity for shopping, and he arrived in Edinburgh
without this important badge of a bishop's office.

He was obliged to wait six weeks in the Scottish capital because Bishop
Gordon had been called to the Highlands and no arrangements could be
made for the consecration until his return. In that time he must have
come to know the town well, with its mile-long main street that descended
like a fish's spine from the castle at its head to the palace at its tail,
narrowing as it went, and the scores of tunnel wynds that led off it rib-like,
encasing the body on either side.

   The date finally fixed for the ceremony was 20 October. Bishop Gordon
acted as promotary, assisted by Bishop Wallace, and with Hugh's old
Scalan master, Alexander Smith, in attendance as witness.[16] The rite,
which under normal circumstances was essentially a public ritual initiating
a public office, was concluded quickly and quietly, behind closed doors
and with no other person present. Only three men heard Hugh's pro-
fession of faith and promise of commitment; recited the Litany of the
Saints over his prone body; witnessed his head bound with the white
cloth and anointed with oil; sung a thin Veni Creator Spiritus for want
of a full choir; watched as he received the ring as bishop of the Church,
the Spouse of God; concluded with the Te Deum as the mitre was placed
upon his head. The privacy of the ceremony seemed to presage an
episcopate that would itself all too often need to be conducted behind
closed doors.

Clement XII's brief approving Hugh's nomination had included a clause
empowering him to define the limits of his district, in consultation with
Bishop Gordon. The two men spent the next few days discussing the
matter and writing up their conclusions in terms comprehensible to
Propaganda. Strictly speaking, their proposed division of the Mission was
not geographical but linguistic: the Lowland vicariate was to be English
speaking, the Highland Gaelic. Though the border between the two
broadly followed the Highland Fault Line, it did so not *per se* but because
at this date the linguistic and geological boundaries roughly coincided.
Counties that straddled the language boundary were to be split: thus
Gaelic Upper Banffshire (which included Glenlivet and Strathavon) was
assigned to the Highland vicariate, but the Anglophone areas of the county
nearer to the coast were made a part of the Lowland.[17] It was a sensible
and workable division that sought to reflect the two quite different cultures

within the Scottish Mission, and also to make for a rational deployment of its Gaelic- and English-speaking clergy.

Bishop Hugh had now been nine months away from home and he was anxious to conclude his business in the capital as soon as possible. By the end of the month he was ready to begin his journey. He carried in his trunk a formal letter of introduction from Bishop Gordon 'to all Churchmen and Honourable Catholic Gentlemen in the Highlands of Scotland', enjoining them to be 'ever obedient and submissive' to him.[18] The letter reminded them that the pope himself upheld the new bishop's authority and threatened 'the most severe censures against any such as were so wicked as to be disobedient or refractory': to obey him was to be faithful to the Holy Father.

It is clear that Bishop Gordon's purpose was to throw the greatest weight of support possible behind his new colleague from the outset, knowing that in the present contentious times his youth and local background might not work wholly in his favour, and that he might be hard put to control the wayward elements among his priests. Unfortunately, his words of exhortation and warning were to fall upon some deaf ears.

On 7 January Rome published its *Decretum* creating the two vicariates and defining their boundaries. It assigned the following districts to the Highland vicariate:

> the town of Inverness, Badenoch, Lochaber, and whatever other districts lie within the shire of Inverness, Ross, Sutherland, Strathnaver, Caithness, the Orkney and Shetland Isles, Argyll, Kintyre, Lorne, Cowal, Atholl, Breadalbane, Menteith, Strathearn, Glenurquhart, Glen Lyon, Strath Ardle, Rannoch, Balquhidder, and the highland parts of Dunbartonshire, Angus, Perth, Stirling, Marr and Moray in which the inhabitants normally use the Highland language, with the Isles of Bute and Arran and all those others which are called Western or Hebrides.[19]

It thus followed the bishops' principle of division by language, and all their specific proposals, including those for dividing the counties that straddled the linguistic boundary. For convenience sake it included as 'Highland' the town of Inverness – the only town of any size within the whole vicariate – which, though largely English-speaking, was surrounded by Gaeldom,[20] and also the isles of Orkney and Shetland which had never been Gaelic-speaking and where remnants of the Norse tongue were still to be heard. The inclusion of the latter, and many of the other districts of Sutherland, Argyll and elsewhere, was in fact purely academic since no Catholics lived there. This was Propaganda dividing up Mission territory: Bishop Hugh would have no call to visit such areas and his authority over them was purely theoretical and provisional.[21]

In one particular only did the *Decretum* differ from the bishops' proposal – in reference to the division of borderline counties by language it made no specific mention of Banffshire. It was a small change but a vital one, for in effect it assigned the populous Catholic districts of Strathavon and Glenlivet to the Lowland vicariate, despite their being upland and Gaelic-speaking. Rev. John Thomson, who had his information from people who knew Bishop Gordon personally, claimed that Propaganda made the change at the request of the bishop himself, his object being to keep these two key districts, and particularly the seminary at Scalan, within his own vicariate.[22]

The other areas of substantial Catholic population in the Gaelic Eastern Highlands, Upper Deeside, Glengairn and Corgarff, were retained within the Highland vicariate. They formed its farthest outposts, cut off from its heartlands by some of Scotland's highest mountains and even less accessible from the West than from the Lowlands.

Map 5 shows the extent of the district that in theory now came under Bishop Hugh's authority, and the areas of Catholic population that were his to administer in practice.[23]

After his consecration he travelled to Laggan in Glen Garry and made it his home for the winter. From this base he was able to make visitations to the Catholic communities in Glenmoriston, Strathglass, BraeLochaber, and Glen Garry itself. Then at the first whiff of spring he headed over the mountain watershed to the west coast and the islands.[24] This was his first view of his vicariate in its entirety, and the shortage of priests, the impossibility of their covering the ground, and the spiritual starvation of the people – which hitherto he had really only heard as talk – now came as a rude shock to him.

Serving the whole area he had a team of just six, including two reluctant Lowlanders. Between ill health and ill will, it was a team that had sorely taxed Bishop Gordon's authority, but Hugh at least had the advantage of being their own unanimous choice as bishop,[25] and could perhaps expect at least a honeymoon period of support. The most troublesome of them, the Benedictine Gregor MacGregor whom Bishop Gordon considered 'one of the men in the world the most unfitt for trade' and the focus of dissent, had been removed from his station and sent abroad shortly before Hugh's arrival.[26] With his departure it was hoped that others who had been infected by his turbulent spirit might now fall into line.

Financially at least the vicariate was healthy. Hugh still had the bulk of the 600 livres from Paris. Bishop Gordon, who had received two extraordinary grants from Propaganda the previous year, had also made a donation to him while he was in Edinburgh.[27] And the Scots agent William Stuart had sent word that Propaganda were to grant him an

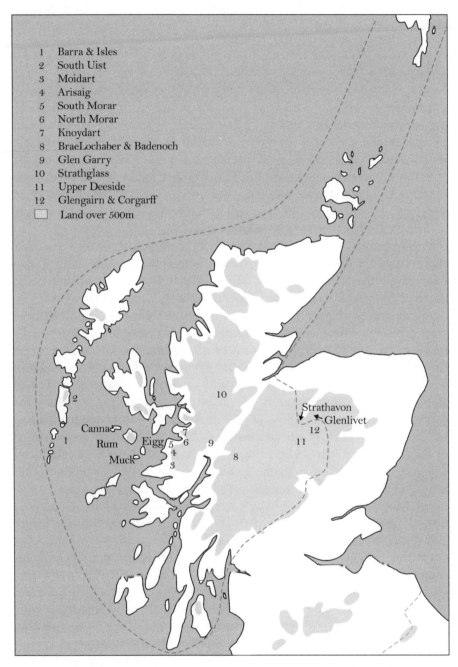

1 Barra & Isles
2 South Uist
3 Moidart
4 Arisaig
5 South Morar
6 North Morar
7 Knoydart
8 BraeLochaber & Badenoch
9 Glen Garry
10 Strathglass
11 Upper Deeside
12 Glengairn & Corgarff
☐ Land over 500m

Map 5. The Highland Vicariate (1732): extent in theory and actual stations

annual pension of 200 crowns, with a further one-off donation of 100 crowns to purchase liturgical vessels.[28]

Mr Stuart had also learned from the Inneses of Hugh's plans for a separate Highland seminary, and had himself put a strong case for it to Propaganda. The cardinals were sympathetic in principle, he reported, but unable to support with hard cash. He promised to continue pressing the issue, which he believed had a fair chance of success if Hugh himself put in a strong request for it. But this would need to be tactically worded. In particular, he cautioned, 'he must have a care not make the least mention of the old seminarie of Scalan, for that might hinder them from granting any help to it let him write only what concern's his own district, for I hope by riff, or by raff at length we may squize somthing from them to help it, if right measurs be takn.'[29]

If the cardinals of Propaganda were to be reminded of Scalan's existence they would probably refuse a second seminary, arguing that Scalan had served the whole Mission quite adequately until now, and could comfortably accommodate the students of both vicariates.

In fact, the problems at Scalan and its unsuitability for Highland boys were central to Hugh's case for a seminary of his own. It had never really been able to serve the cultural needs of its Gaelic-speaking students. And for several years now it had been a doubly divided house. The arrival of several older students, 'failures' from the Scots colleges abroad, had created a polarised community of adults and young boys, in which the former resented working alongside children and the latter were scandalised by their elders' critical attitude to the Church.[30] The most disenchanted of the newcomers was a Highlander, who had drawn the other Highland students into a secretive Gaelic-speaking clique at odds with the other boys and resentful of the master's authority. So fraught had the atmosphere become that the seminary's very survival seemed in doubt, and Bishop Gordon had been forced to clear the air by expelling the leader and three of the other Highland students.[31]

On this occasion the immediate cause of dissension lay with particular personalities. But underlying it, the age-old incompatibility between Highlander and Lowlander [32] presented a deeper and more permanent problem less easily resolved. For the young people, the gulf had proved too wide to be bridged by appeals either to their Christian charity or to the common cause of their oppressed Church. As an alumnus Hugh understood this better than most, and it was this above all that had prompted him to seek his own independent seminary. To him, indeed, the arguments for a separate vicariate and for a separate seminary were really one and the same: both were necessary in order to serve the unique conditions and needs of the Highlands. Unfortunately, he was very soon to find that the creation of two vicariates had itself widened the divide that it was intended to reflect.

Nonetheless, when he wrote his first report to Propaganda in March[33] he heeded the agent's tactical advice and made no mention of Scalan. He began his letter by thanking the cardinals for their annual grant and advising them of the grave shortage of priests throughout the Highlands, in language that showed a thorough mastery of the effusive diplomatic style he had learned in the library of the Scots College Paris. He pointed to the number of Highlanders who had abandoned their vocations while studying abroad, seduced by 'the world's vanities', and proposed that the most effective remedy would be to establish a seminary in the Highlands for the Highlands. But in view of the poverty of the people such a step would require Propaganda's help. He was now departing for the West, he concluded, where he intended to move ahead with his plans, 'trusting in their Eminences' generosity'.

Young and enthusiastic, he did not wait to hear from Rome. He had already learned through the Inneses that William Stuart had promised to release 300 livres annually for the new seminary from funds held in Paris, in addition to anything that might come from Propaganda.[34] Judging that this would enable him to make a start whatever the cardinals' decision, he arranged for the refurbishment of the house on Eilean Bàn in which he had begun his own training nearly twenty years before. In June he saw it opened for students.

At the end of the year James III gifted 200 crowns for the Highland seminary and schools,[35] but Hugh had still received nothing from Propaganda or the agent. His note to the latter appealing for assistance provides the best account we have of the new seminary:

> I have begun that good work haveing made up a large house in a place called the I,le of Moror which seems to be the most proper place for that purpose in all this Nation considering present circumstances, it being situated in the heart of our best and surest freinds, where by boat all necessaries can be brought, and all unecessary distractions can be keept off; I have already gott three or four boys together which is perhaps more than I am able to maintain without some help.[36]

Eilean Bàn was indeed the safest place for a seminary, among the Church's best and surest friends. There were other wholly or predominantly Catholic districts, but perhaps none so safe. BraeLochaber and Glen Garry were too close to the garrison at Fort William; Glenmoriston too accessible from the new barracks at Killiechumen. In Inveroy, Benbecula, Eigg and Canna, Knoydart and Barra, SSPCK schools had recently been set up, whose resident masters and visiting directors would be only too ready to report the existence of a Catholic school in their areas.[37] South Morar was nearly forty miles from the nearest garrison and had no parish or society school. Forming the northernmost tip of the parish of

Ardnamurchan, its minister lived two days' journey away. Nor was there any danger from king's bounty ministers or catechists now, for they had been withdrawn to work elsewhere.[38]

A further advantage of Eilean Bàn was that it belonged to Hugh's own family, and so was readily available without delay and negotiation, and unlikely to be withdrawn at whim. The fact that he 'made up a large house' on it – probably extending and renovating the existing buildings – suggests that he saw it as more than a stop-gap solution: given his own and the Mission's limited means it was likely to be in use for the foreseeable future.

Whether or not the idea of a Highland seminary originated with himself, it was certainly to his credit that he embraced it with a will and made it his top priority. In doing so he rightly identified the most urgent problem confronting the Church in the Highlands, and took the step that offered the best promise of solving it. His vicariate would now have the where-withal to train its own home-grown priests, independently, according to its own needs, and through the medium of Gaelic. At the same time, by freeing Scalan from a task it could not really fulfil his action would also benefit the Lowland vicariate and the Mission as a whole. As the opening gambit of his episcopate the bishop's move was the correct one.

Certain of the priests of the Highlands had long been waiting for the creation of their own vicariate, and the appointment of their own bishop, as the chance to redress what they saw as their second-class standing within the Mission. Their main grievance was their intolerable burden of work, with a far greater number of people to serve than in the Lowlands, and fewer priests to serve them. The inequality was an old one, but the creation of the two vicariates had thrown it into stark relief.

When Hugh met them that summer they seized this first opportunity to press him to arrange a meeting with representatives of the Lowland vicariate in order to put their case. In particular, they argued that their workload should be reflected in their recompense, and therefore that the Mission's quota funds should be divided between the two vicariates not according to the number of priests in each, but the number of the faithful.[39]

Hugh contacted Bishop Gordon and arranged a meeting for mid-August at the latter's home at Glastirim. When Bishop Gordon sounded out his own priests in advance of the meeting he not surprisingly found them dismayed at the proposal, which would in effect be robbing the Lowlands to pay the Highlands, and which also flew in the face of long tradition and the intention of the original donors. He could only hope that on the day the Highlanders would show themselves 'too wise, reasonable, just and zealous for the common good to be obstinate in such wild pretensions', which would merely lead to dissent among friends and the ridicule of their enemies.

Representing the Highlands at the meeting were Colin Campbell,

Alexander Paterson and Bishop Hugh himself. Between argument, the weight of his own authority, and Hugh's reasonableness, Bishop Gordon successfully warded off the calls for change. The Highland priests were forced to accept the *status quo*, but they did so with ill grace. They took back a bitterness to report to their colleagues in the West.

At the meeting the two representatives also aired the proposal, favoured by most of the Highland clergy, that every priest on the Mission should be compelled to subscribe in writing to the constitution *Unigenitus*. But neither Hugh nor Bishop Gordon was prepared to commit himself to such a course of action, which was certain to breed fierce disagreement among their clergy. News of the proposal horrified the community at the Scots College Paris, where Lewis Innes feared that if implemented it would 'kindle a fire of division that could never be quenched but by the ruin of trade'.[40]

Thus it was that within nine months of Hugh's taking office differences were already emerging between Highlands and Lowlands, centring upon both administrative and doctrinal issues. There was a real danger of a wedge being driven between the two vicariates, which could prove highly delicate for the two vicars apostolic, in regard to their relationships with their priests and, not least, with each other.

Notes

1. Bishops Gordon and Wallace to Propaganda, 4.7.1730, BL, SCA (in Latin); translation also printed in Belleslieim A. (1890), vol. IV, appendix XII.
2. Charles Whyteford had been principal for almost twenty years, but was little more than a figurehead. Vice-principal Thomas Innes was now the real power in the College. Lewis Innes, who had been principal from 1682 to 1713 and was now close to eighty, lived in and to many people 'still appeared to be head of the College' – Halloran B. M. (1997), p. 149.
3. A further advantage of Paris was that it could be reached at less cost than Rome.
4. This, we know, was the route he took on the return journey.
5. The present description based on Halloran B. M. op. cit., p. 24, with illustrations of the exterior on jacket and plate 4. Interior of chapel, plate 5a; of painting, plate 5b. Re the library, ibid., p. 177ff., and Cherry A. (1984 J), pp. 327ff.
6. Thomas Innes to Bishop Gordon, 23.11.1731, BL.
7. Lewis Innes to Bishop Gordon, 21.9.1731, BL. He advised that Hugh would require an allowance comparable to that of the Scots agent himself. Some months before this, Thomas Innes had contacted James III, urging him to use his influence in Rome to get Hugh the same grant as Bishop Gordon – Thomas Innes to Bishop Gordon, 26.5.1731, BL.
8. Lewis Innes to Bishop Gordon, 23.11.1731, BL.
9. Halloran B. M. op. cit., p. 116.
10. Since the mid-1720s, when Bishop Gordon had first pressed the argument

for a Highland bishop, they had stressed that his most urgent priority upon appointment should be the setting up of a separate seminary – Thomas Innes to William Stuart, 15.7.1726, BL.

11. Lewis Innes to Bishop Gordon, and Thomas Innes to same, 21.9.1731, BL.

12. This bishop was the nephew of his more famous namesake, Jacques Bénigne Bossuet, bishop of Meaux (1627–1704), known as the 'Eagle of Meaux' on account of his eloquence in the pulpit.

13. Ibid. Their action was particularly dangerous in that the prior of the local chartreuse, who had final authority over the Scots College and its principal, was vigilantly anti-Jansenist and had long harboured concerns regarding the college staff: cf. e.g. Thomas Innes to Bishop Gordon, 12.2.1727, copy SM 3/22, SCA, telling him of the new prior's threat to put a proctor in the college *ex officio*; he only held off out of regard for Lewis Innes.

14. Ibid.

15. Thomas Innes to Bishop Gordon, 23.11.31, BL.

16. Bishops Gordon and Wallace to Propaganda, 20.10.1731 (in Latin), BL. The date has traditionally been stated as 18 October, the Feast of St Luke. But the bishops' letter, which states that the consecration took place 'today', is dated 13 Kal. Nov. – i.e. 20 October.

17. 'Divisio variarum in Scoticae Regno regionum inter duos Vicarios Apostolicos', Edinburgh, 20.10.31 (in Latin), SM 3/26/2, SCA.

18. *The Scots Magazine*, appendix for the year 1747, pp. 614ff. Bishop Gordon's letter, dated 29.11.1731, was among the papers of HMD confiscated by Government troops on Eilean Bàn in summer 1746 and subsequently published as above.

19. *Decretum Sacrae Congregationis de Propaganda Fide*, 7.1.1732 (in Latin), SM 3/26/2, and typescript copy SM 3/26/4, SCA. Previous commentators have failed to identify two of the districts named, Glen Lyon and Strath Ardle, due to a mis-transcription of their Latin names in the text, in which 'Glenleo' has been copied as 'Glenlea' and 'Strathardalia' as 'Strathandalia'.

20. Cf. Burt E. (1754; 1998 edn), Letter III, p. 19.

21. When Bishop Geddes planned to visit Orkney in 1790, to meet the one Catholic family now living there, neither he nor his vicar apostolic George Hay knew which vicariate the islands belonged to – Bishop Hay to Bishop Geddes, 9.4.1790, BL. From 1862 to *c.* 1870, Orkney, Shetland and Caithness were actually taken out of the Scottish Mission and made a part of the Catholic Church's Mission to the polar regions, along with Greenland, Lapland, Iceland, the Faeroes and parts of Hudson's Bay! – For the fullest account of the Polar Mission, see Ciamberlani X. (1865); also 'Prefecture of the Arctic Missions', *Catholic Directory*, 1868; Anson P. F. 'An Outpost of the Faith', *The Month*, March 1938, pp. 247f; and Gray A. (2000), p. 60.

22. Thomson J. 'Some Account', etc., Th/10, p. 3, SCA – 'these [Glenlivet and Strathavon] Bishop Gordon designedly kept in his own Vicariate, though the Erse at that time was the only language spoken in them, on account of his seminary being settled at Scalan'.

23. The map in Forbes F. and Anderson W. J. (1966 J), p. 130, though otherwise

accurate, makes no mention of Glenlivet, and includes Strathavon within the Highland vicariate.

24. According to a joint letter from Bishop Gordon and himself written the following year, he visited 'all the farthest Hebridean islands and many other districts committed to to his care' – Bishop Gordon and HMD to Cardinal Falconieri, 27.8.1733 (in Latin), SM 4/4/19, SCA.
25. Bishop Gordon to William Stuart, 5.4.1732, BL.
26. Ibid. Fr MacGregor had transferred to the Benedictine monastery at Würzburg, where he continued to speak calumnies against many of his former colleagues, including Bishop Gordon and Hugh MacDonald himself.
27. Bishop Gordon received 400 crowns from Propaganda for the use of the Mission early in 1731, and a similar amount towards the end of the year – Thomson J., Th/10, SCA, also in Forbes Leith W. op. cit., p. 319.
28. William Stuart to James Carnegy, 10.1.1732, BL. (The following year Propaganda agreed to forward an additional 500 scudi [equiv. £125 sterling] to the Mission, in recognition of the increased expenses involved in administering two vicariates – Propaganda archives, cited in Bellesheim A. (1890), vol. IV, p. 190).
29. Ibid.
30. Bishop Gordon to Lewis Innes, 12.8.1732, BL. For a fuller account see Watts J. (1999), espec. p. 65.
31. William Reid to Bishop Grant, 16.12.1763, BL, recalling events when he was one of the Lowland students. The leader of the Highland dissidents was Ranald MacDonald.
32. This issue would arise again more than once in later years, when the enrolment of Highland boys at Scalan was mooted, and the advice was always that Highland and Lowland boys simply could not get on together in a close community – cf. e.g. John Paterson to William Reid, 14.10.1778, BL; and Bishop Hay notes on back of letter of 26.6.1778, CS 1/1/4, SCA; both letters quoted in Watts J. op. cit., pp. 163f.
33. HMD to Cardinals of Propaganda, 20.3.1732 (in Latin), BL.
34. HMD to William Stuart, 20.8.1733, BL.
35. The grant was made via Lewis Innes, the Queen's Almoner in James' court – Lewis Innes to William Stuart, 1.12.1732, BL.
36. Ibid.
37. Inveroy – 1720; Benbecula – 1725; Eigg-Canna – 1728; Barra – 1732: SSPCK Records, GD 91/9/1, NAS; Knoydart – 1731: GD 95/91 p. 68, NAS. The expansion of the SSPCK into the traditionally Catholic areas had in fact given an added urgency to opening a seminary in the West.
38. In 1729 the SSPCK had decided to concentrate its resources in supporting Protestant areas suffering a shortage of permanent ministers, or which were in danger of Catholic expansion – King's Bounty Committee Records 1725–30, Meeting of 27.2.1729, recommendation to the General Assembly, CH 1/5/51. p. 420, NAS.
39. Bishop Gordon to Lewis Innes, 12.8.1732, BL.
40. Lewis Innes to Bishop Gordon, 1.11.1732, copy SM 3/22, SCA.

7

Schisms and Most Scandalous Divisions (1733–45)

In the autumn of 1732 accusations of Jansenism were levelled by Highland priests against a number of their Lowland colleagues. From this time on the differences that were already growing between the two vicariates would crystallise around the issue of doctrine, as charges of heresy became entwined with complaints about working conditions, and in some cases were made a convenient peg to hang old jealousies on. As it developed, the rift broadly followed the Highland–Lowland divide, but not exactly, for its edge was blurred by individual friendships, animosities, ambitions and past histories, and by the regular and Jesuit clergy, all of whom allied themselves with the accusers.

The following spring a national conference of clergy was held at Preshome at which Bishop Gordon insisted that the whole Mission 'should keep together united as one body', and that the existence of two vicariates must in no way alter this.[1] During a part of the meeting chaired by his assistant, Bishop Wallace, Colin Campbell tried to present a motion that all Mission priests should be obliged to sign the constitution *Unigenitus*. Not wishing to take responsibility for such a far-reaching decision, Bishop Wallace ruled the motion out of order.[2] Shortly afterwards Campbell went down to Edinburgh, where he met Bishop Gordon and persuaded him to convene a meeting of representatives of the two vicariates at Scalan that June to discuss Jansenism and other issues affecting the Mission.

How much Hugh knew of or was involved in these developments is not entirely clear. Colin Campbell claimed that it was the Highland bishop who had requested him to propose his *Unigenitus* motion, and it was a common belief among the clergy that Hugh had also instructed him to raise the question of Jansenism with Bishop Gordon in Edinburgh and to request him to make investigations.

On the other hand, Bishop Hugh's own recollection of events gave a very different account:

> Its certain that, before Mr Colin went off from the Highlands for Ed^r in spring that year, our people had no thoughts of Jansanism nor did we suspect any body in this Kingdome about it, much less did we supose that ther was any necessity of subscriving the Constitution, but when Mr Colin returned from Ed^r after his circuit thorough the North, he brought me a verball comission

from B: Gordon desiring that I and the most principal Laburers in the Highlands shoud meet him that Summer at Glenlivet [Scalan] to concert measurs aganst Jansennism which he affirmed was spraeding south and north, and this did give me the alarm who never heard of any such thing before that time. Now as I am informed that it was said that Mr Colin had a commission from me before he left the Highlands that year to desire Doctor James Gordon to inquir into that affair; I solemly declare that I never gave any such commission.[3]

We can believe his solemn declaration that he did not actually instruct Colin Campbell to request an investigation, and probably also his assertion that Mr Campbell relayed Bishop Gordon's request for the Scalan meeting to him. But his claim that he and the Highland clergy had no thoughts of Jansenism, and suspected no-one of it, before Colin Campbell's visit to Edinburgh in spring 1733 will not hold water. He must have been aware that Jansenism was an issue at least since the meeting of August 1732, when Campbell had first proposed the compulsory signing of the constitution.[4] And there is evidence that he was aware of the accusations against particular Lowland priests by autumn 1732 at the latest.[5] His account was written twelve years after the event, after Colin Campbell had been discredited, and was clearly an attempt to dissociate himself as far as possible from the Campbell faction and indeed from the whole controversy.

Several weeks before the meeting at Scalan was due to take place, Colin Campbell's brother James travelled to Aberdeen and took lodgings there. Though his visit was purportedly for reasons of health, some thought his real intention was to meet the priests of the North-East and prime them prior to the meeting. For similar reasons, it was alleged, he arrived at Scalan ten days early in order to 'sift' Bishop Gordon.[6]

The meeting took place on 6 June (1733). Both brothers attended, Colin as one of the three Highland representatives accompanying Hugh, and James as an observer.[7] The Lowlands were represented by four priests of the North-East, John Tyrie from Huntly, the Scalan master, George J. Gordon and his assistant George Duncan, and the Benedictine, Thomas Brockie. All four had been approached by James Campbell beforehand and could be counted on to take the 'Highland' side in any discussion of Jansenism.[8]

According to Bishop Gordon the delegates' approach was aggressive throughout. They 'disturbed him very much with the clamours and compleants and could not be persuaded to act or let him act with the sedatness and maturity that weighty affair required'.[9] Their invective was directed not so much at their fellow missioners as at the Scots College Paris where they had trained, whose teaching had led them astray.

The harassed bishop finally agreed to the publication of a circular from himself and Bishop Hugh instructing all priests in Scotland, secular and regular, to sign the constitution *Unigenitus*. To set an example and begin the process a form of acceptance was drawn up, to which the two bishops and the seven priests present appended their names.[10]

It was also agreed that letters should be sent to Rome, one from the two bishops to the pope, a second from the bishops to the cardinal protector, and a third to the cardinal from the priests present on behalf of 'the whole clergy' of Scotland.[11] The contents of the three were in essence the same – a searing attack on the senior staff at Paris for infecting their students despite repeated warnings from home, and a call for them to be removed from office as part of a wholesale reformation of the college. By implication Thomas Innes came under the greatest censure, though he was not actually named.

We may perhaps question Hugh's prudence in involving Rome directly at this stage by putting his name to the letters, but we cannot doubt his sincerity. He knew the Scots College Paris well enough to realise that the accusations were not without foundation. In addition, Thomas Innes had been rash enough to divulge his personal opposition to *Unigenitus* to James Campbell while the latter was a student there,[12] and it is certain that Campbell would have discussed this with Hugh in France or on their journey home together.

Bishop Gordon later claimed that he himself was a reluctant participant at the meeting,[13] and he was certainly harried by the priests into making hurried decisions. But the letters to the pope and cardinal protector from himself and Hugh were unequivocal as to where he stood. It was he who penned them, and as senior bishop he bore the chief responsibility for them. He must have known that Rome would be bound to follow them up, and that this must have serious consequences for the Scots College and the Mission. We can only assume, indeed, that this was his intention, in order to bring the matter to a head. That he was by now deeply worried that Jansenism might be taking a hold upon the Scottish Mission is clear from the pastoral letter that he issued jointly with Bishop Hugh on the subject that autumn.[14] He perhaps vainly hoped that a stand taken now regarding Paris might serve to unite the Scottish clergy and prevent the situation deteriorating further, for he saw a real danger of the Mission 'falling into schisms and most scandalous divisions'.[15] But the Scalan meeting must have left him doubting whether his action or any action could now stem the tide.

Two days later a second, private meeting was held at the house of Alexander Grant at Clashnoir four miles down the glen. Bishop Gordon and the two Scalan masters were not invited, but – perhaps through inexperience – Hugh agreed to attend. Without the restraining influence of the older bishop those present gave free rein to intemperate debate, in the current of which Hugh found himself swept along.

Their targets were a number of fellow priests whom they accused by name of Jansenist heresy. These men, dubbed the 'Paris Club' because of their association with the Scots College, they pronounced unfit for promotion on the Mission. Among those condemned were Alexander Smith, Hugh's one-time master at Scalan, and the present master, Hugh's fellow 'heather priest', George J. Gordon who, ironically, had signed the constitution along with them just two days before.[16]

After the meeting Hugh returned to Scalan, where he confided to Bishop Gordon the decisions taken at Clashnoir. If the older man doubted the younger's wisdom in allowing himself to be a party to them, he did not allow it to impair their relationship. He in fact penned a further letter to Rome on behalf of them both, reiterating the stance they had taken in their previous joint letters.[17]

James Campbell was the man chosen to carry the Scalan letters to Rome.[18] On arrival he was refused permission to present them to Propaganda, but before leaving entrusted them to the care of Æneas MacGillis, a Highland student at the Scots College, through whom they finally came into the hands of the cardinal protector.[19]

The death of Bishop Wallace on the last day of June brought the question of a successor to the fore again. The consensus at Scalan and Clashnoir had been for Colin Campbell, but in the meantime a caucus had turned against him. The instigator seems to have been Alexander Grant, who not only withdrew his own support but conspired to persuade others in the North-East to do the same.[20] The clique argued that Campbell had proved himself unsuited for office by his 'fury and madness' at the Scalan meeting (where he had pled the special hardships of the Highland vicariate with great warmth). Their further arguments, that no Highlander if appointed would have the Lowland vicariate at heart, and that only Lowland clergy should have a vote in the election, only served to widen the Highland–Lowland divide.

Hugh had also become the butt of their invective. His youth and dynamism were a threat to them,[21] and they were now speaking openly of him as the leader of 'a Caballing Club of Highlanders' who were trying to wreck the Mission by their inordinate demands. When they made this accusation in circular letters to the clergy of the South, Hugh was shaken by their attack: 'I did not expect that Churchmen whom I saw att Scalan in june last and w^t whom I parted in grace union and charity, should begin to write a libell against me without provocation,' he wrote.[22] He was particularly hurt that George J. Gordon, whom he had considered his friend since their student days at Scalan, had put his name to the documents. So upset was he that he wrote to the priests of the Lowland vicariate, defending his position and uging them to sign the constitution.[23] But his action probably did more harm than good, since it was construed as an encroachment upon Bishop Gordon's domain and apparently left the latter 'not a litle nettled'.

The situation was threatening to slide out of control. Letters of the clergy were now filled with conspiracy, mutual recrimination and the worst spiteful language of *odium theologicum*. 'Schismatical Simoniacal', 'Mad-Cap', 'Simon Magus', 'Gall of Bitterness', 'Enimys of God', 'Monster' were among the phrases used to describe fellow Christians of the other camp.[24]

The election of a Lowland coadjutor bishop had become for the time being the main focus of the power struggle. When Bishop Gordon announced that there would be a meeting of his priests in August at which the election would take place, his decision to invite Bishop Hugh and several of the Highland clergy was viewed by the North-East faction as a ploy to ensure victory for Colin Campbell.[25] Had they known it, he did not in fact favour Campbell as his coadjutor, and had not done so for several years past.[26] Because of his own doubts, and the opposition whipped up by the North-East clergy, no clear name emerged at the meeting and the election was postponed.

The meeting also saw skirmishing between the Highland and Lowland priests regarding their unequal working conditions, from which the Highlanders came away entirely frustrated. On the journey home they warned Hugh that discussion was fruitless and that they would be content with nothing less than a deputation to represent their case in person in Rome. Their insistence on this course of action developed into a trial of strength between him and them that was to last for more than a year.

They at first proposed that he should make the journey himself, accompanied by someone able to speak Italian. By his own account this sudden and quite unexpected suggestion caught him off guard:

> M^r McAlister [himself] was att a stand how to answer directly a proposal so new, and attended with so many deficulties, especialy when the most solide objections could get no hearing; but as he had alwais had a strong inclination to satisfi them, and to gain their hearts and affections, to make them the more submissive and chearfull in going about their laborious functions, he did not flatly deny to give himself that trouble, and as little did he promise to goe, but gave them a general answer, that he was willing to do any thing that might contribut to the advantage of trade.[27]

In this, the first real test of his episcopal authority, he surely made the wrong decision. His own character was naturally generous, reasonable and pliant, but he was wrong to assume that his priests were the same and that his desire to please would win their hearts. His failure to give them a firm 'yes' or 'no' at the outset left them no more submissive and not a whit more cheerful: they merely saw it as temporising and a weakness that they might exploit. In his defence, it must be doubted whether a heavier or more decisive hand would have succeeded any better with priests so wayward and intransigent.[28]

Once back in the West he wrote to the Scots agent to seek his advice regarding sending a deputation to Rome. The agent's reply never reached him and was, he believed, probably intercepted by one of his own priests. They themselves were meantime using 'all their rethorick' to win over the rest of the Highland clergy. He continued to play for time, pointing out that he could not give a decision until he had heard the views of the priests of the Outer Isles.

His lack of enthusiasm for the whole idea was clear to see, and its proponents realised that even if he agreed to travel he would make a tepid advocate of their cause. They therefore now proposed that he remain at home and that two of their number be deputed to make the journey. This he felt obliged to refuse, since it would have taken all control over the discussions in Rome out of his hands. But taking a firm stand and speaking strong words at this late juncture only had the effect of breeding resentment and secrecy, even among those who had been open with him up to now.

That autumn John Tyrie arrived in the West. Certain scandals involving himself and a woman in Huntly had come to the ear of Bishop Gordon,[29] and a private arrangement had been agreed that he should be transferred to the Highland vicariate to avoid further damage to the Church. Hugh decided to put him in charge of the seminary on Eilean Bàn, where he would be away from women's company and at the same time solve the ongoing staffing problem there, and where he himself was well placed to keep a vigilant eye on him.[30]

Word now came back from the Outer Isles that the messenger sent to consult with the priests there had been taken ill and would be unable to return for some months. With his usual disregard for self Bishop Hugh went at once to cover his mainland station. His own constitution had never been robust and now, wearied by long travel and lashed by the Highland winter already setting in, he too succumbed. His illness lasted from December until March (1735) and so deep was his decline that for a while the surgeon despaired of his recovery.

Colin Campbell and John Tyrie, who were tending him in his sickbed, urged him to make his will while there was still time, name a successor, and compose letters to Rome representing the hardships of the Highland district. Too weak even to dictate the letters, he gave them permission to compose them on his behalf. But when, with great effort, he read them over he found that they contained damaging slanders against Bishop Gordon and accusations of heresy against a number of well-respected priests. He refused to countenance them; for how could he, about to face judgment and most in need of mercy, judge others with so little mercy? Totally isolated, desperately ill and believing his death was near, he was now actually hoping it would come, merely 'to be free of present troubles'.

When the messenger finally returned from the Hebrides in April Hugh was all but back to full health again and able to accept his priests' request for a meeting. But as they gathered at his house he discovered that most of them had met privately beforehand, 'so that everything was already concerted'. They were determined to have a decision, and threatened that unless the deputation to Rome went ahead they would abandon the Mission and publicly denounce him as an enemy of the Highlands. They had touched the weak point of his whole position as a bishop, his ultimate dependence upon their goodwill. He was forced to accede, and even failed to secure the right to choose his companion. When the meeting pushed through the appointment of John Tyrie, his worst fears were confirmed.[31]

He at least got agreement that Mr Tyrie must promise on oath to act entirely under his direction, and included this in a document of 'Instructions' drawn up before the meeting closed. The latter defined the issues open to discussion in Rome. Though these could include the question of Jansenism and the reformation of the Scots College Paris, the main emphasis was to be on the problems of the Highland vicariate and proposals for solving them.[32]

The priests now pressed Hugh to request a coadjutor while in Rome, to put the Highlands in line with the Lowlands. Their own choice for the post was Colin Campbell. It was accepted procedure that such requests were only ever made at the discretion of the vicar apostolic himself, if his own age and/or infirmity rendered it necessary.[33] Hugh considered that these conditions did not apply, and that losing a priest to create a bishop would only deplete an already overstretched team. He therefore stood firm against it. He also refused to set a date for travelling, making it his excuse that he must first confer with Bishop Gordon. Though the priests received this rebuff 'in a most seditious manner, pressing solicitations and even threatnings', they had no choice but to accept it.

He left for the low country at the beginning of May, visiting the eastern extremes of his vicariate – Upper Deeside, Glengairn and Corgarff – *en route*. His detour only aroused the suspicions of the North-East clergy, who believed that he had ambitions to annexe the nearby Gaelic-speaking stations of Strathavon and Glenlivet in order to tip the balance of power in favour of the Highland vicariate.[34] The fact was, he had problems enough in his own territory without thinking of adding to it.

His position had become impossible. He had behaved honourably (if perhaps rather weakly) throughout, but had succeeded in pleasing no-one and incurring the suspicion of all, within and without his vicariate. In the loneliness of his life as a bishop never perhaps was he more alone than now. The one person in Scotland in whom he could confide was James Gordon, his compeer in Edinburgh, and he was glad to be staying some days with him. He found him if anything even more opposed to the Rome visit than himself.

On the very day that he arrived home the priests appeared unannounced at his door 'as if they had fallen out of the clouds'. They were now demanding that he should send two of themselves, to the point of threatening that if they did not have his permission they would go without it. 'I know not what to do,' he wrote in anguish to Bishop Gordon, 'for I see dangers in whatever method I take, either in venturing my self, or entrust affairs to others who seem to be in a more violent humor. I hop you will be mindfull of me.'[35]

In the end he agreed to let Colin Campbell and John Tyrie travel, with a remit strictly confined to the temporal affairs of the vicariate as set out in letters from himself to the pope, the cardinal protector, the agent and King James, which they carried with them, and of which he was careful to keep copies.[36] He enjoined them to speak ill of no fellow missioner and to act in all things under the direction of the Scots agent. Unfortunately, though the intention of the letters was to restrict the scope of their competence, their effect was to give them an official authority and a credibility without which they would have got nowhere in Rome.

The two deputies – they would later be dubbed the 'Pilgrims' – left Morar on 8 August.[37] They were the last people Hugh would have chosen, for he had come to recognise them for what they were, the root cause of the challenge to his authority and the 'primum mobile of mischief'. The turning point in his judgment of them must have been the time of his great illness, when their ruthless behaviour had revealed their true colours. Most of all he feared Colin Campbell, whom he had once counted as a close friend. Ambition had changed him, and now he could only say of him '*cum bene nemo melius, cum male nemo pejus*' ('when he acted well there was no-one better, and no-one worse when he acted ill'). Yet even now he was ready to forgive him, and 'breathed no revenge'.

Their departure left more Highland stations vacant. No-one could be spared to take Mr Tyrie's place at the seminary, and since Hugh himself was only able to keep half an eye on it, being away more often than not, trying to support his priests, he seriously considered closing it. 'My young plants will goe to nought, after spending so much upon them,' he feared.[38] The deputation to Rome was also a huge financial drain, the whole of which had to be borne by the Highland vicariate. The one bright note in an otherwise dark affair was that throughout it he had managed to keep 'constant good freindship' with Bishop Gordon.

Some weeks before the departure of the pilgrims, Alexander Smith had been recalled from his post at the Scots College Paris in order to be consecrated coadjutor bishop for the Lowlands.[39] There were many on the Mission who opposed his election. Some Lowland clergy thought his physical appearance should have disqualified him, while to most Highlanders he remained one of the 'Paris Club' condemned as unfit for office at Clashnoir two years before. The latter made it very clear to Hugh that he should not attend the consecration, even if appointed to participate by the pope himself.[40] Colin Campbell actually had the impertinence to 'forbid' him to attend, threatening to denounce him to Rome as a Jansenist if he did. He ignored their threats and made the journey down to Edinburgh, where on 2 November Alexander Smith was consecrated by Bishop Gordon in his presence.

Once back in the West he spent the last weeks of 1735 on the road, covering for his depleted team. He had been forced to send Neil MacFie to Uist, having no-one else to spare, though he knew that the alcoholic would be almost useless in that large and populous station. The Kirk was at this time targeting Uist and Barra for evangelisation and had recently placed a minister, schoolmaster and catechist on each island.[41] Word now came back to Hugh that there was a real danger of some islanders on Uist being drawn over to Protestantism by their efforts. The case seemed urgent enough to require his presence, even if that meant hazarding the Minch and its notorious moods in mid-winter.[42]

As soon as the Christmas season was over he left for Arisaig, where he hired a boat and, amazingly, four men willing to row her. Setting out from Rhu they stayed as long as possible in the lea of the Small Isles, skirting Eigg, nosing out into the treacherous currents off the western point of Rum, and keeping as close as they safely could to the rocky coast of Canna, before battling the south-west wind in a dash to the shelter of Lochboisdale. Hugh remained on Uist until April, cut off from all contact with the outside world.

On his return to Morar he learned to his 'mortification' that Campbell and Tyrie had broken their commission in Rome and were actively accusing Bishop Smith and a number of the Lowland clergy of heresy, and Bishop Gordon of collusion.[43] They had borrowed the Scalan letters from Æneas MacGillis and made copies of them to use as evidence. He at once wrote to the cardinal protector, defending the new bishop and repeating his condemnation of the two deputies.[44] The noise they had made, he told him, had already done untold harm in Scotland, scandalising the faithful and discouraging many a would-be convert. It was no coincidence that the Church was enjoying a degree of peace and harmony again in their absence.

What he did not know was that they had actually called for Bishop Smith's removal, and for the amalgamation of the two vicariates, and, unforgivably, had claimed that in these matters they were speaking on his behalf.[45] It must have appeared to Rome that Hugh was working against his colleague Bishop Gordon, while he, being ignorant of their lies, did not know how to defend himself.

Although the document drawn up at the Scalan meeting of June 1733 had instructed all priests of the Mission to register their acceptance of the constitution *Unigenitus*, the two bishops had later reduced this to a *request*.[46] As a result several of the Lowland clergy had declined to sign it and Bishop Gordon had been obliged to send it to Rome incomplete.[47] In addition, some had apparently petitioned for a dispensation from certain clauses, and had been allowed to sign what was in effect a less stringent document. (Campbell and Tyrie later brought this to the Vatican's attention, claiming that as a result the whole purpose of the formula had been frustrated.[48]) Now, in the autumn of 1736, following a specially convened meeting of Propaganda, Clement XII issued a brief, making signature of the full formula compulsory for all.

At the same time the papal nuncio in Paris, Mgr Niccolò Lercari, was instructed to conduct an examination of the Scots college in that city. Though he met with obstruction and something of a wall of silence he gathered what evidence he could and issued his report in March 1737. It was a devastating document.[49] He found the staff, and in particular Thomas, Lewis and George Innes, guilty of Jansenism and recommended their removal as a necessary first step in the complete reformation of the college. He also found 'a large proportion' of the clergy in Scotland itself infected with the heresy, singling out several for mention by name. Most damaging of all, he reported that Bishop Gordon himself appeared to share the infection, and raised a range of circumstantial evidence to support the claim, not least his choice of Alexander Smith as coadjutor. Lercari judged that Bishop Smith might be the cause of great harm to the Mission should he ever succeed to the position of vicar apostolic. Of the three bishops only Hugh escaped censure, and indeed enhanced his reputation: 'Mgr Magdonol has been spoken of to me with the highest praise, in regard to both doctrine and true zeal for religion, so that complete reliance may be placed on his orthodoxy,' Lercari wrote.

He recommended that all the priests of Scotland should be instructed to sign the formula again. He also noted that the division of the Mission into two vicariates had not brought the benefits that had been hoped, and that 'the most fervent missionaries' – how he identified them is not clear – now favoured reunification.

The three bishops arranged to meet at Scalan in June to discuss the implications of the report.[50] It must have been a delicate meeting. The Lowland bishops were deeply hurt and aggrieved at the accusations against them, which left their authority totally undermined. If Rome were to order the reunification of the Mission the only possible choice for vicar apostolic would be Hugh MacDonald, despite his being the youngest of the three. The Lercari report had put a strain on their relationship, but it is to their great credit that – as far as we know – their friendship and co-operation remained unimpaired.

At the meeting Hugh also reminded his colleagues of the dearth of priests in the Highlands, and appealed for their help. As a gesture of support Bishop Gordon offered to let him have Francis MacDonell, since the young priest really belonged to the Highland district.[51] He had entered Scalan when it was still the seminary for the whole Mission, and had remained there instead of transferring to Eilean Bàn after the creation of the two vicariates. He had received his entire training there – the only student to do so since Hugh himself – and was now assistant master following his ordination there the previous year. Bishop Hugh was grateful to add him to his small team, and posted him to the station at Moidart which at the time was without a priest. He thought him a God-sent acquisition, but it was one that within five years he would come to bitterly regret.

Hugh remained at Scalan for several days after his fellow bishops had left. On the night before his departure an express letter arrived from Bishop Gordon giving news of the brutal murder of William Stuart, the Scots agent, who had been bludgeoned to death in his appartment in Rome.[52] Hastily changing his itinerary Hugh set off at once to meet his Lowland colleagues at Aberlour in order to decide upon a successor. Before his death William Stuart had named Peter Grant as his own preferred choice. Mr Grant was only two years ordained, really too young and inexperienced for such a post. But there was also much to be said in his favour: as an alumnus of the Scots College Rome he knew the city and the Italian language well; he was acceptable to King James; he was untouched by Paris; and (as regards domestic politics) he was a Gaelic speaker, but from Glenlivet in the Lowland vicariate, who moreover had been abroad during the height of the Highland–Lowland disputes. Hugh, who knew him from their student days at Scalan, was happy to agree to his nomination. But he did so with a real sense of sacrifice, for Mr Grant had been doing excellent work in Glen Garry and could not easily be spared.[53] The young man set out for Rome early in

September, hardly imagining that he would be remaining there as agent for close to half a century, long after the deaths of those who appointed him.

At about this time Hugh approached his younger brother John concerning the possibility of moving the seminary from Eilean Bàn. John had the tack of Gaothdail (*anglice* Gaotal or Guidale) [54] a farm which formed part of the seven merklands of Arisaig still in the possession of the MacDonalds of Morar, which Hugh saw as a more suitable site.

He had several reasons for making the change. The land at Gaotal was better and more extensive, and directly accessible by sea (plate 5). But its real benefit was that John's family lived close by and could look after the board and maintenance of the students. [55] When Hugh had opened the seminary on Eilean Bàn five years before he had thought it the best site available in the existing circumstances, having at that time received no outside funding to support it. [56] But ideally he would have preferred to keep it as a priest's house, serving Morar, or even as his own residence. He had perhaps never seen it as more than a stop-gap, and had always intended moving as soon as he was able.

Now he had the finance to do so, for though he had never received the grant promised by Propaganda he had received 500 crowns from Rome, as his share of the bequest of the late Cardinal Protector Falconieri, which, on King James' instruction, was to be divided between the High-land and Lowland seminaries. He was in a position to seal an arrangement for Gaotal with his brother in principle, with a view to making the move the following year.

In spring 1738, only a few weeks before the transfer, promise of more funding came his way just when he needed it. The administrators of the Mission met in March to decide on the best use for two recent gifts from abroad. The first, a grant of 2,000 crowns from Pope Clement XII, they decided should be placed in secure stocks, with the interest used to provide annual support for the two seminaries. The second, the legacy of Lewis Innes (his final gesture after a life-time of generosity, for he was to die that June), they agreed to divide equally between the two vicariates. [57]

At the beginning of May the students and master made the short boat journey round the Rhu peninsula to their new home. Finance had always put a bar on their number, but now for the meantime that bar was lifted. Within a few weeks Gaotal was more than full, with eight boys studying for the priesthood, several other lay boarders, and – with the master and servants – a total community of sixteen, far more than had ever been possible before. [58]

Once the new seminary was open Hugh set sail for the Outer Isles, where he remained until early October. While in Uist he visited Clanranald's house at Nunton, for he particularly wanted to meet Neil MacEachan, the tutor to Clanranald's sons. Neil was a Uist man himself who had been dismissed from the Scots College Rome, and Hugh was thinking of appointing him as the master at Gaotal. But what he saw disappointed him. The young man seemed to have little interest in either study or teaching and was leading a life of indolence. Clanranald had formed a similar impression, and had decided not to retain his services.[59]

Hugh had no choice but to appoint Allan MacDonald, his old friend from their Eilean Bàn days, to the Gaotal post, at least for the time being. Allan was now over forty and had enjoyed a very chequered career since leaving Eilean Bàn for the Scots College Rome in 1715. He was still only a deacon. He had been dismissed from Rome *re infecta*; unsuccessfully sought admission to Madrid; entered Douai, whence he was dismissed within a year; begged for a final chance at Scalan, where, after a promising start, he was one of the four Highland students dismissed in 1730; since when he had been teaching in Catholic schools in the West Highlands, still harbouring hopes of ordination. His appointment to Gaotal was strictly temporary, under Hugh's own direct supervision, and dependent upon good behaviour. The early signs were good at least: Allan appeared far more serious and determined to succeed than Hugh had ever seen him before.[60]

When he arrived in Edinburgh Hugh found a letter waiting for him from Peter Grant, the new Scots agent. Enclosed with it was a dictat from Mgr Rivera, the recently appointed cardinal protector, written on behalf of the pope, instructing the Scottish bishops to arrange for all priests to sign the constitution *Unigenitus*. (The order followed the recommendation in the Lercari report of the previous year). Hugh wrote back to Mr Grant, assuring him that the instruction would be obeyed, but objecting to having to repeat the process yet again.[61] It seemed totally unnecessary and incomprehensible; a 'most mortifying stroak' to the Mission that its integrity was still doubted in Rome; a cause of scandal to the Catholic laity and the loss of many potential converts; and difficult and dangerous to accomplish in the Highlands, where signatories and witnesses must be gathered and where any gathering was at once suspected and exaggerated by their enemies. And all on account of two mischief-makers who 'endeavour'd to ruin the reputation of their innocent brothers, without any appearance of reason but their owne ambitious vews'. As he aptly pointed out, if the priests were honest men the proofs they had already given should suffice, and if they were not another round of signatures would prove nothing.

The dictat had of course been drawn up by men who had no concept of the conditions of the Highland Church. How could Rome's bureaucrats in their sun-filled offices begin to understand the daily lives of its priests?

Priests like William Harrison, who had the whole of North and South Morar to serve, and must borrow a boat whenever he travelled; who never got word from the outside world, and had celebrated Easter that year without even knowing for sure whether it had been on the right date; who for want of a table wrote his letters on his knee, and for want of ink used gunpowder mixed in water.[62] And his was by no means the remotest station in the vicariate.

Between the challenges to his authority at home, Rome's lack of confidence in the Mission, and his own desperate shortage of priests, Hugh's morale was shattered. Some of his clergy were on the point of quitting, he warned the Scots agent, and he was near breaking point himself: 'The few laburers we have are so tired with troubles, that some of them are threatening to forsaik the western trade, but if any more of them follow the example of those who have already left us, you may exspect to hear, that Mr Sandison [himself] has doon the saime for it,s imposible for him to stand out alon.'

The reply he received[63] must have brought him satisfaction on one point at least, for the agent assured him that Propaganda was now on its guard against the deputies. The cardinal protector had taken careful note of Hugh's original letters commissioning them, and his letter of 1736, and was now fully aware of the true purpose of their visit, the motives behind it, and 'what sort of gentles' they really were.[64] He recognised that Hugh himself was in no way implicated in their machinations, and indeed had been betrayed by them.

Hugh's testimony had been accepted by the key people in the Vatican, as that of a man of proven integrity and the one best placed in all the Mission to know the truth, and had in fact been the crucial evidence in the exposure of the Pilgrims' true designs. If therefore he is to be blamed for allowing them to take their mission to Rome in the first place, and inadvertently lending it credibility, he must also be acknowledged as the one who more than any other ensured its ultimate failure.

Colin Campbell left Rome in late January 1739.[65] On reaching Scotland he took it upon himself to stay in Edinburgh until Easter, sending no word to his bishop nor seeking his permission to remain out of the vicariate. He then headed for Aberdeen. When Hugh travelled to the North-East in August to visit his stations at Braemar and Glengairn he met Mr Campbell by pure chance on the road through Glenlivet. It was the first time he had seen or heard from him in four years. He found him cool and guarded and reluctant to take charge of a station, preferring to be free to travel round the country.

There were still priests in the Highlands only too ready to listen to him – men like William Harrison, who had assumed his mantle of chief inquisitor during his absence. Mr Harrison had been writing to Rome on his own account, and had even had the temerity to enter Hugh's house while the bishop was away, carrying off and burning several books that he considered heretical.[66]

Such effrontery and treachery at home, and its apparent credence in Rome, seemed to leave Hugh's authority in tatters. His position appeared to him now barely tenable, and he even suggested to his friend Thomas Innes that he should resign and leave the field to Mr Campbell: 'If his callumnies will gett better hearing (as I hop they will not) than my real greivances, I am truly tempted to give him the long wished for satisfaction, which is, to leave all to himself and to retire to some place where I can live and dy in pace, for we have so many cridicts now that we know not how to behave.'[67]

How changed his tone from the buoyancy and energy of the newly consecrated bishop! Seven years of unrelieved struggle against enemies within and without, a keen sense of betrayal, the apparent impossibility of finding acceptable solutions, and illness that had brought him to the face of death, all these had taken their toll. He decided to stay on in the North-East for the autumn, far longer than he had originally intended; probably he was just too weary to return home.

On the day he visited Corgarff, a distant adjunct of the Glengairn station, he found himself in the company of the local priest, James Leslie, and Patrick Gordon the Jesuit who served nearby Upper Deeside. The latter waited until he could speak to Hugh privately and then showed him a letter he had written. It concerned the continuing threat of Jansenism within the Mission, and targeted eleven priests by name as well as Bishop Gordon himself. It referred in particular to the latter's support for the condemned Montpellier Catechism, claiming that he had supported it at the Scalan meeting of 1733 and had even threatened to suspend any priest who presumed to censure it. Fr Gordon wanted Hugh to confirm his account of the events at Scalan.

While they were talking the Jesuit noticed that James Leslie had slipped into his bedroom and appeared to be searching it. He then came out to join them. Fr Gordon now felt a tug at his clothing and felt sure that Mr Leslie was trying to pick his pocket. He rounded on him, only to be met with a 'jesting smile'. He could prove nothing; but the letter was gone. It eventually found its way to Bishop Gordon, with a note appended – 'Found by Mr J. Lesley in Corgarff dropt by Mr P. Gordon Jes:'. Patrick Gordon wrote to the bishop giving an account of the whole incident,[68] but the damage could not be undone. It put further strain on relations among the clergy, and left Hugh himself – innocent bystander though he was – in a delicate position.

The winter of 1739–40 was the longest and hardest of the century to date, reawakening among the older generation memories of the horrors of the 1690s. Snow, frost and storms lasted from late November until the end of May. So severe was the cold that the two-mile-wide estuary of the Tay froze from bank to bank. So late was the crop that Kirk ministers allowed the farmers to work on the Sabbath in order to save it. Meal prices rose to unheard-of levels.[69] Two boys whom Bishop Hugh had selected to join the Scots College Rome were unable to sail until June.

The boys concerned were the sons of Scottas and Glenaladale. Choosing students for the colleges posed problems for Hugh. He was under pressure from the college principals to fill places as soon as they became vacant, since this brought them income, and with the colleges dictating the arrangements he often had to send boys before they were ready. At the best of times it was difficult to find candidates with the required educational background in the Highlands, as he reminded the Scots agent: 'Youth have no opportunity of being taught unless they be sent to Prespiterian Masters which our people look upon to be much the saime as to compliment them to the Devil, therefore they think it much better for their Children to have religion without learning, than learning without religion.'[70]

Sending them was also a severe drain on his funds, since he had to find the money for their fees in the first instance and – in the Highland tradition of letting debt lie – the parents were often very slow to reimburse him. Only when they did so could he balance his books, or even pay his priests their quotas.

Yet sending them was essential to the future of the Church. Those bound for the priesthood were his long-term hope for solving the clergy crisis. But almost as important were those sent for a secular education. They were the next generation of Highland gentlemen. Some of them were the children of mixed marriages, or even of well disposed Protestant parents, and it was crucial that they receive an education in the faith.[71] Hugh even hinted to the principal of the Scots College Paris that he should create extra places beyond capacity for these gentlemen's sons and give them priority over other applicants, knowing 'what credite and advantage such persons might bring to our trade if rightly educated, and what harm they may do to it when they are not so'.[72] Bishop Nicolson had made a similar point to Rome at the end of the previous century, and now forty years on the chiefs and chieftains remained a key to the well-being and future of the Highland Church.

In the meantime Hugh was searching for anyone to add to his team. One possibility was Antony Kelly, the Recollect friar with whom he had begun his own priestly career, who had been recalled to Ireland but wished to return. He knew him as a friend and held him in high regard: 'For my part,' he told the Scots agent, 'if poor Antony Kelly should com I wold willingly dispence with all the rest.'[73] And one definite recruit was Æneas (Angus) MacGillis, who had completed his training in Rome and was now on his way home: Hugh intended placing him in the care of an experienced priest for his first year, 'to learn the practical part of the Trade'.

The following summer (1741) he was able to add Alexander Cameron to the workforce. Alexander was a younger son of Cameron of Lochiel and of Isobel Campbell of Lochnell, the sister of the convert priest Colin Campbell and his brother James. He had served as an officer in the French army, and had converted to Catholicism in 1730 after visiting the court of James in Rome. At the time he had written a lengthy *Apologia* to his older brother, in which he set out the arguments in favour of his new-found faith and urged him to follow his lead.[74] Soon afterwards he had joined the Society of Jesus, and had now returned to Scotland an ordained priest.

Hugh sent him to serve the Catholic parts of Strathglass and Glen-strathfarrar on the estates of Lovat and Chisholm. With no priest's house in the area he set up home in a shieling hut in Glen Cannich which offered so little shelter that he almost died of exposure in his first winter there. His *Apologia* of ten years before had obviously made little impression upon his family, for when he approached his father for permission to preach and celebrate Mass among the Camerons, promising to wean the tenantry away from their traditional practice of cattle rustling, Lochiel refused. The Catholics of Glen Garry, Knoydart and Arisaig, he pointed out, were even worse thieves than the Camerons; if Alexander could turn them from rieving he would allow him in, but until then he forbade him to 'middle with his people'.[75]

Hugh spent much of 1741 struggling to contain a long-running scandal involving one of his priests that was threatening to get out of hand.[76] When Francis MacDonell had transferred from Scalan to the Highland vicariate in 1737, Hugh had placed him in the Moidart station, where he built himself a one-roomed house. The following year he had brought his sister Catherine, young and recently widowed, to keep house for him, but there was much about their behaviour together that made the local people uneasy. They were often seen kissing and caressing, and used to sleep at the same end of the house, separated from the man-servant by a partition. In February 1739 she gave birth to a still-born child. There were suspicious circumstances surrounding the birth, for it was apparently brought on by use of the herb *miosachan* ('Fairy Flax', a recognised abortifacient) which her brother had gathered himself. The baby was buried that same night in a secret place. Though the women attending Catherine were sworn to secrecy, the word got out that summer. She had told them that Donald MacDonald of Kinlochmoidart was the father, but rumour at once laid the responsibility on her brother.

Because he had been away at Scalan when the news broke, Hugh had only heard of it on his return to the west at the end of October (1739). He had confronted Mr MacDonell at once, insisting that Catherine be sent away to scotch further scandal. The priest promised to comply and the following summer took her to the Raws of Huntly in the north-east of Scotland. But about Martinmas he sent his servant with a horse to bring her home. Hugh, who was in Glenlivet at the time, heard of what was happening and sent word to her forbidding her to travel. Francis then sent a second servant, who brought her, now obviously pregnant again, back to Moidart. For the next few months brother and sister moved from house to house in the countries of Moidart, Arisiag, Morar and Knoydart, everywhere living as a couple.

On 2 February 1741 Catherine gave birth to a baby boy at Barrisdale. Again strange circumstances attended the delivery. When the placenta failed to come away Francis brought her a silver tass filled with his own urine to drink, which those present took as a tacit admission of guilt, since drinking the father's urine was a known remedy in such a case. The child died a few days later, though he had shown none of the usual symptoms of infantile sickness.

Soon afterwards Francis arranged for her to marry one Ranald Mac-Donald, a widower, in Ardnamurchan. The unfortunate man knew nothing of past events, and when he finally found out he very under-standably accused Mr MacDonell of entrapping him. The latter continued to visit his sister, against the strict orders of his bishop and to the scandal of the Protestant community of Ardnamurchan. Finally about Christmas he plucked her from her husband's home and set up house with her on the island of Eigg, from where he sent Hugh a long letter pleading his innocence. No way persuaded, the bishop ordered him to return to the mainland to discuss the matter formally.

They met on 17 February (1742) at Gaotal, in the presence of a panel of five priests that included Colin Campbell and William Harrison. Hugh invited him to name the father before the witnesses present, but this he declined to do. Nor could his apparent willingness to give an answer in the secrecy of the confessional satisfy them, since the affair had long since become a public matter and required a public resolution. Hugh had no choice but to withdraw his priestly faculties.

Mr MacDonell demanded a second hearing and in the weeks that followed tried to put pressure on the bishop by smearing his name – he may even have hinted that he was the father of the second child – and by enlisting some of the old Campbell faction priests against him. Hugh agreed to meet him again on Holy Thursday, in the presence of six clergy.[77] At that meeting their unanimous verdict remained the same.

Once more the accused appealed, and asked that his case be brought before Bishop Gordon as the senior bishop of the Mission. Hugh was determined that justice be seen to be done, and arranged a meeting for 2 August at Scalan, with the bishop and seven priests. There Mr MacDonell again failed to offer a convincing denial of his guilt, and when asked outright turned away from his questioners in tears. The panel upheld the previous decisions and his suspension from priestly duties. Since he could have no future in the Scottish Mission the bishops advised him to go abroad and perhaps join a religious order there.

He returned to Ardnamurchan, where he stayed for three weeks with Catherine, sharing her bed during her husband's absence. While there he showed the local people a letter supposedly written by William Rattray, a shoemaker from Glenlivet, admitting to be the father of both Catherine's children. Rattray, whom he had met while at Scalan and had bribed with a guinea to sign the letter, later retracted his statement under oath. Francis also met Hugh in Moidart, where he assured him that he was now fully resolved to retire to a monastery in Germany and there end his days in penance. Hugh perhaps naively agreed to write to Bishop Gordon on his behalf, requesting a letter of recommendation and the money for his fare. The young man then set out for the capital, where Bishop Gordon gave him all that he required.

The bishops had long recognised the damage done to the Church in Scotland by the divisions of the past decade, and they felt a bitterness towards Rome. They told Propaganda candidly that if it had acted decisively at the beginning the problem would have evaporated long since.[78] But they had never received any official statement of support and felt their own position undermined. Some of their priests were threatening to resign and they were now even considering the same themselves. That a man of Bishop Gordon's years and experience could make such a statement in writing to Rome tells us better than anything the desperate state of the Mission at this time.

It was in fact tragic and unbelievable that such sores had been allowed to fester, when in the face of outside enemies internal unity was needed above all. Tragic that men, who had dedicated their whole lives to the cause of their Church at great personal cost, could have so set back that cause through failing in the virtues of humility, charity and obedience. And for Hugh personally, a matter of deep regret that the Mission's self-inflicted wounds had coincided with his own episcopate.

The only hope for the future lay with the next generation of priests. And fortunately Gaotal was already beginning to bear fruit. That summer two of its students were sent to the Scots College Rome, one of them Hugh's own fifteen-year-old nephew, his sister's son John.[79] And the future of the seminary itself was also secure, for Hugh had clinched an agreement with his brother John that May for part of the house to remain at the disposal of the Church for the next five years, and for John's family to continue to board and maintain the students and master.[80]

Francis MacDonell did not go abroad. He remained in Edinburgh, where soon afterwards he approached the local presbytery, confessed his former popish errors and asked to be admitted into the Church of Scotland. The recent scandals were unknown to them, and in February 1743 they accepted him in good faith.

So damaging had his actions, lies and false accusations been to the Church that Hugh now decided to publish a full account of the whole saga.[81] In doing so he sought to scotch the rumours and half-truths that had spread among the Catholic and Protestant laity, and also to justify his decision to withdraw Mr MacDonell's priestly faculties, an action that some had judged unwarranted. His account was verified as accurate by the five missionary priests who had been present at all three meetings, and were better placed than any to know the full facts.

Since Francis was already trained in divinity and a Gaelic speaker the Kirk readily granted him a licence to preach and recommended him for work in the West. Worse, because of his knowledge of Catholicism they considered him an ideal controversialist, equipped to defend Protestantism in districts where the Catholic Church was threatening to make advances, and as such assigned him to Strontian, of all places, just a few miles from the home of his sister's husband.

Inevitably, it was not long before his past reached the ears of the local presbytery. Word came to them that Donald Kinlochmoidart intended to make application to them to dispel the continued slanders on his name. In August 1743 they reported their concern to the synod of Argyll.[82]

The following March Donald Kinlochmoidart and Bishop Hugh took the unheard-of step of attending the presbytery's meeting at Aros on the isle of Mull, where they presented a lengthy written 'Complaint' against Mr MacDonell. Though the local Kirk might easily have dismissed the evidence of a Catholic bishop, the story was too public and too patently true to ignore. On the other hand, to accept it would be a serious embarrassment to them. At a loss they turned to the Royal Bounty Commission, who paid MacDonell's salary, for a way out of the dilemma. The latter judged it most prudent to remove the cause of their embarrassment to Skye, where he might start afresh. He was transferred to Duirinish accordingly, and the presbytery of Mull could now write in clear conscience and some relief to the complainants that he and his past deeds were no longer their business. Francis MacDonell settled well in Duirinish, where he apparently served without controversy until his death thirty-seven years later.[83]

The person who had actually penned the 'Complaint' to the presbytery of Mull was the bard Alasdair mac Mhaighstir Alasdair (Alexander MacDonald of Dalilea), whom posterity would judge the greatest Gaelic poet of the century. His father had been the Episcopalian minister of Ardnamurchan for some forty years until his death in 1724, famous throughout the Rough Bounds for his strength of body and character, and so popular with his congregation that they had resisted all attempts by the Presbyterian establishment to unseat him. Tradition tells of him making the sixty-mile round trip to his church at Kilchoan on foot every summer Sunday.[84] Young Alasdair was brought up in his father's faith, but later joined the Church of Scotland, and from 1729 was employed as a schoolmaster by the SSPCK and as a catechist by the Royal Bounty Committee in several parts of Ardnamurchan.

If Alasdair was known for his poetry, his older brother Angus was renowned for his enormous strength. It was said of him, and believed by all the local people, that his torso enclosed not ribs but a single breastplate of solid bone, and his feats of strength were legendary. At some stage he had become interested in Catholicism, and had his children educated in Catholic schools while still a Protestant himself. He probably converted about 1740, the year that his own son Angus left to train for the priesthood in Rome.[85]

Alasdair must have been influenced by his brother, and also by his association with Bishop Hugh and his friendship with Donald Kinlochmoidart. When he followed Angus into the Catholic Church we do not know, because at first he kept his new faith private to safeguard his job. Certainly by 1744 his position as schoolmaster at Corryvullin was becoming more and more strained, because of his open Jacobitism and through suspicions as to his religious leanings. For some weeks that summer he actually absented himself from the school, touring the country as a Jacobite agent. Further complaints were levelled against him that autumn, and by the spring of 1745 the SSPCK were on the point of dismissing him. On 15 May he beat them to it by resigning his post.[86] Like his fellow Jacobites he was awaiting the expected coming of the prince.

Notes

1. HMD to Bishop Gordon, 17.11.1733, BL, SCA.
2. Halloran B. M. (1997), p. 109.
3. HMD to Bishop Smith, 24.7.1744, BL.

4. Cf. chap. 6, p. 79 supra.
5. Thomas Innes to Bishop Gordon, 19.12.1732, BL. Hugh identified Alexander Paterson as the chief instigator of the accusations. Ironically, Mr Paterson was a Lowlander, unwillingly serving in a Highland station.
6. James Carnegy to William Stuart, 31.8.1733, BL. Bishop Gordon was staying at Scalan that summer, as he often did, to convalesce on the bracing climate and a diet of goats' milk.
7. James Campbell could not attend as an official representative because he was not an ordained priest.
8. George J. Gordon and George Duncan were invited because they were on the premises, and really attended to make up the numbers. Mr Tyrie was already in the Campbell camp, as would become clear later. Fr Brockie had close connections with the Scots Monastery at Ratisbon, and supported the accusations made by that house against supposed Jansenism on the Scottish Mission. The two other representatives of the Highland vicariate were Iain Mór MacDonald and James Leslie.
9. James Carnegy to William Stuart, 31.8.1733, BL, quoting Bishop Gordon's letter to him.
10. Thomas Innes to Lewis Innes, 27.7.1733, BL, quoting Bishop Gordon's account to him.
11. Bishops Gordon and HMD to the pope, Propaganda Archives CP 86 ff. 269 and 274; Bishops Gordon and HMD to cardinal protector, CP 86, f. 270; priests to cardinal protector, CP 86, ff. 271f.; (in Latin); translated in full in Halloran B. M. op. cit., pp. 110ff., as part of a detailed account of the meeting. For an account as it particularly affected the Scalan master see Watts J. (1999), pp. 73f.
12. Halloran B. M. op. cit., p. 115. The whole question of the Scots College's involvement with Jansenism is discussed at length in chap. 7, 'The College and the Jansenist Controversy'.
13. Thomas Innes to Lewis Innes, 27.7.1733, BL, which includes a transcript of Bishop Gordon's account of the meeting to him.
14. Pastoral Letter 'to the Clergy and faithful of the kingdom, concerning the errors of Bajus, Quesnellus, Jansenius, etc., AD 1733', full text in Clapperton W. (c. 1870), (revised and transcribed by Wilson G., 1901).
15. James Carnegy to William Stuart, 31.8.1733, quoting Bishop Gordon's account to him.
16. 'Intended Resolutions for Meeting at Clashnoir Glenlivet', 8.6.1733, transcribed 5.7.1733, signed John Tyrie, SM 4/1/4, SCA. George J. Gordon had incautiously put his thoughts on *Unigenitus* in writing to James Campbell in May of the previous year, where he had stated that he believed the bull to have been published under pressure, and refused to condemn the 101 Propositions of Quesnel. His letter was later taken to Rome by Colin Campbell and used to discredit him; on the strength of it he was explicitly condemned for Jansenist heresy in the 'Lercari' report of 1737 (see pp. 91f.).
17. Bishops Gordon and HMD to the cardinals of Propaganda, 13.6.1733, BL (in Latin).

18. HMD to William Stuart, 20.8.1788, BL. The documents have always been referred to as the 'Clashnoir Letters', since it was long believed that they were drawn up at the meeting at Clashnoir. Halloran has convincingly demonstrated that they were in fact written at the first meeting at Scalan – Halloran B. M. op. cit., pp. 109f.

19. Cf. account in the brief biography of Æneas MacGillis in Gordon J. F. S. (1867), p. 592.

20. HMD to Bishop Gordon, 17.11.1733, BL. The cause of Alexander Grant's *volte face* was the choice of James Campbell to visit Rome as a delegate for the Mission. The choice was Bishop Gordon's, but Mr Grant (wrongly) believed that Colin Campbell was behind it. Mr Grant, whose name had been proposed at the Scalan meeting by Colin Campbell himself, had been very keen to go.

21. Explicitly stated in, e.g. George J. Gordon, Scalan, to George Gordon, Mortlach, 18.12.1734, BL, on the subject of 'the Westerns' young D".

22. HMD to Bishop Gordon, 17.11.1733, BL.

23. George J. Gordon, Scalan to George Gordon, Mortlach, 10.12.1733, BL. Hugh's letter itself has not survived.

24. George J. Gordon, Scalan to George Gordon, Mortlach, 14.5.1734, BL, quoting words used by Alexander Drummond.

25. George J. Gordon, Scalan to Robert Gordon, Edinburgh, 8.6.1734, BL.

26. Cf. e.g. Bishop Gordon to William Stuart, 5.4.1732, BL, writing of Colin Campbell and John Tyrie – 'who knows thorowly those 2 laborers will never judge them fitt for the station [of coadjutor bishop]'.

27. HMD to William Stuart, 10.11.1735, BL. Much of the present author's account of the whole long-drawn-out episode is based on this important letter.

28. It is relevant to note that the Mission's first vicar apostolic, Thomas Nicolson, also incurred criticism from some of his clergy for a perceived lack of decisiveness and resolution in exerting his authority – cf. e.g. George Anderson to Paris, 20.7.1704, BL. Like Hugh, he had no predecessor, and it must have been particularly difficult to strike the right note where there were no precedents.

29. Bishop Gordon to Scots agent, 7.1.1740, BL (in French). This important letter also gives a detailed account of the Jansenist dispute in Scotland as Bishop Gordon saw it, including the parts played by individual priests, and the machinations and ambition of Colin Campbell.

30. Cf. HMD to Bishop Gordon, 17.11.1733, BL, in which he states that because a priest whom he expected had not arrived 'I am obliged to keep my boyes att the scool taught by Allan McDonald'. Allan Macdonald was at this time a deacon. (For his career since leaving Eilean Bàn see p. 94). Whether HMD's statement above implies that he was teaching at Eilean Bàn, or that the seminary students were sent to a school where he was master, is not clear, though the second is the more likely. In any event, it indicates a staff problem at the seminary at this time. Hugh was based mainly at Bunacaimb and sometimes Eilean Bàn at this date.

31. The Campbell-Tyrie camp had taken it upon themselves to invite two regulars to the meeting, 'contrary to the usual custome, who had no tittle to be present', and their presence ensured that the voting went against Hugh.

32. 'Instructions for Mr John Tyrie, who, with the consent and approbation of his fellow Missionaries, in a meeting held at the Isle of Morar, in montanis, on the 14th and following days of April, 1735, was chosen by our most Rev. Bishop Hugh MacDonald, Vicar Apostolic in montanis Scotiæ, to accompany him to the Old Town [Rome], in prosecution of the affairs spiritual and temporal of our Highland Mission'; the original which had been kept by Bishop Hugh was discovered by Government soldiers at his house on Eilean Bàn after Culloden. Part of it was printed in *The Scots Magazine*, appendix for 1747, pp. 614ff. The main problems of the Highland vicariate were identified as its chronic shortage of priests, and aggressive missionary activity by the Kirk in Catholic areas. To address the first, the case was to be put for the Highlands being allocated two-thirds of all student places at the Scots Colleges, and for financial support for Eilean Bàn. It was noted that Paris had not provided a single priest for the Highlands in twenty years.

33. Cf. Bishop George Hay to Alexander Fraser, Tytler, 2.1.1792, in Report Laing MSS, (1925), vol. II, pp. 595f.

34. George J. Gordon, Scalan, to George Gordon, Mortlach, 4.5.1735, BL. 'We have to do with Subtle men that will overreach and outwitt us if they can,' he warned.

35. HMD to Bishop Gordon, 16.7.1735, BL.

36. HMD to Bishop Gordon, 15.8.1735, BL. A copy of the document to William Stuart the Scots agent, counter-signed by the nine priests present, and dated Lochailort, 3.8.1735, is extant – (in Latin, with a brief covering letter in English from Hugh), SM 4/5/10, SCA.

37. Ibid.

38. HMD to Bishop Gordon, 13.8.1735, BL.

39. His journey home was monitored by British Government Intelligence who believed that he was carrying letters from the Pretender to supporters in Scotland, and orders were sent to the Sheriff of Aberdeen to arrest him as soon as he disembarked – Lord Advocate to the Sheriff of Aberdeen, 17.6.1735, in Warrand D. ed. (1927), vol. III, pp. 109f.

40. HMD to Bishop Gordon, 13.8.1735 and 15.8.1735, BL.: 'Laburers [priests of the Mission] being informed of Mr Smellum's [Alexander Smith's] promotion declair'd I shoud not be present att the Cerimony otherwais that it shoud be lookt upon as Crimen Irremissibile, even tho Mr Cant [the pope] should mention me in his Comission'.

41. 'A more particular but brieff Condescendance of the State of Popery within the bounds of the several Synods of Scotland', n.d. but 1737, CH 1/5/119, pp. 6ff.

42. HMD to William Stuart, for the Cardinal Protector, 1736 (n.d.), BL 3/24/14.

43. Dorrian is surely correct in arguing that the particular denigration of Bishop Smith gives a clue to Campbell's real underlying motive in the whole Jansenism controversy and the 'Pilgrim' adventure: his own ambition for

the mitre. Campbell had always opposed Bishop Smith's appointment, describing it as giving the Lowland vicariate a coadjutor 'to perpetuate the poison' of Jansenism – SM 4/4/4, SCA. Cf. Dorrian G. (1990 Th), pp. 111f. In a document addressed to the pope, they described Bishop Smith as 'a man no ways fitt att any time for being B', and claimed that Bishop Gordon had 'used no means to redress or stop the evil' – SM 4/4/5, SCA (no title) (in Latin, followed by English version). They also claimed that the true motive for dividing the Mission into two vicariates was to further the cause of Jansenism by creating a Lowland District where the majority of clergy favoured it. The Superior of the Jesuits in Scotland, Fr James Hudson, supported the visit of Campbell and Tyrie to Rome, and had encouraged his contacts in the city to give them hospitality – Fr James Hudson to Mr Wolf, 16.9.1735, Propaganda Archives CP 86, f. 299, cited in Halloran B. M. (2001 J), p. 86.

44. HMD to William Stuart, 1736 (n.d.), BL 3/24/14.
45. Colin Campbell to Iain MacDonald, n.d., and same to Alexander Grant, 12.4.1736, both in SM 4/4/6, SCA. Campbell told his colleagues that the Scots agent William Stuart refused his requests, saying that he would follow Bishop Gordon's wishes rather than Bishop Hugh's. He urged them to write to Rome with the same demands, confident that if they did so they would be granted.
46. 'Subscription to the Unigenitus Formula', 1733, SM 4/1/23, SCA (in Latin).
47. Bellesheim A. (1890), vol. IV, pp. 202f., citing Propaganda Archives, 29.3.1734.
48. Colin Campbell and John Tyrie to Pope Benedict XIII, n.d., SM 4/4/5 (no title) (in Latin, followed by English version).
49. Report of Mgr Lercari to Propaganda, 4.3.1737 (in Latin), partial translation in Bellesheim A. op. cit., appendix XVIII.
50. George J. Gordon, Scalan, to George Gordon, Mortlach, 13.5.1737, BL. The accusations against Bishops Gordon and Smith were certainly the least fair and well substantiated parts of the report.
51. Bishop Smith to Thomas Innes, 20.8.1737, BL. Francis was born and raised at Keitry, Glen Garry.
52. HMD to Thomas Innes, 4.9.1737, BL, upon which this and the following paragraph are based. William Leslie's murder was apparently the unpremeditated act of an intruder.
53. Peter Grant hailed from Blairfindy, Glenlivet, which at the division of the Mission had been included in the Lowland vicariate. He had studied at Scalan 1724–25, and at Rome 1725–35.
54. Gaothdail, *gaoth dail* (windy field), well named since it faces the sea and forms a wind tunnel between the hills on either side. Pronounced 'Gaochel'. The form 'Gaoideal' is also found. The normal eighteenth-century English version was 'Guidale'; the modern 'Gaotal' is a rather closer rendition.
55. We know that board and lodging by John of Guidale were part of the arrangement, from Articles of Agreement drawn up in 1742, when that arrangement was extended – see p. 101 and note 80 infra.

56. HMD to William Stuart, 20.8.1733, BL; cf. p. 77 supra.
57. George Gordon (Kirkhill), Procurator for the Mission, to Thomas Innes, 1.5.1738, BL; and Thomson J. 'Some Account of the Mission in Scotland', etc., TH/10, pp. 60 and 109, SCA. Pope Clement's gift was obtained through 'the interest of King James'. These monies were not actually paid until 1738. Two years previously, the Mission had also received 1,000 crowns from the bequest of Cardinal Falconieri who had died in 1734, to be spent 'in the manner his Majesty should judge best'.
58. HMD to Peter Grant, 19.10.1738, BL.
59. HMD to Thomas Innes, 21.10.1738, BL. Neil MacEachen appears several times later in the narrative (especially in the events following Culloden, chap. 8). Apart from his own claim to fame as guide and confidant of Prince Charles Edward Stuart, he was the father of 'Marshal MacDonald' who served as Marshal in the army of Napoleon and was made a duke by the French emperor.
60. Ibid.
61. HMD to Peter Grant, 19.10.1738, BL. Bishop Gordon had also received a letter from Pope Clement to himself and Hugh on the same theme, which included also a summary of the Vatican's perception of Jansenism and recent developments – Clement XII to Bishops Gordon and MacDonald, 21.7.1738 (in Latin), BL.
62. William Harrison to Robert Gordon, 1.4.1738, BL.
63. As was the follow-up letter of Bishops Gordon, Smith and HMD to Pope Clement XII, 13.11.1738 (in Latin), copy, BL. The latter assured the pope that the signatures were being gathered, thanked him for his grant of 2,000 crowns (plus the *Bona Hereditaria* of the late William Stuart), and strongly criticised Colin Campbell and John Tyrie whilst also expressing their own willingness to forgive them.
64. Peter Grant to George Innes, 23.1.1738, BL
65. HMD to Peter Grant, 1.9.1739, BL. John Tyrie had stayed on in Rome.
66. A further reason for vigilance was the long-standing rumour, by now pretty well substantiated, of a scandal in which Colin Campbell had tried to seduce a woman of virtue and good family – cf. Bishop Gordon to Peter Grant, 7.1.1740 (in French), BL.
67. HMD to Thomas Innes, 1.9.1739, BL.
68. Patrick Gordon SJ to Bishop Gordon, 26.11.1739, BL.
69. Flinn M. (1977), pp. 216ff.
70. HMD to Peter Grant, 20.6.1740, BL.
71. Hugh had recently made arrangements for Clanranald's heir Ranald, whose mother's family were Protestant, to complete his education at the Scots College Rome; and he was anxious to make similar arrangements for the sons of Glengarry and MacNeil of Barra – see HMD to Thomas Innes, 1.9.1739, BL.
72. HMD to George Innes, 2.9.1739, BL.
73. Ibid; and HMD to same, 19.10.1738, BL. He hoped that Mr Grant could

influence the Superior of the Franciscan order, then resident in Rome, to release Fr Kelly.

74. The document is untitled, and runs to 48pp. of octavo – MS 20310, NLS.

75. Based on Wynne T. (1994 J and 2001 UnP); and the contemporary account by Rev. Alexander Macbean, 'Memorial concerning the Highlands', in Blaikie W. B. (1916), p. 87.

76. The present account based on three sources: HMD to Peter Grant, 10.8.1742, BL, which gives a full account up to that date; HMD, 'Reasons for Laying on and continuing Mr Francis McDonells suspension, and why they are published', n.d., but from internal evidence late 1743, SM 4/11/3, SCA; and the written 'Complaint' by HMD and Donald MacDonald of Kinlochmoidart presented to meeting of Presbytery of Mull, 7.3.1744, in Registered Acts of the Presbytery of Mull, CH 2/273/1, pp. 83ff., NAS.

77. The panel was the same as at the previous meeting – Æneas MacLachlan, Colin Campbell, William Harrison, Dominic McColgan and Allan MacDonald – plus Archibald MacDonell.

78. Bishops Gordon and Smith to Propaganda, 5.2.1743 (in Latin), translation in Bellesheim A. (1980), vol. IV, appendix XV.

79. HMD to Peter Grant, 10.8.1742, BL; John would later become Hugh's assistant bishop, and succeed him as vicar apostolic of the Highlands.

80. Paper IV of the documents in the possession of HMD confiscated at Eilean Bàn in 1746, printed in *The Scots Magazine*, appendix for 1747, pp. 614ff.

81. HMD, 'Reasons' etc., SM 4/11/3, SCA.

82. Synod of Argyll meeting of 1.8.1743, CH 2/557/6, p. 241, NAS, cited in Ferguson W. (1969–71 J), p. 26.

83. Letter to Kinlochmoidart, 6.3.1745, minuted in Records of Presbytery of Mull, cited in Ferguson W. loc. cit.; death of Francis MacDonell reported in Royal Bounty Records, 22.11.1781, CH 1/5/59, NAS.

84. The present account of Alasdair and his son Angus is based on MacDonald C. (1889; 1997 edn), espec. pp. 118, 125 and 138 n.

85. Cf. HMD to Thomas Innes, 1.9.1739, BL, which suggests that he himself had not converted by this date, especially as the sentence is written in the context of other well-disposed Protestant parents.

86. Black R. (1986), pp. 34f.

8

The Coming and the Going of the Prince (1745–46)

On 25 July, as the summer sun was at its height, the frigate *Du Taillet* nosed round the point of Rhu and headed east into the sparkling blue waters of Loch nan Uamh.[1] She was a fine eighty-footer, with three masts.[2] As she passed behind the islands in Gaotal Bay perhaps the seminarians at their after-lunch recreation gave her a brief glance, taking her for a trading vessel; but none had any idea that the cargo she was carrying was Charles Edward Stuart, the Young Pretender himself.[3]

At 3 p.m. the captain cast anchor near the head of the loch. Before them was a shingle strand, a stretch of lush meadow covered with cattle, and the poor-looking houses of a farm-town. The prince and several of his men were put ashore by row-boat, where they were met by the local proprietor Angus MacDonald of Borrodale. Not being certain of their host's politics they at first let it be known that they were 'rich smugglers come upon a jobb of trade'. The story hardly squared with the prince's appearance, dressed as he was in the clerical attire of a student of the Scots College Paris, with black coat, stockings and hat, and black shoes with brass buckles.[4]

Borrodale's son Ronald returned to the ship with them that evening, and over the next few days a number of the local gentlemen came aboard, where they were made privy to the prince's identity and the purpose of his coming and were then sent back to their districts to raise their people. One of the prince's visitors was the pocket Hercules, Angus MacDonald of Dalilea. Another was his brother Alasdair the bard who, when he drank Charles' health in Gaelic, was at once made his official tutor in the language and sent to raise men in Ardnamurchan.[5] A third was Donald Kinlochmoidart, for whom Alasdair had penned the 'Complaint' to the presbytery of Mull. Learning that Donald was a son of the sister of Cameron of Lochiel the prince asked him to find Lochiel and try to persuade him to join them, since his support was considered crucial to the enterprise. Donald at once set off for Achnacarry House, Lochiel's seat close to the lower end of Loch Arkaig.

Bishop Hugh was at this time on his way home from an administrators' meeting in Edinburgh. His route took him through Glen Spean, with the corries of the Aonach range to his left still under snow, and down to the ferry at the broad River Lochy. There he chanced upon Donald Kinlochmoidart disembarking, fresh from his visit to Lochiel and now on his way to give news of the landing to the duke of Perth.

'De an naidheachd a th'agad?' asked Donald – 'What news have you?'[6]

'I have none, ' Hugh answered.

'Then I will give you news. This night at my house you may see the prince.'

'What prince do you mean?'

'Who but Tearlach himself?'

'You are jesting for certain,' said Hugh.

When Donald had convinced him, Hugh quizzed him further:

'How many men has he along with him?'

'Only seven.'

'And what is his stock of money and arms then?'

'A very small stock.'

'And what generals or officers fit for command are with him?'

'There are none at all.'

Hugh could only see the attempt failing. 'I cannot help it, I am committed to it,' Donald answered, and added prophetically, 'If it does fail I shall certainly be hanged.'

They parted and Hugh continued on his journey west. But instead of making for his home at Bunacaimb[7] he struck off south for Kinlochmoidart House. There he found no prince, but Donald's brother Angus who had accompanied Charles from France, who confirmed the news. He agreed to take Hugh to the ship, but warned him that for security's sake Charles was maintaining the disguise of a French cleric, and that he must play along with the charade.

The following day, Saturday 3 August, Angus brought Hugh on board and introduced him to the prince in a tent set up on deck. Each man played his part. The bishop welcomed the visiting 'priest'; the 'priest' paid due honour to the bishop, kneeling to kiss his ring. They then retired to his private cabin where they were able to throw off the pretence. Charles spelled out his plans and hopes and asked for Hugh's opinion.[8] Hugh warned him that because he had not been expected that year the country was not prepared, and that to proceed would be to put himself and his followers in jeopardy: better surely to return to France and await the opportune moment. This was not the answer the prince wanted and he rejected it out of hand. Never let it be said, he cried, his face working with passion, that by turning their backs on him his friends had forced him to abandon the enterprise. If he could get but six good men to follow him he would choose to skulk with them among the mountains of his homeland rather than return to France.

Hugh's advice was not sought again, but within a day messengers arrived with news that seemed to confirm the wisdom of it. On Skye Sir Alexander MacDonald and MacLeod of Dunvegan were refusing to join the prince, dismissing the whole affair as a 'Don Quixote expedition'. Cameron of Lochiel had also declined to bring out his men, and Young Clanranald remained undecided. Hugh pointed out that their coolness would certainly deter the lesser chiefs. Now even Charles' own advisers who had sailed with him from France urged him to desist. But he was adamant to continue.

When it became clear that he intended to leave the ship and set up base at Borrodale House, Hugh took Young Clanranald aside and begged him to at least mobilise enough of his men to provide a bodyguard, and this he agreed to do. On Monday the 5th the whole party were rowed ashore, whence Charles and his companions took the short road to Borrodale and the local gentlemen made their way to Kinlochmoidart. Hugh disembarked with them and headed for Bunacaimb on the West coast.

The crew of the *Du Taillet* spent the next two days landing the swivel guns and other ordnance, and taking in supplies. Then early on Thursday the 8th they weighed anchor and set her course for the Sound of Sleat.[9] As she disappeared round the Point of Rhu everyone knew that the die was cast for the Rising.

During the following week the prince's party finalised their plans, first at Borrodale and later at the house of Donald Kinlochmoidart. The date fixed to proclaim the Rising was Monday 19 August; the place Glenfinnan. For all their precautions, place and date were somehow leaked and reported to the authorities before the week was out.[10]

On the eve of the appointed day the party arrived with their bodyguard of Clanranalds at the house of MacDonald of Glenaladale on the west bank of Loch Shiel. There they made their last overnight stay, ready for the short sail to Glenfinnan on the morrow. On the same day Hugh set out from Bunacaimb, his destination the same as theirs.[11]

On the 19th the prince rose early, and by 6 a.m. his party were aboard the three boats that were to take them up the loch.[12] The distance was less than seven miles, but they made slow headway into the wind; they were in no hurry, and even paused for a while at the place known since as 'The Prince's Bay'. When at last they moored in the little bay, Camus t-Sladaich, and disembarked it was already eleven o'clock.

The whole place was eerily quiet. The wet flat land at the head of the loch, the valley closing in beyond, the hills to north, east and west, all were empty of men. Not one man-in-arms was there to greet them. Charles strode through the curious onlookers of the Slatach farm-town and retired into the chief tenant's house to see what the afternoon would bring.[13]

The first to his door was Allan Ruadh MacDonald, Hugh's half-brother, with 150 men.[14] A start, but hardly an army. For three hours nothing more happened. Then he caught from the east the sound of the pipes, rising and falling among the hills but growing ever closer, until two columns of men came into sight out of the trees. It was Lochiel at the head of 700 Camerons, zigzagging down the hill. They halted at the Finnan river, for etiquette demanded that Lochiel should not encroach beyond the boundary of his land without invitation. The prince crossed the river, reviewed his men and then brought them over. Minutes later, from the same direction, MacDonald of Keppoch marched in with 300 of his clan. By this time Hugh had also arrived and was among those gathered by the river bank.

The whole party now moved some distance west onto the eminence of a knoll, the leaders crowding upon the rocks atop it and their men spread out about its slopes.[15] Here the prematurely old marquis of Tullibardine, bowing to his prince, unfurled and held aloft the *bratach bhàn*, the silken banner of crimson and white, which was then set upon a pole at the topmost point of the knoll. As it fluttered there Bishop Hugh stepped forward, raised his right hand, and blessed it and those who were to march with it. His blessing, given first in Latin, and repeated in Gaelic, English and perhaps French, came only as disjointed snatches to those at the back of the crowd.

Hugh's blessing of the standard raises several questions. The first concerns his own position vis-à-vis the Rising. Strictly speaking, like all bishops of the Mission countries he was under a general instruction from Propaganda not to become involved in domestic politics, and as such should not have been near Glenfinnan.[16] But he was a Highlander and a Jacobite as much as a bishop, and long before he became bishop. And in fact, whatever the official line he saw no contradiction of roles. Indeed, the opposite was the case. To him 19 August was *kairos*, as the Gospel writers had used the word, the opportune day marked out by providence, and he rejoiced to be part of it. Furthermore, he had a pastoral duty to his people. In every way, therefore, he saw his proper place as with the prince and the army.

The second question concerns the impression that his action would have had upon the authorities and the country at large. It seems that at the time they were barely aware of it.[17] Had they been, it must have strengthened their case that this was a rebellion by a popish pretender seeking to destroy their hard-won religious freedom, and much political capital might have been made of it.

Thirdly, what was its effect on those present? It was customary and entirely natural in the culture of the Catholic Highlands to begin every significant activity with a blessing. The particular intention in this case was to symbolise the rightness of the cause, its sacredness indeed and the certainty that it was approved by God. Whether it was received in this spirit by the Protestant majority in the crowd – for nearly all the Camerons were Presbyterian or Episcopalian[18] – we do not know. Why, they may have asked, was there not more than one clergyman to perform the blessing? Their own regiment, after all, had three chaplains, Presbyterian, Episcopalian and Catholic, while an Episcopalian priest George Kelly, one of the prince's seven companions on the journey from France, was also at the front of the gathered crowd. But perhaps the unity of their cause lent a spirit of ecumenism to the day.

The Camerons' Catholic chaplain was Lochiel's brother Alexander, the convert who had joined the Jesuit order and returned to the Mission in 1741. Within the army as a whole three of the regiments were entirely or mainly Catholic, and each had its chaplain. Serving the Clanranalds was Allan MacDonald, Hugh's old fellow student on Eilean Bàn whose subsequent career had been so chequered, and who had finally been ordained by Bishop Hugh in 1742. As well as chaplain he was also made the prince's personal confessor. Serving Glengarry's regiment was the islander Æneas (Angus) MacGillis, another priest of only three years' standing. And appointed to Glenbuchat's, the regiment drawn mainly from the Catholic Banffshire uplands, was John Tyrie the 'Pilgrim': he won the honour after drawing lots with the priest of Strathavon.[19]

As chaplains these men were given the rank of captain, and bore arms accordingly (though again such military standing and arms-bearing flew in the face of the rules of Propaganda). They were appointed by their respective colonels-in-chief, not by their bishop, whose only role – if communication of any sort was possible in the haste of the time – was to give them permission to leave their stations.[20]

Hugh was inevitably and inextricably a part of the Rising, in fact, not only pastorally and in sentiment, but by ties of blood. When Clanranald had called out his people, the MacDonalds of Morar answered as they had always done. Hugh's half brother Allan Ruadh had been appointed lieutenant-colonel (effectively third in command) of the regiment, and as we saw was the first of all the officers to join the prince at Glenfinnan.[21] His two sons, John and Ranald, each held the rank of lieutenant and fought throughout the campaign. Hugh's full brother, John 'of Guidale' (the tacksman of Gaotal who was still maintaining the students at the seminary there), was given the rank of captain. And his mother's brothers, the MacDonalds of Kinlochmoidart, also all held commissions in the regiment, Donald as colonel and aide-de-camp, Dr John and Allan as captains, and James with the rank of lieutenant. In such a family environment it was unthinkable that Hugh himself would not be involved.

At the same time his episcopal duties required his presence in the Highlands and – other considerations apart – precluded any thought of military activity. He perhaps accompanied the army for a few miles on their first day's march, before hastening home. But thereafter, during the eight months of their campaigns until their final defeat at Culloden, his involvement was necessarily restricted to moral and spiritual support among those left behind.

His movements during those eight months remain a matter of surmise, for no oral or written word of them has come down to us. But we can be sure that he and his people followed the army's every move, as word filtered back to them. He heard of the taking of Linlithgow and Edinburgh, and the victory at Prestonpans; of the £30,000 reward upon the prince's head, and of his unaccountable and damaging delay in the Scottish capital before the advance into England; of the failure of the English Jacobites to come out in numbers, and his decision taken in late December to turn back, when he seemed to be within reach of London. And from the New Year of '46, as ever more clansmen (Allan Ruadh among them) abandoned the enterprise and drifted home, he learned from these eyewitnesses that the army had dwindled to less than 5,000 men and, despite a brief flourish at Falkirk, was now in retreat. Through the early waxing of its fortunes, the crisis, and the decline to inevitable defeat, Hugh's task was to pass on the news, bolster morale, welcome back the stragglers, and comfort the bereaved. Towards the end of February, almost lost among his other disappointments, word came to him of the death of his friend and counsellor, Bishop Gordon.

Early in the afternoon of 16 April the prince was led off sleet-swept Culloden field. The battle had lasted less than an hour and his outnumbered forces were scattered. With just four aides he made his way south and west, and on the evening of the 17th found shelter and a few hours' respite in the relative safety of Glen Pean. Among his party was his private confessor Allan MacDonald.[22]

Shortly after midnight they struck out west to the head of the glen, taking the cattle drovers' path through the saddle between Carn Mór and Sgurr nan Coireachan and down to Oban farm at the head of Loch Morar, where they found grateful rest in a shieling hut. The next morning they picked their way along the steep south shore of the loch as far as the Meoble river. There they turned up the glen past Hugh's old boyhood home, to a house where they were kept out of sight and well entertained.

That night they were on the road again, using the dark hours to reach the home of Angus MacDonald of Borrodale, the first house that the prince had set foot in on his arrival in mainland Scotland the previous summer. Here the party remained for five days, debating the best way forward.

Their hosts advised their staying put, and perhaps regrouping. But the prince's own companions were for abandoning the enterprise, at least for the meantime; Allan MacDonald, himself a Uist man, suggested that if so they should head for the Outer Isles. The latter counsel prevailed.[23]

A boat of eight oars was secured with experienced local sailors to man her, and with the prince impatient of delay the party set their course for Eriskay on the night of the 26th, a night on which no sane man would have ventured on the Minch. As he himself later recalled the sea was running with 'monstrouse waves' which threatened to fill the boat and capsize her.[24] The night seemed endless. The boat was driven far to the north, its huddled passengers glimpsing now and then shadowy headlands on Skye and South Uist, until somehow by sheer skill and nerve the crew got her into the lea of the land. They beached at last on the east coast of Benbecula and scrambled ashore. Fingers of the broken landscape thrust into the sea on every side, treeless and utterly barren. Eagles flew and nested at sea level there.

Word of their arrival reached Clanranald at Nunton and he came to find them. He brought with him Neil MacEachan, the one-time tutor of his children whom Bishop Hugh had once hoped to make the master at Gaotal. For the next two months, while Charles hid in the Outer Isles, Neil acted as his companion, guide and intermediary, his fluency in French allowing him to pass on the latest news without their conversations being understood.[25] Almost every day they were on the move. For one fortnight only had they respite, when Neil hid the prince in Glen Corodale and he watched from the safety of the Uist hills his pursuers scouring the Minch for him. In the last week of June Neil was the prince's go-between with Flora MacDonald as the plan was hatched to get him off the island. On the 28th he was his companion in the row-boat with Flora, as the five-man crew shoved off from Loch Uisgebhagh to make the dash to Skye in the short hours of night.

Immediately after Culloden the Government forces had begun the operation to consolidate their victory. Orders were at once given for the surrender of the rebels' weapons and several centres were assigned for their collection. Mingary Castle on Ardnamurchan was the reception centre for the Catholic west coast and Islands.[26] At the same time Cumberland set about the systematic destruction of enemy property. By his own report he and his men 'demolished all Mass houses and Meeting houses as [they] marched allong', and before they were finished every single place of Catholic worship throughout the Highlands lay in ruins.[27] Homes of the leading Jacobites and their tenants were treated in the same way. Lord Lovat's Downie Castle and Lochiel's house at Achnacarry were destroyed in the first month, and in the following weeks, in what came to be known as the 'wasting of Lochaber', nearly all the farm-towns in Glen Nevis and Loch Arkaigside and on the estates of Lochiel and MacDonald of Keppoch met the same fate.[28]

On the west coast the vessels searching for the prince sent raiding parties ashore with instructions to burn villages. On 9 May troops from Capt. Fergussone's bomb ketch *Furnace* burned Barrisdale's mansion to the ground, returning to South Morar the following week to put Cross, the home of Hugh's half-brother Allan Ruadh, to the torch.[29] They then sailed round the coast and laid waste the farm-towns around Borrodale.

There were other ships in the Minch too. The French were also searching for the prince, to bring him out of Scotland. *Le Mars* and *La Bellone* had entered Loch nan Uamh and were enquiring of the local people as to his whereabouts. A sub-lieutenant on *Le Mars* noted in his diary that many of the Highlanders who came aboard their ships were in a state of starvation. Taking the opportunity to go ashore he saw for himself their thin cattle, wretched fields and poverty-stricken homes (and this before the arrival of Fergussone's men). Even Angus MacDonald of Borrodale, the landlord, was living in a one-roomed house. Walking further along the coast he came upon a somewhat larger house, the only one with a garden, which he was told belonged to the bishop. This was the seminary at Gaotal, though he did not know it, and within he noted with admiration the library of some 200 books in Scots, English, French, Greek and Latin that Hugh had acquired for his own and the boys' use. Hugh himself was elsewhere but his sister, whom the gallant Frenchman thought a 'very pretty, handsome lady', gave him and his companions a generous Highland welcome.[30]

It was in the hope of contacting one of the French rescue ships that the prince sent Allan MacDonald back to the mainland about mid-May, with a message for Lochiel. On the 23rd Allan met up with Lochiel and Murray of Broughton by the head of Loch Arkaig, where it was arranged that he would return to Uist and bring the prince over for a rendezvous on 1 June. He then headed west with Murray, sleeping that night – according to the latter's account – 'upon the Coast in a little house belonging to Bishop Mcdonald',[31] before taking sail for Uist.

The house where they slept was Bunacaimb. On another occasion around this time Murray mentions using Hugh's house on 'the Island of Lochmorror',[32] and it seems likely that both Eilean Bàn and Bunacaimb were used as rendezvous by leading Jacobites in the months after Culloden.

Hugh's half-brother Allan Ruadh was certainly using Eilean Bàn as one of his temporary homes after his house at Cross was destroyed, and in mid-June he was joined there by Hugh, Dr John MacDonald and Lord Lovat. The latter, now eighty years old, overweight and lame, had spent his life hedging his political bets, and even after Glenfinnan had still affected to side with the Government.[33] But for all his trimming he had lost his castle, and his capture was one of the Government's top priorities. Eilean Bàn offered a refuge, and a meeting-place to consider the possibility of the remnant army regrouping.[34]

While raiding the coast of Arisaig Capt. Fergussone arrested several of the locals, who under duress divulged the whereabouts of Lovat and his friends. He at once took 300 men overland to Glen Meoble and along the south shore of Loch Morar until they came level with Eilean Bàn. Hugh and the others watched them coming, but having previously commandeered every boat on the loch they thought themselves safe from attack. According to one of the officers the four men actually fired several volleys at the troops, 'at the same time calling them by insulting and opprobrious names'.[35] What they did not know was that Fergussone had sent the *Furnace* round the coast into the Morar estuary, from where soldiers were at that moment carrying two row-boats the half mile overland to the loch. Once they realised the danger they took one of their own boats and, rowing for life up the loch, managed to reach the strand at the mouth of Glen Meoble ahead of their pursuers. From there they took refuge in the hills. Lord Lovat, who could now barely walk, remained hidden in the glen for three days and nights before he was discovered.[36] The soldiers rowed him back down the loch, from where they carried him at a run on their shoulders to the ship.

Searching Eilean Bàn for any other fugitives who might still be hiding there the troops came upon Bishop Hugh's house and chapel, the buildings of the former seminary. They burned both to the ground, leaving only the smoke-stained foundation stones, some of which lie there to this day. Several then put on the vestments and took up the sacred vessels, and cavorting about performed a grotesque popish rite for the amusement of their fellows. Nearly all Hugh's books and papers were tossed onto the fire, or scattered on the loch, just a few being saved by an alert officer. Their burning was an irreplaceable loss both for the eighteenth-century Church and the scholar of today.

Hugh and Allan Ruadh both escaped from Glen Meoble. Later that month and throughout July, following Government intelligence reports that the prince had returned to the mainland, searches were made of South Morar and Arisaig during which every beast in the country was rounded up or slaughtered in an attempt to starve him and his followers out.[37] In the tightening cordon Allan was eventually captured, but Hugh contrived to avoid arrest. Where he hid in the fifteen weeks between leaving Eilean Bàn and making his final escape we do not know. According to his own account he simply 'lurked the best way he could'.[38]

The intelligence reports of the prince's return to the mainland were accurate. On 5 July he had crossed from Skye in a row-boat in the company of MacKinnon of Elgol and his son John and put ashore at Mallaigbheag in North Morar.[39] After waiting three days in vain for news the party headed out into Loch Nevis, with the intention of making for Clanranald country. Rounding the point they almost locked oars with a boat whose occupants, they could see by the red crosses on their bonnets, were members of the Skye militia. There was no chance of evading them. With great presence of mind John MacKinnon pushed the prince down between his knees and covered him with his plaid, while the rest answered the questions put to them, each with his gun cocked ready in case their identity was discovered.

Once ashore they cut inland, crossing Loch Morar by the ford at its shallow lower end, and headed for Cross farm in the hope of finding shelter with Hugh's half-brother Allan Ruadh. His own house and all its outbuildings were in ruins, but he received the fugitives with whatever hospitality he could offer. He housed them for the night in a cave above the estuary,[40] promising them all the provisions and support they might need, and then set out to alert Young Clanranald of their arrival.

When the party woke the next day they found a great change in their host's mood. He was altogether cooler, claiming that he could provide neither food nor shelter for them, and making it abundantly clear that he would prefer to be rid of them. They were sure that Young Clanranald was behind the change. The prince decided to move on to Borrodale and put himself in the hands of Angus MacDonald, his 'faithfull old Landlord' who had been the first to welcome him ashore the previous year, and who he was sure would welcome him now. With Morar's son as a guide he and John MacKinnon set out that night. At dawn they arrived at Borrodale's house, only to find it too in ruins. Angus, as frank as Morar had been grudging, took them to a wood close by and offered them a hut to rest in until he could arrange something better.

Between the ruins of his house and the shingle strand on Loch nan Uamh lay the flat, verdant meadow where Charles had first set foot on his arrival from France. From its edge, some way back from the shore, a steep cliff rose among trees. One third of the way up it there was a cleft, so narrow and overhung with timber as to be quite hidden from view and unknown even to many of the local people. If you squeezed inside and stretched down in the blackness until your foot touched solid rock you would find yourself standing in a narrow, cold-sweating cave that led back thirty feet into the hill,[41] (plate 6). This was the place that Angus found for him. From its mouth he could see over the loch to Ardnish and the domed peaks of Roshven beyond. Invisible to all, yet himself able to watch the movements of his pursuers, he made it his home and hideout while friends made plans to spirit him away.

ABOVE. Aerial view of Loch Morar, looking east, with the estuary in the foreground, Eilean Bàn the nearest of the islands, and the bay of Glen Meoble half-way up the loch (Simmons Aerofilms)

LEFT. Glen Meoble: view up the glen, with the hills of Moidart in the distance to the south (Mairead MacDonald, Kinsadel)

RIGHT. Scalan: the burn and well, all that remains of the original site (John Watts)

BELOW. The Scots College Paris (*Innes Review*)

BOTTOM. Gaotal and Loch nan Uamh, looking south towards Moidart (John Watts)

LEFT. Interior of the cave at Borrodale, taken some 3 m in from the entrance, with figure to give idea of dimensions (John Watts)

BELOW. Traquair House, Innerleithen, Borders (Pádraig Watts)

As the Government forces had used the pretext of consolidation-after-victory to destroy all Catholic places of worship, so they used it as their excuse to make a general trawl of priests, whether or not they had participated in the Rising. In doing so they appear to have been acting on official orders.[42] Colin Campbell was one for whom they made particular search, following up rumours of sightings of him,[43] unaware that he had in fact been killed at Culloden.

Their first capture was the Jesuit, Fr Alexander Gordon, who had been on the field at Culloden and whom they seized in Glengairn. Lying in irons in the damp of Inverness Gaol he contracted pleurisy and died in agony in May.[44] On 5 July Allan MacDonald, the prince's confessor who had returned to Uist to bring him off the island, was captured there by his kinsman Lieutenant MacDonald of Knock. His captor relieved him of sixty guineas, all that he possessed. On the same day Knock also picked up Alexander Forrester, the resident priest on Uist who had played no part whatever in the Rising. The two men were put aboard a vessel searching the islands, until finally shipped to Applecross and thence taken overland to Inverness.[45]

About 12 July Captain Fergussone of the *Furnace*, scouring the coast of Morar for the prince, arrested Fr Alexander Cameron, the convert brother of Lochiel who had followed the army throughout the campaign as Catholic chaplain to the Cameron regiment. Fergussone, notorious for his cruelty in the West, treated his prisoner with the same inhumanity and contempt for authority that he displayed throughout. Despite his gentle birth the priest was made to sleep among the ship's cables, until he became so ill that the physician declared his life in danger. When the earl of Albermarle sent orders for him to be put ashore Fergussone ignored the instruction. He also turned away friends of the priest who had brought him bedding, swearing that if they tried to bring it aboard he would sink their boat. In this state Fr Cameron was brought to the gaol at Inverness.[46]

At the end of July, James Grant, the priest of Barra, was captured and shipped across the Minch. He arrived at the garrison at Fort William on 9 August, one of nine prisoners that included Hugh's half-brother Allan Ruadh. They were conveyed to Fort Augustus, and thence to Inverness.[47] Allan had never had much enthusiasm for the Rising and had excused himself from the army some weeks before Culloden,[48] but he would spend the better part of a year a prisoner. His wife and family were left destitute, their plight the worse for knowing that the estate lay under threat of forfeiture.[49]

On 13 August the armed privateers *L'Heureux* and *Le Prince de Conti*, with 500 men aboard, set sail from St Malo bound for the Scottish

Highlands. Their coming was the sixth attempt by the French to rescue the prince. They reached the Western Isles at the beginning of September, whence they crossed the Minch and put down anchor in Loch nan Uamh on the 6th.[50] There they waited a full fortnight while word went out of their arrival. Fortunately, gales in the Minch and the absence of British ships (sent elsewhere on false intelligence) saved them from confrontation with the enemy.

By the 15th officers of the Jacobite army were arriving on the shore and being taken aboard: Young Clanranald, Lochiel, Lieutenants John and Ronald the sons of Morar among many others.[51] Shortly after, Bishop Hugh emerged from his hiding place, slipped through Arisaig to Borrodale, easily avoiding the skeleton force of troops still stationed there, and came aboard the *Conti*.[52] The prince himself was still on the road, making his way by night from his hideout on Ben Alder far to the east. He arrived at last as night fell on the 19th and was taken on board *L'Heureux*.

The following day the two ships, with upwards of a hundred Scotsmen aboard, weighed anchor and headed for the open sea. At the end of the month they made the harbour of Roscoff on the north coast of Brittany, from where the fugitives made their way towards Paris.

Like several of the others Hugh intended to take lodgings in the Scots College, at least for a while, and then perhaps move on to Rome. The journey to the capital took him a good two weeks,[53] and before the end of it the little money he had brought with him was spent. He landed on the college doorstep exhausted and destitute, his arrival vividly described to Rome by the principal, his old teacher George Innes, who took him in: 'You may tell y'm [the Cardinals of Propaganda] y't as he came hither without one farthing of mony, or so much as cloths upon his back to appear in; he behoavd certainly to live in ye streets during night, and beg his bread all ye day long, if we had not receivd him.'[54]

He left behind a Mission in distress. No less than thirteen priests were in captivity.[55] Alexander Cameron, his fellow Jesuits the brothers John and Charles Farquharson, Alexander Forrester the priest of Uist, Allan MacDonald the prince's confessor, and James Grant the priest of Barra were all held in Inverness Gaol, in a single large cell with three dozen other men. (John Farquharson had actually been arrested twice. He had originally been apprehended while saying Mass, and dragged away in his vestments. Released through the influence of his landlord Chisholm of Strathglass, he had returned to his station and taken refuge with his brother in a cave in Glen Cannich, eluding all attempts of the local garrison to find them. The two men had finally given themselves up when the commanding officer threatened to burn down every Catholic home in the glen unless they revealed their whereabouts).[56]

In the gaol James Grant was chained by the leg to another prisoner, in such a way that if one turned in his sleep he must pass over the body of the other; he was denied all comforts, even his water bottle being seized on the ridiculous pretext that it might be used as a weapon in a break-out.[57]

In October all but Mr Grant were moved by sea to the Thames, there to await trial in the prison ships anchored off Tilbury Fort. For Alexander Cameron, whose health had been broken at the hands of Capt. Fergussone even before his imprisonment, the voyage was an agony. On arrival, close to death, he found himself separated from his fellow clergy. His cries for a priest were heard by the captain of one of the other prison ships, who had the goodness of heart to tell Fr John Farquharson, one of his own prisoners. Fr Farquharson went aboard, brought his dying friend back to his own ship, heard his confession and cared for him in his last hours.

On the day Hugh arrived in Paris, his uncle Donald Kinlochmoidart was lying in the cell at Carlisle Castle, under sentence of death. On 18 October he was executed by hanging, just as he had prophesied to Hugh at the Lochy ferry, and thereafter disembowelled and his head fixed upon the city gate. His estate was later forfeited to the Crown and his large family reduced to penury.[58]

Lovat was in the Tower of London, awaiting trial and subsequent execution. Forty of the most prominent Jacobites had already been attainted for high treason, following the passing of the Act of Attainder in June, and more were to be added to the list. The Disarming Act had effectively put every Jacobite clansman outside the law.[59] The general fear that the Government was considering the mass transportation of entire clans to the colonies was not groundless. The notion had been mooted in the highest places, and though it had since been abandoned there was still serious talk of all priests and some Catholic laity being banished 'as a people whose principles were inconsistent with the safety of the State'.[60]

Banishment was in fact to be the fate of some. Others had already escaped abroad, or were about to. The leaders of the Mission estimated that, in all, up to 1,000 Scots Catholics either died, suffered banishment or fled the country during and after the '45.[61]

For Hugh himself – we can see with hindsight – the Rising was to be the critical episode in his life. In it the main defining forces of his person, as Highlander, Jacobite and bishop, the main determinants of his life for more than forty years, were brought together in a uniquely charged tension. The '45 and its aftermath would prove a watershed for all that he stood for and held dear. They would give the *coup de grâce* to the clan system, inflict irreparable defeat on the House of Stuart, spell the end of Highland autonomy, scatter his own family, and deal a wound to the Church that at the time must have seemed mortal.

For him personally also it would prove a watershed. Hitherto he had lived his religious vocation among his people; henceforth, for more than half his remaining years, he would have to play his part in exile. Despite the painful disputes that had dogged his episcopate he had gone into the '45 still young; he would return old from the '46.

If we take his adult life as beginning when he first left home for Scalan in autumn 1716, then the blessing of the Standard in summer 1745 was the exact mid-point of it. The Rising was his climacteric, the pivotal chapter in his life. It is fitting, therefore, that it forms the mid-chapter of his biography.

Notes

1. The present account of the arrival based on the captain's log – Robertson J. L. transl. 'The Log of the *Dutillet*' (1904–07 J). pp. 23ff. Where there are discrepancies re dates between the various accounts of the prince's stay at Loch nan Uamh I have followed those of the captain's log.
2. There is a scale drawing of the *Du Taillet* in Gibson J. S. (1967), between pp. 54–55.
3. Prince Charles had landed first on Eriskay, from where he had visited South Uist to meet Clanranald and MacDonald of Boisdale. Neither had been willing to join his expedition, and had advised him to return to France – see the 'Journal of the Prince's Imbarkation and Arrival', etc., by Angus MacDonald, the 'Paris Banker', one of his companions and a close relative of Hugh, in Forbes R. ed. Paton H. (1896; 1975 edn), vol. I, pp. 281ff.
4. Information by Ronald MacDonald, son of Borrodale, 13.10.1748, in Forbes R. op. cit., vol. II, pp. 198ff.; and 'Journall and Memoirs of P—C— Expedition into Scotland', etc., by a Highland Officer in his Army (Alasdair mac Mhaighstir Alasdair), in *Lockhart Papers* (1817), vol. II, pp. 479ff.
5. Alasdair mac Mhaighstir Alasdair, loc. cit.
6. The present account based on HMD's own verbal narrative, 15.6.1750, in Forbes R. op. cit., vol. III, pp. 5of. I have made Donald use the familiar singular '*agad*' rather than the more formal '*agaibh*' in addressing Hugh, despite the fact that he was speaking to his bishop, since he was Hugh's uncle and considerably older than him, and had known him since he was a baby.
7. The local tradition is that at this time Hugh had the use of the house at Bunacaimb, which certainly belonged to the family. The discovery of foundation stones close by two generations ago suggests that there may have been a farm or farm-town attached – Peter MacDonald (Bunacaimb) and Alasdair MacDonald (Port na Dòbhrain) verbal communications. The south-facing house, with views across to Rum and Eigg, would have been a relaxation after Gaotal or Eilean Bàn, away from clergy, students and the day-to-day concerns of the vicariate.
8. Present account based on HMD's verbal narrative in Forbes R. loc. cit.; and

Bishop J. Geddes 'Some Account of the Catholic Religion in Scotland during the Years 1745–6–7', copy B JG 2/5, SCA, the relevant part based on conversations with HMD.

9. From where she headed north through the Minch, rounded Cape Wrath, sailed along the north coast of Scotland, through the Pentland Firth and on to Holland.

10. Lord President Forbes to Sir John Cope, Culloden 17.8.1745, CCCCII, giving a general location as the coast of Arisaig; Norman MacLeod to Lord President Forbes, 17.8.1745, CCLII, confirming Glenfinnan; both in *Culloden Papers* (London, 1815), pp. 373 and 208 respectively.

11. This according to the local tradition – Peter MacDonald (Bunacaimb) and Alasdair MacDonald (Port na Dòbhrain) verbal communications.

12. Present account based in particular upon Alasdair mac Mhaighstir Alasdair, op. cit., p. 484; and Browne J. (1838), vol. III, pp. 19f.

13. Several details in the present account, though probably accurate, cannot be verified: Camus t-Sladaich is the most obvious place in the vicinity for the landing. The traditional description of the hut that Charles entered – a 'hovel' – is one often used to refer to a tenant's house, and it would almost certainly be the chief tenant's home that the prince would choose; the foundations of such a house may still be seen close to the present Slatach House. Likewise, the tradition that the prince crossed a river could be explained by Lochiel halting his men on its east bank at the boundary of his own land – Tearlach MacFarlane, verbal communication.

14. Capt. Alexander MacDonald's Observations on the Journal of Angus Mac-Donald 'Banker', 29.12.1747, in Forbes R. op. cit., vol. I, p. 352.

15. Several sites have been proposed for the raising of the Standard. One, the site of the nineteenth-century monument, can almost certainly be discounted since it is on flat land where tradition and documentary evidence speak of a knoll. The most persuasive case is for the small hill behind the present-day presbytery across the road from the RC church; the one argument against – that the prince crossed to the *east* bank of the Finnan river – can be explained as in note 14; this knoll was also claimed as the site in the nineteenth century when the rocks at the top of it were carved with a message marking the spot, which remained hidden until the late 1980s when a heather fire uncovered it – see Thornber I. 'On this Spot' (1988 J) – though some doubt has been cast on the veracity of the claim. A persuasive case for the site being on the east side of the river was made by Donald B. MacCulloch and published by the 1745 Association (1963 J). As to the sequence of events, the present account can be no more than surmise. It is quite possible, for instance, that the banner was blessed *before* it was unfurled and hoisted.

16. Binding instructions on this and other issues had been issued to vicars apostolic in 1659 – cf. *Instructiones*, in *Codex Juris Canonici Fontes* (ed. Seredi), no. 4463, instr. 21, including 'Distance yourselves from all politics and affairs of State' and 'Instruct your people to obey their rulers, even those who are hostile, to avoid criticising their actions, and to suffer in

silence'. These refs in Dorrian G. (1991 Th), who offers a detailed discussion in chaps 1 and 7, and a translation in appendix 3.

17. The fact that the blessing was never raised as an issue later, and particularly at Hugh's trial in 1755 (see p. 151ff infra.), strongly suggests that the authorities were unaware of it.

18. Cf. Cameron W. (1971–2 J).

19. Details from Bishop John Geddes, op. cit.; Livingstone A., Aikman W. H. and Hart B. S. (eds) (1984), Lists; and Seton B. G. and Arnot J. G. (1928), vols II and III, alphabetical lists.

20. *Pace* Anson, the historian of the Catholic Church in penal times – cf. Anson P. F. (1970), p. 145. Two other Catholic priests who fought in the prince's army were Robert Leith, later abbot of the Benedictine monastery at Ratisbon, and John Tyrie's fellow 'pilgrim', Colin Campbell.

21. He later claimed in court that he was drawn into the army against his will by Young Clanranald, and never held a commission – Allan MacDonald to ?, 15.4.1747, MS 1306, f. 125, NLS, quoting his own confession after capture; but this was merely an attempt to minimise his punishment.

22. Account based on Edward Bourk [Burke] 'A Short but Genuine Account of Prince Charlie's Wanderings from Culloden etc', in Forbes R. op. cit., vol. I, pp. 189ff.

23. Neil MacEachan 'Narrative of the Wanderings of Prince Charles in the Hebrides', in Blaikie W. B. (ed.) (1916), pp. 227–66.

24. 'A Journal of the Prince's transaction since the batle of Culloden to this day as taken from his own mouth', in Tayler H. (ed.) (1948), pp. 115ff.

25. Neil MacEachan 'Wanderings of Prince Charles', in Blaikie W. B. (ed.) op. cit., pp. 227–66. The prince's wanderings in search of a way of escape were complex. For a full account, based on the above and other primary sources as well as local knowledge and tradition, see MacLean A. (1982; rev. edn 1990), chaps 2–6.

26. Maj. John Campbell to Glengarry, enclosed with letter John MacDonell of Glengarry to Lord President Forbes, 6.5.1746, in Warrand D. (ed.) (1930), p. 82.

27. Duke of Cumberland to duke of Newcastle, 30.4.1746, postscript; Newcastle Papers, in Warrand D. op. cit., p. 72. Re the fact that every place of worship was destroyed – Bishop John Geddes 'Some Account of the State of the Catholic religion in Scotland during the Years 1745-6–7', copy B JG 2/5, SCA, based on first-hand knowledge.

28. Intelligence report Lord Albermarle to duke of Newcastle, 15.12.1746, CLXXXIV S. P. Scotland Geo II, in Terry C. S. (ed.) (1902), vol. I, pp. 333f.

29. Gibson J. S. (1967), pp. 49, based on Capt. Fergussone's Log. Fergussone then sailed round the coast and destroyed the farm-towns around Borrodale and Glenuig.

30. Guillaume Frogier de Kermadec, Diary, in Gibson J. S. (1967), pp. 33f. According to local tradition HMD had a rose garden at Bunacaimb (Peter MacDonald, Bunacaimb, verbal communication). But the house visited by Frogier must have been Gaotal, Bunacaimb and Eilean Bàn both being too distant for an on-shore expedition.

31. 'Memorials of Murray of Broughton', in Bell R. F. (ed.) (1898), p. 288.

32. Ibid., p. 274.

33. Lord Lovat to lord advocate, 23.8.1745, *Culloden Papers* (1815), CCLV, pp. 210 f., in which he asked for 'a thousand stand of arms' so that his clan could aid the Government against 'the pretended Prince of Wales ... that mad and unaccountable Gentleman'.

34. Following the landing of a huge sum of money in *Louis d'Or* on the west coast a summer campaign still seemed a real possibility.

35. Letter to duke of Newcastle by one of Fergussone's officers, of which an extract was printed along with other documents in *The Scots Magazine*, appendix for 1747, pp. 614ff. The present account is based on this source.

36. According to the officer's account Lovat was found lying on two feather beds. Local tradition has it that he was discovered hiding in a hollow tree. That tree was remembered by Æneas MacDonald of Morar as still standing in the 1840s, and was identified by him as being at Druim a' Chuirn – Fraser Mackintosh C. (1888–9 J).

37. Captain John Campbell to ?, Loch na Nua, 25.7.1746, MS 3736, f. 449, NLS, and same to earl of Albermarle, Loch ne Houa bay, 30.7.1746, MS 3736, f. 455, NLS. On receiving intelligence the search was abandoned on 29 July.

38. Bishop John Geddes loc. cit., based on HMD's account to him in numerous conversations.

39. The present account based mainly on the prince's own recollections – 'A Journal of the Princes transactions since the batle of Culloden to this day as taken from his own mouth', in Tayler H. (ed.) (1948), pp. 115ff.; Narrative by Capt. Alexander MacDonald, Young Clanranald and MacDonald of Glenaladale, in Forbes R. op. cit., vol. I, pp. 320ff.; 'A Genuine Account, etc.' by James Elphinston, in ibid., vol. II, pp. 249ff., and Additions to the Above, given verbally by John MacKinnon, in ibid., vol. III, pp. 184ff.; John MacDonald, son of Borrodale 'A true and real state of Prince Charles Stuart's miraculous escape after the batle of Cullodden', in *Blackwood's Magazine*, October 1873; John MacKinnon, additions to account compiled by James Elphinston, in Forbes R. op. cit., vol. III, pp. 183ff.; John MacKinnon of Elgol 'Declaration', 12.7.1746, MS 3736, f. 430, NLS; 'Journal and Memoirs of P— C— Expedition into Scotland Etc. 1745–46', by a Highland Officer in his army, *Lockhart Papers*, vol II (1817). The prince's landing is variously located at Glasnacardoch, Buorblach and Little Mallaik (Mallaigbheag), but the last makes the most sense.

40. One tradition has the cave at Scamadale on the south side of Loch Morar, which surely is too distant from Cross (assuming that Morar's temporary home was itself near to Cross, though convenient if he was at this time living temporarily on Eilean Bàn). The cave above high tide on the south shore of the estuary, on the other hand, is just over the hill from Cross, and a far more convenient place of refuge.

41. The cave is between 3'–5' wide, tapering to a point at its far end, with a shallow downward slope, and varies in height between 5' and 12'.

42. It was certainly the recommendation of Lord President Forbes of Culloden

that all priests should be arrested and held in custody, even where there was no evidence against them – Lord President Forbes of Culloden 'Some Considerations on the Present state of the Highlands of Scotland', *c.* June 1746, in Warrand D. (ed.) (1930), vol. V, p. 102.

43. William Duthie to Bishop Smith, 1.5.1748, BL, giving news of troops searching for Colin Campbell in BraeLochaber and other parts of the West.
44. Bishop John Geddes loc. cit.
45. Journal of Donald MacLeod, 17.8.1747, in Forbes R. op. cit., vol. I, p. 178; also 'The Journal of Mr Anderson Aid-de-Camp to General Campbell', in Terry C. S. (ed.) op. cit., vol. II, appendix VIII, p. 409; and 'A List of Prisoners taken at the Island of South Uist', 28.7.1746, MS 3736, f. 430, NLS. Mac-Donald of Knock held the rank of lieutenant in the MacDonald Independent Company (O/C Capt. James MacDonald of Airds) – see Warrand D. (ed.) (1930), vol. V., p. 92. According to Paul McPherson, who may possibly have had his information first-hand from the captive, Allan MacDonald willingly gave the money to Knock for safe-keeping, considering him a friend, and Knock promised to restore it on demand to him or anyone deputed by him – McPherson P., Continuation of J. Thomson's Account of the Mission, Th/10, SCA, also printed in Forbes Leith W. (ed.) (1905), vol. II, p. 354. The episode would have repercussions for the Morar family and for Bishop Hugh at a later date – cf. pp. 145 and 148f. below.
46. 'The Journal of Mr Anderson' loc. cit., p. 407; and 'Copy of several remarkable Narratives taken from the mouth of Dr Archibald Cameron's Lady', by Dr John Burton, in Forbes R. op. cit., vol. I, pp. 312f. Archibald Cameron was Fr Alexander's brother.
47. Alexander Campbell to earl of Albermarle, Fort William, 9.8.1746, in Terry C. S. (ed.) op. cit., appendix LXII, p. 85; and earl of Albermarle to duke of Newcastle, Fort Augustus, 12.8.1746, in ibid., appendix LXXII, p. 98.
48. Letter Allan MacDonald of Morar, 15.4.1747, MS 1306, f. 125, NLS.
49. Estate proposed for forfeiture – Lord President Forbes of Culloden, Notes attached to List of Prisoners loc. cit., p. 102.
50. For a detailed account of their route, see Gibson J. S. (1967), pp. 51f.
51. Intelligence from Donald MacDonald, 16.9.1746, 6 am, in Terry C. S. (ed.) (1902), vol. II, appendix CLXIV, pp. 241f.
52. Intelligence Received from the Hills by Lord Albermarle, 229.9.1746, MS 3736, f. 494; and Copy of a letter from another person to Lord Albermarle, 22.9.1746, MS 3736, f. 495; both NLS. The former source also printed in Terry C. S. (ed.) op. cit., vol. I, p. 268.
53. We know that he had not arrived by 7 October – George Innes to Peter Grant, 7.10.1746, BL. Innes had apparently not even heard of the arrival of the prince in France, and thought he must still be in hiding in Badenoch or Lochaber.
54. George Innes to Peter Grant, 21.1. 1747, BL.
55. Details in Seton B. G. and Arnot J. G. (1928), vol. I, p. 224, and vols II and III, alphabetical lists. In addition to the 13, James Gordon, imprisoned since

December 1745, had been acquitted the previous month; John Godsman had been held and released after one day.

56. Account based on Mackenzie A. (1846 J), and MacWilliam A. (1973 J).

57. Bishop John Geddes loc. cit.

58. See Alexander MacDonald (his eldest son) to John Gordon, 2.6.1755, in Tayler H. (ed.) (1941), pp. 190f.

59. 'An Act to attaint [n. n.] of High Treason, if they shall not render themselves to one of his Majesty's Justices of the Peace, on or before the twelfth day of July ... and submit to Justice', 19 Geo II c. 46. The list of names attainted included the following who appear in the present work – Young Clanranald, Donald MacDonald of Lochgarry, Alexander MacDonald of Keppoch, Archibald MacDonald of Barrisdale, John MacKinnon of Skye, Lord Lovat, John Gordon of Glenbuchat, John Murray of Broughton, and Donald Cameron Younger of Lochiel. The list also printed in Seton B. G. and Arnot J. G. op. cit., vol. I, appendix A, pp. 294f.; subsequent lists in appendices B and D, pp. 297f. and 299 respectively. 'An Act for the more effectual disarming the Highlands in Scotland; and for more effectually securing the Peace of the said Highlands; and for restraining the Use of the Highland Dress', etc., 19 Geo II c. 39. The most detailed account of the post-'45 Acts is in Jewell B. F. (1975; facsimile 1978).

60. Re proposal to transport entire clans – duke of Newcastle to duke of Cumberland, 23.5.1746, and duke of Cumberland to duke of Newcastle, 5.6.1746, in Seton B. G. and Arnot J. G. op. cit., vol. I, p. 5. The proposal was Cumberland's. Re recommendation for banishment of priests and other RCs – earl of Albermarle to duke of Newcastle, 15.11.1746, including Enclosure 'Memorial concerning the Disaffected Highlands', proposals 7 and 11, CLXXVII, in Terry C. S. (ed.) op. cit., vol. I, pp. 305ff. The laity proposed for banishment were those refusing to attend Protestant worship.

61. Thomson J. 'Some Account of the Mission in Scotland, etc', Th/10, SCA, also printed in Forbes Leith W. (1909), vol. II, p. 359.

9

Fugitive Abroad
(1746–49)

Since Hugh was penniless he was given free board at the Scots College Paris. Propaganda questioned this use of college funds, but the principal, George Innes, justified it as an act of mercy.[1] Hugh was not the only recipient of his charity. By the end of the year Innes reckoned that at least 140 of the prince's followers were already in Paris, with more on their way, and many of them were knocking on his door. He urged Propaganda to send him money to help pay for these émigrés, and also if possible find something for the Scottish Mission to ease the misery at home.[2] Though he was giving his guests what hospitality he could the living was Spartan.

Propaganda responded by sending a small grant to Hugh, with an indication that a further donation to him and an 'extraordinary' for the Mission were likely to follow. The gift was especially welcome since he had received nothing whatever from the French Government, despite a personal recommendation on his behalf from the prince.

He was now anxious to return to Scotland and in April 1747 wrote to seek Bishop Smith's advice as to whether it would be safe to make the journey, and if so whether he would be allowed to pursue his work freely at home.[3] Alexander Smith had succeeded to the office of vicar apostolic of the Lowland vicariate on the death of Bishop Gordon in February 1746. Hugh now gave him authority for the Highland vicariate during his own absence and asked him to do what he could for his people. He was less than sanguine of either of them receiving more help from Rome in the foreseeable future, despite the pleas and half-promises. He believed that any further funding would be blocked at the very highest level: 'Mr Cant [the pope] is impregnable when it's a question of giveing money,' he assured his colleague.

Though Bishop Smith had been mainly confined to Edinburgh due to travel restrictions after Culloden, he had managed a brief visit to the North-East in the autumn of 1746. Shortly after receiving Hugh's letter he made a second, longer visit to the same area, using a travel pass acquired under a false name and including the Highland stations of Upper Deeside and Glengairn in his itinerary. Unable to reach the West personally he at least sent letters of comfort and support to the priests there.[4]

That summer the prince's younger brother Henry was made a cardinal of the Catholic Church. It was a step that Charles himself had opposed, since it further weakened his hopes of restoring the Stuart line, and the news was greeted with dismay in the Highlands. But Henry's elevation, in which he also became a member of Propaganda, at least augured well for the Scottish Mission. Hugh and Principal Innes sent him letters of congratulation, which he acknowledged with thanks, assuring them of his 'particular regard and consideration' for them personally and promising to miss no opportunity to help the work of the Church in Scotland.[5]

Allan MacDonald, Alexander Forrester and the brothers John and Charles Farquharson had been taken off the prison ship at Tilbury Fort in the autumn of 1746 and moved to London to await trial. When their hearing finally came up in June 1747 they found the whole atmosphere totally different from what they could have expected in Scotland. They were fully expecting to be transported to the Plantations.[6] But the chairman, the duke of Newcastle, ruled that they should simply be banished from Britain, on payment of £1,000 surety each. When they protested that they were penniless he smiled; because he could see that they were honest men, he answered, they might stand as surety for one another. As they were leaving one of his colleagues leaned across and murmered with the hint of a wink that to get to Scotland via Holland would not be so very far out of their way.[7] They took sail for Rotterdam, whence the Farquharsons travelled overland to Flanders, and Mr MacDonald and Mr Forrester to the Scots College Paris.

There were now only three priests to cover the entire West Highlands and Islands, one of whom was quite unfit for any work.[8] For Hugh the position was the more frustrating in that, though his programme for training priests had now begun to bear fruit with two men already ordained, neither had yet been able to return to the Mission: Alexander MacDonald from Uist and Dugald MacDonald, son of Kinlochmoidart, had been ordained in Rome a year before, but had never received their fare home from Propaganda. To him this was but one more example of the cardinals' neglect.

He now received news that James Grant, who had served in Barra for a decade before the Rising, was unwilling to return to the Highland vicariate. He had suffered ill health even before his arrest and imprisonment, and now wished to work in a less remote and barren station in the Lowlands.[9] For Hugh his loss was a 'dead stroke', the final straw which seemed to make his own work now virtually impossible:

> I see clearly it,s needless for me to attempt the North Country any more being
> destitute of all those that could do me any service, I am resolved to represent
> all these deficulties to the Merchants att Hamburg [the Cardinals in Rome],

and if no redress be given, I shall give up my charge, it being impossible for
me alon to do any thing in it, as every body may see, if they consider the
situation of trade in that Country.

He had made similar threats in the past, of course. But this time he was
not crying 'wolf'. His task as Highland bishop really must have seemed
utterly impossible. He knew better than anyone the vast distances to be
covered in all weathers, the constant danger from the garrisons, the
devotion and spiritual hunger of the people, and the impossibility of
satisfying them with the remnants of a team and himself so far away. He
was nearly forty-nine. How tempting to pass the rest of his days in the
safety, sunshine and comfort of Paris or Rome!

Ironically, the reasons the cardinals put forward for refusing to support
the Scottish Mission – the dislocation in the country and the virtual
destruction of Church organisation – were the very conditions that should
have elicited their help. Instead they were insisting that they would not
provide any funds until they received evidence of more settled conditions,
as well as a detailed account of the number of priests active in Scotland
and the scale of their activity.

Hugh therefore urged Bishop Smith to pen a report covering the
Lowland vicariate and to post it to him. Meantime he himself would
compile a report for the Highlands, and either send the two together or
even go with them in person to Rome.[10] He pieced his own report together
from the scraps of news brought from Britain by the trickle of Highland
fugitives still finding their way to Paris. But he waited in vain for Bishop
Smith's report, until he felt his own could be delayed no longer. Knowing
that Allan MacDonald was travelling to Rome at the end of November,
having found friends in Paris willing to loan him money for the journey,
he took the opportunity to send the report with him. With it he enclosed
a strong recommendation to the cardinal protector for a pension for both
Allan and Alexander Forrester. The latter had no source of income
whatever and was unable to stir from Paris, where he remained entirely
dependent on the college's charity and fast disappearing funds.[11]

Hugh had now recovered his courage and was determined to return to
the Mission as soon as possible, whatever the danger.[12] He was also under
pressure to do so from his fellow vicar apostolic. Bishop Smith had never
enjoyed good health. Since the death of Bishop Gordon he had been
carrying the Lowland vicariate alone, and now he was trying to cover the
Highland also, with insufficient priests in either. In the aftermath of
Culloden many of the laity had abandoned the faith or turned crypto-
Catholic. The Mission was penniless and some of his priests were holding
him responsible, since they believed that he had not fought Rome hard
enough on their behalf. He too was now warning Propaganda that unless

help came his way soon he would have no choice but to give up his charge.[13]

The past eighteen months had seen a number of laws enacted in Scotland tightening the noose upon the Jacobite Highlands. The Heritable Jurisdictions, the traditional foundation of the chiefs' legal authority, had been abolished. The Highland dress had been outlawed. The Vesting Act had opened the way for the annexation of Jacobite estates by the Crown, annexation that as far as anyone knew might be permanent.[14]

In December 1747 the Government instructed the Highland magistrates to follow the letter of these and earlier laws against 'Jacobites, Papists and Nonjurors', and issued instructions to the army to ensure that they did so.[15] As a part of an overall strategy plans were drawn up for a more effective deployment of troops in the Highlands and Islands. In all, five additional Highland companies were to be used. One of them, numbering 100 men, would be based at Bernera barracks on the west coast, from where detatchments would be sent to Knoydart, Morar, Arisaig, Moidart and Glenfinnan, key districts considered 'the most to be suspected for landing Money, Arms or French Emissaries'. The outposts were to patrol these areas constantly and provide weekly reports via Bernera to the control centre at Fort Augustus.[16]

Intelligence coming in to the lord justice clerk's office at Fort William during the autumn had warned that confidence among the West Highland Jacobites was now running high again. They were anticipating news of a second attempt by the prince, in connection with which couriers were expected to arrive with despatches from the Continent any day. One of the couriers identified by name was Hugh MacDonald.[17]

We have no way of knowing whether there were in fact serious plans for using Hugh as a courier. He was corresponding with the West Highlands and Islands, certainly, but as far as we know only with letters of pastoral support for his priests.[18] Travelling as a paid courier would ironically have been his one chance of returning home, for he had no funds of his own. Already by this date the French Crown had awarded 'gratifications' to more than sixty prominent Jacobite fugitives, many of whom had travelled with Hugh in *L'Heureux* and *Le Prince de Conti*. But his name had not been among them.[19]

Nor could he expect help from his family at home, for they were destitute. His brother Allan Ruadh had only recently been released from gaol, his house was a charred shell, and he had no way to support his wife and eight children, never mind anyone else.[20] He was reduced to selling his lands on Uist to MacDonald of Boisdale, and feuing the farm of Retland in South Morar, in order to put bread into their mouths.[21]

A second obstacle to Hugh's return was the problem of his entering

Britain. Bishop Smith had suggested that the court of Vienna might issue
a recommendation through its ambassador in London, but this he thought
impracticable.[22] Several foreign envoys in Paris were already under orders
not to issue such recommendations, particularly for persons who had fled
Britain in the company of the prince. As he saw it, the only possibility
was that the Viennese ambassador might obtain a passport for him under
an assumed name. Failing that he might be able to get in by sailing from
Lisbon, a safer but hugely more expensive option.

By April 1748 he had more or less decided upon the latter solution. He
had heard from Cardinal Rohan that the French Government had at last
agreed to award him an annual life pension of 1,000 livres, the amount
granted to captains in Prince Charles' army.[23] It was to be issued to him
under the name 'Marolle' – could this simply have been a French clerk's
attempt to render the name mac Dhomhnaill? – with the first instalment
to be paid the following year. He particularly asked the Scots agent not
to mention his windfall to Propaganda, for he was still hoping for income
from that source also.[24] The cardinals had finally issued a grant to the
Scottish Mission worth 1,428 livres (about £62 10s. sterling), to be used
for the purchase of sacred vessels destroyed in the burning of Mass houses
after Culloden. But there was no sign of them moving on viatics, and
until they did so no-one could return to the Mission.

In May he wrote to the Scots agent again, urging him to put more
pressure upon Propaganda: James Leslie and Alexander Forrester were
ready to travel and put their lives to any hazard in Scotland, but they
remained stranded in Paris; Dugald MacDonald was still in Rome, though
now two years ordained. Let Propaganda not plead poverty, he wrote,
for no-one would believe them: rather they would believe that they simply
did not care about the Mission.[25]

It was an angry letter, written by a frustrated man. He no doubt
suspected that the fact that he and the two priests were staying at the
Scots College Paris would be held against them in Rome, particularly by
the cardinal protector, Domenico Rivera, who had been in post since the
time of the Lercari report. Hugh knew that some stations at home had
been without a priest for two years, and that a number of the faithful
were beginning to turn to the Protestant Church for want of services of
their own.[26] He wanted to be home himself so that he could begin to
rebuild, and was already making plans for a late August departure. But
he needed his exiled priests.

Rome came up with nothing that summer, though Peter Grant, the
Scots agent, did send a small donation from his own funds. It was 'only
a mite', a fraction of the amount needed to cover even one man's travel.
But George Innes again dug into the meagre resources of the Scots College

Paris and found enough to pay Alexander Forrester across. Mr Forrester sailed from Le Havre in August and after disembarking at Ayr made his way secretly to Uist. There was still no way to send the others.[27]

Some priests had already contrived to make their own way back to the Highlands and pick up the threads again. Æneas MacGillis had never been captured, despite his prominent role as chaplain to MacDonell's regiment, and had returned to work in Glen Garry at an early date. Since then he had also been trying to support Strathglass and the other stations nearby that had no priest, celebrating Mass whenever and wherever he could.[28] John Farquharson had returned from banishment and had himself been in Strathglass for a while in 1747, before being forced to take refuge in Edinburgh. In the autumn of 1748 he slipped back and began working – in the words of the local presbytery – 'more openly and insolently than before', carrying the sacraments far beyond Strathglass, despite a warrant for his arrest from the sheriff of Inverness.[29] At about the same date Alexander MacDonald, who had also been confined to Edinburgh by the restrictions on travel still in force, at last managed to get back to Knoydart.

Mr MacDonald had caused some mischief while in the capital, by trying to resurrect the old ghost of Jansenism and dropping accusations against fellow priests into the ear of Bishop Smith. His action threatened to set back a Mission that, whatever else, was now enjoying harmony. When Hugh heard of it he judged it 'a very unseasonable time for renewing such old stories that ought to be buryed in oblivon, when we have so manny things to take up our thoughts'.[30] And it seems this opinion was general. In the hardship of the times the old enmities, the internecine quarrels that for close to two decades had threatened to pull the Mission apart, had been overtaken by greater external events and problems. With Colin Campbell dead on the field of Culloden there was now a tacit resolve among nearly all the clergy to let the Jansenist issue die with him, and after Alexander MacDonald returned to the Highlands no more was heard about it. For the Scottish Catholic Church this was the one good outcome of the tragedy of the '45.

On 18 October 1748 the plenipotentiaries of Britain and France signed the Treaty of Aix-la-Chapelle, bringing to an end the war of the Austrian succession. Under its terms France finally recognised the claim of the House of Hanover to the British Crown, and cancelled the right of the Stuart Pretender to asylum within her own borders. Charles Edward Stuart was formally requested to leave the country and when he continued to ignore the request, counting on his personal popularity among the citizens of Paris, he suffered the indignity of public arrest on 10 December. Freed on condition of leaving France immediately he sought sanctuary at

Avignon, a city under the jurisdiction of the papacy at this time, and set up house there before the end of the year. But his stay lasted a mere two months, for the pope, under duress from Britain, in turn requested him to leave. On the last day of February he departed the city and disappeared from the public eye.

The New Year of 1749 found Hugh still in Paris, and still awaiting the grant promised by Rome. A fellow exile with him at the Scots College was his nephew Ranald, the younger son of his half-brother Allan, who had seen service in Clanranald's regiment and had escaped to France in the same vessel as himself. The young man was one of the living casualties of war. At a time when he should have been at school he had been subjected first to the sight of slaughter and then to a life on the run. So scarred had he been by the trauma that he had become – in Hugh's words – 'in a manner wild so that he could hardly bear the sight of men'. He was fortunate to have found understanding and support from the college staff, under whose care he was now beginning to recover his health of mind and body and salvage his education.[31]

At home Bishop Smith was still carrying the whole Mission. He had written to the cardinal protector begging for a coadjutor, but because of the restrictions on travel his letter had not yet been conveyed to Rome. Hugh therefore wrote to Cardinal Rivera on his colleague's behalf, urging his need for an assistant, and at the same time warning that the Mission could no longer afford to send students abroad unless Propaganda was prepared to grant a special viatic for them.[32] The reply he received was 'very civil but nowaise encourageing': the cardinal did not consider this the proper time for a coadjutor, nor would he promise extra money for students. He also pointed out that one of Hugh's own Highland priests, Allan MacDonald, the prince's personal chaplain in the '45, was now in Rome eating up funds set aside for the Scottish Mission.[33]

The news that there would be no assistant for Bishop Smith made it all the more imperative that Hugh himself return to Scotland. He had put back his plans too many times already. He had also learned that his own long-awaited grant from Rome was to be forwarded to him in April, which therefore seemed the fittest time to go. He arranged with the Scots agent for the money to be sent direct to Edinburgh to await him on arrival, rather than to Paris, where he might be tempted to spend it. But it was essential, he stressed, that it reach him in the Scottish capital, since once he entered the Highlands there would certainly be a further delay of at least six months before he would see it, for that was the way things were done there.[34] And there would be no way of getting hold of ready cash locally, for the Highlanders dealt almost entirely by bills of promise and thought nothing of running up long-standing debts. As soon as they knew he was back, in fact, some of them would no doubt be looking to borrow from him.

No details have survived of his journey home, except that he reached England in May and remained in London before making his way to Edinburgh in August.[35] He stayed some weeks in the Scottish capital, awaiting both the arrival of his grant from Rome and an opportune moment for returning to the Highlands in safety.

Notes

1. George Innes to Peter Grant, Scots agent, 21.1. 1747, BL in which he gives a description of Hugh's poverty in order 'to pacyfy Padrons about B. Mdls staying in this College'.
2. George Innes to Peter Grant, 7.10.1746, BL.
3. HMD to Bishop Smith, 17.4.1747, BL. The pope referred to was Benedict XIV.
4. Bishop Smith, Report to Propaganda, 13.12.1747, Propaganda Archives (in Latin), transl. in Bellesheim A. (1890), vol. IV, appendix XVI, pp. 399ff. The passport, carrying the name 'Brown', was acquired through the influence of the sister of Lord Leuchars, a convert – Bishop John Geddes 'Some Account of the State of the Catholic Religion in Scotland During the Years 1745, 1746 and 1747', copy B JG 2/5, SCA; also printed in Forbes Leith W. (1905), vol. II, p. 338.
5. George Innes's letter of congratulation, with covering letter, 31.7.1747; reply of Mr Edgar on behalf of Henry Cardinal York, 22.8.1747, in Browne J. (1838), vol. IV, CX (p. 16), CIX (p. 15), and CXVI (p. 19) respectively.
6. Cf. George Innes to Peter Grant 5.6.1747, BL, written just before their trial.
7. Bishop John Geddes op. cit.
8. The three were William Harrison, Angus MacGillis and Angus MacLachlan. The first, having pled his non-participation in the '45, had received a pass giving him virtual immunity in the West. The third was inactive at Scottas in Knoydart. In addition to these three Fr Gordon SJ was serving in Upper Deeside in the East Highlands cf. Bishop Smith Report to Propaganda, 13.12.47, loc. cit.
9. HMD to Bishop Smith, 1747 (no precise date), BL 3/89/4. His use of the term 'North Country' here is unusual. It was normally used in Mission correspondence in reference to the North-East, the main Catholic areas of the Highlands and Islands being referred to as the 'West'. But he here clearly uses the 'North' to refer to the Highlands and Islands in general.
10. Ibid.
11. HMD to Peter Grant, 24.11.1747, BL.
12. Ibid.
13. Bishop Smith Report to Propaganda, 13.12.1747, loc. cit.
14. 'An Act for taking away and abolishing the Heretable Jurisdictions in that part of Great Britain called Scotland; and for making satisfaction to the proprietors thereof; and for restoring such Jurisdictions to the Crown; and

for making more effectual Provision for the Administration of Justice throughout that Part of the United Kingdom, by the King's Courts and Judges there', etc., 1747, 20 Geo II c. 43. 'An Act for more effectual disarming the Highlands in Scotland; and for more effectually securing the Peace of the said Highlands; and for restraining the Use of the Highland Dress', etc., 1746, 19 Geo II c. 39; 'An Act for vesting in his Majesty the Estates of certain Traitors, and for more effectually discovering the same, and applying the Produce thereof to the Use of his Majesty', etc., 1747, 20 Geo II c. 41. Re the process of annexation, see Smith A. (1982), passim. In the Catholic West Highlands the estates of Lochgarry, Kinlochmoidart and Barrisdale were annexed. The Keppoch estate was surveyed with a view to annexation, but eventually exempted. Clanranald's estate was saved on a technicality, through the Crown's mis-spelling of the landlord's forename.

15. Extract of letter, General Bland to Capt. White, Edinburgh, 14.12.1747, MS 3044, f. 123, NLS.

16. Lt. Col. D. Watson, 'Proposals for Cantoning the five Highland Add^l. Company's in the Western Isles, and Remoter Parts of the Highlands', Fort Augustus, 4.12.1747, RH 2/5/12, pp. 68f., NAS. Intelligence was to be gathered through bribes and whisky. It was considered the key to the success of the operation.

17. Lord justice clerk to duke of Newcastle, 3.11.1747, including 'enclosure' collector of customs, Fort William, 26.10.1747, in Terry C. S. (ed.) (1902), vol. II, appendix XXXVI, p. 470. The confidence of the Jacobites had been particularly boosted by news of the taking of Bergen-op-Zoom.

18. Cf. Intelligence, enclosed with letter lord justice clerk to duke of Newcastle, 28.1.1748, in Terry C. S. op. cit., vol. II, pp. 524ff, in which a priest on Barra incautiously let slip receiving letters from Hugh.

19. Browne J. (1838), vol. III, appendix doc. XLVII, p. 469; and vol. IV, appendix doc. CXXIV, p. 22. There had been two lists to date, the second awarded in new year 1748. In all nearly 63,000 livres were dispensed (24 livres = 1 guinea; i.e., 1 livre = 10½d.).

20. Allan MacDonald to ?, Inverness 15.4.1747, MS 1036, f. 125, NLS.

21. Cf. Fraser Macintosh C. (1888–89 J), p. 66.

22. HMD to Peter Grant, 24.3.1748, BL.

23. In sterling the pension's value was approx. £41 13s. 0d. It may well be that Cardinal Rohan was himself instrumental in the award being made, since only the previous year James III had petitioned Pope Benedict XIV to have him elevated to the college of cardinals – Dorrian G (1991 Th), p. 72.

24. HMD to Peter Grant, 19.4.1748, BL.

25. HMD to Peter Grant, 26.5.1748, BL.

26. There is some evidence that this was the case on South Uist and Barra – cf. 'Report of Doctors Hyndman, Dick, &C, appointed by the General Assembly 1760 to visit the Highlands and Islands', CH 1/5/70, p. 35, NAS.

27. HMD to Peter Grant, 4.8.1748, BL.

28. Letter Patrick Nicolson, Minister of Kiltarlity, 26.1.1748, MS 3431, f. 91, NLS.

29. Presbytery of Dingwall, Report of meeting of 12.4.1749, MS 3431, f. 135, NLS.
30. HMD to Peter Grant, 19.4.1748, BL.
31. HMD to Peter Grant, 24.3.1749, BL.
32. HMD to Peter Grant, 25.1.1749, BL.
33. HMD to Peter Grant, 24.3.1749, BL.
34. Ibid.
35. Re his arrival in England – HMD to Propaganda, July ? 1751, BL 3/106/1 (in Italian); re his arrival in Edinburgh – Geddes J. op. cit.

10

A Little Barque Much Tossed About (1749–56)

When Hugh finally left Edinburgh in November he decided not to return to his own district at once, but to make for Upper Banffshire. He knew that there would be less chance of capture there. The Gordon lands were less under scrutiny than the West. The duke had played no part in the Rising and though troops were stationed close by, their quarry were cattle reivers rather than Jacobite refugees. There were no emissaries from France to be tracked down. Upper Banffshire was far inland and, unlike the west coast, not living in expectation of a new Jacobite attempt by sea. Above all, his own face was not known there.

He took the coast road to Aberdeenshire and then cut west through the hills to the Cabrach. This largely Catholic community was to a good extent isolated from the outside world by its geography. A wide shallow upland glen surrounded by barren hills, dominated by the steep and craggy mountain known as The Buck, accessible only through a narrow throat at its north end and a high hill path to the south-east, rarely visited by outsiders, it offered him the promise of a safe retreat.

The resident priest, the Benedictine Fr Thomas Brockie, welcomed him into his own house at Shenval as a temporary home while he considered his position. From the Cabrach he could reach the most easterly stations of his own vicariate, Glengairn and Upper Deeside, and also the stations of the Lowland district in the North-East that Bishop Smith could not risk visiting.

He wrote more than once to his Lowland colleague during the autumn seeking any word from the capital as to the situation in the West, but heard nothing. In December he decided to find out for himself. Borrowing a servant and horse from his host he set out for Moidart, where he spent Christmas and the New Year, keeping as far as possible out of sight. News that lawyers were seeking to recover debts from a man for whom he had stood as guarantor, action that was sure to draw attention to himself, added little to his sense of safety.[1] As soon as the weather eased he returned to the Cabrach.

In May (1750) he wrote again to Bishop Smith. It was now a year since his return to Scotland, yet he was no closer to a decision as to his future. He was inclined to remain where he was at least until he had a clearer idea of the mood of the West Highlands. But he knew he was needed in the West, where there were problems that only he could resolve, and was 'in great hover' whether to go or not.[2]

The position was particularly bad in the Outer Isles, where both Neil MacFie on Barra and Alexander Forrester on Uist were being hunted by the military and would almost certainly be forced to flee the islands. The laity in the West were also suffering harassment, and some of the Catholic gentlemen there had already taken the precaution of sending their sons abroad to avoid the persecution at home.[3] The words used three years before by Bishop Smith to describe the Scottish Mission – 'a little barque much tossed about ... only by the singular grace of God not yet overturned'[4] – still certainly applied to the Highland District. And they also aptly described Bishop Hugh himself, driven as he was from place to place, nowhere settled and rarely safe.

The troops' harassment of the Catholics of the West was a response to orders from a Government in a state of near-panic. After his departure from Avignon in February 1749 Charles Edward Stuart had disappeared entirely from sight, and all attempts to trace him by the governments of Europe had proved vain. Intelligence reports had him sighted as far afield as Sweden and Poland. The British Government received word, much closer to the truth, that he was in hiding in Paris, where one of his main retreats was said to be the Scots College.[5] It was believed, again accurately, that he was about to enter Britain to lay plans for another rising, and that the Catholic priests and gentlemen of the Highlands were among his close associates. That several gentlemen's sons had recently been sent abroad to keep them out of trouble ironically fuelled this suspicion, since they were thought to have been sent as emissaries. It was further reported that certain West Highland gentlemen were now back home from France enlisting men and inciting their tenants to rebellion, with the active assistance of the clergy. Enough weapons were said to be concealed there to arm 6,000 men. Once again Hugh was cited by name as being among those involved.[6]

It was in response to this intelligence, and to recommendations originally made to the Government more than two years before,[7] that troops of General Guise's regiment were posted to the West Highlands in spring 1750. They set up headquarters at the head of Loch Arkaig, with outposts at the foot of the loch and at Glenfinnan, Loch Eil and Strontian. A second force of twenty men was deployed along the west coast, with its base at Traigh on the South Morar estate and posts at Loch Hourn, Beoraid in North Morar and Keppoch in Arisaig. Anyone who knows the terrain will easily see what a limited effect such a force could have. But they were stationed exactly where Hugh's chosen base in the West would have been, and would have had no difficulty finding him.

His arrival at this time would also have caused serious embarrassment to his half-brother Allan Ruadh. The commanding officer at Traigh had demanded a promise from Allan to ensure that his tenants kept the king's peace,[8] and since his estate was under threat of forfeiture to the Crown he had had no choice but to comply. The presence of an outlawed brother on his land would only have increased the likelihood of its confiscation.

Though the harassment of priests was most severe in the West Highlands it was being felt elsewhere in Scotland also, and that autumn Bishop Smith was forced to leave Edinburgh and seek refuge in London. He remained there nine months, in close contact with Bishop Challoner, the leader of the Catholic Church in England. It was through Challoner's approaching the duke of Norfolk, and the latter's influence with the duke of Argyll, that representation was made to ease the persecution in Scotland. At the same time the Scots agent was pleading the case to Propaganda and the pope, at whose prompting the ambassadors of Catholic Europe won from the duke of Newcastle an undertaking that all harassment on grounds of religion *per se* would cease.[9] By the following summer, 1751, Bishop Smith felt free to return.

In response Hugh's enemies now turned to accusing him of political crimes. Their charge that he was enlisting men for the French service was by his own account a pure fabrication, supported by no evidence whatever, and by any account a most improbable story. The Edinburgh justiciary nonetheless saw fit to relay it to London, where the case was taken to court.[10] There the justices were not long in reaching a verdict, neither summoning Hugh to defend himself nor giving the arguments any serious consideration.[11] They ruled him guilty and issued an order to every military post in the country for his arrest. Their ruling was a blatantly political decision only too typical of the times. Their transparently unjust handling of the case can most charitably be ascribed to panic, coming as it did at a time when there were known to be emissaries actively recruiting in the West Highlands and a rising was in the air.[12]

Hugh was now a man on the run. Luckily the approach of winter restricted the movements of troops against him and gave him some respite, but with the coming of spring the searches were resumed. In March and April 1752 he found himself stuck in Moidart, caught between the military posts at Strontian, Glenfinnan and Keppoch, not easily able to get out yet far enough from all of them them to feel reasonably safe from arrest.

Given the formalism of the Catholic Church – its strict rules for liturgical practice in regard to action, word, dress, and even time and place of celebration – running an illegal, underground mission was difficult at the best of times. The Catholicism of the day was not designed for such circumstances, nor had it got round to adapting practice to cope

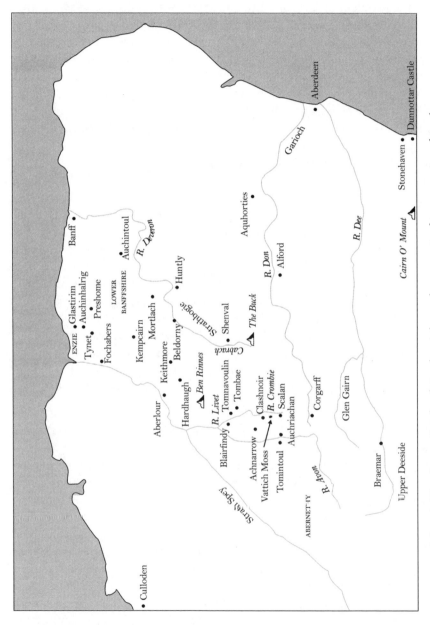

Map 6. North-east Scotland (in the eighteenth century): places mentioned in the text

with them.[13] Thus as a newly ordained priest Hugh had experienced problems finding Communion hosts that complied with the rubric requiring the use of wheaten bread, as we saw,[14] and his fellow clergy constantly faced the problem of lack of vestments, vessels and suitable Mass centres.

Added to these general problems, the difficulty of trying to run his vicariate while himself on the run can well be imagined. Just contacting his priests was dangerous, far less visiting them. Even a normally routine matter such as getting hold of balsam for the blessing of chrism oil on Holy Thursday now became a nightmare. Sending students to the colleges abroad was virtually impossible, for the necessary 'testificat' required the signatures of several priests and a justice of the peace, a thing not easy to organise by a fugitive from the law.[15]

Since it was impossible to 'attend his trade' in any serious way he decided to get out of the West if he could. He wrote to Bishop Smith suggesting that they should try to rendezvous somewhere on the edge of the Highlands – at Crieff perhaps – to compare notes and discuss their next move.[16] The two men were supposed to meet at least annually, but had not been able to get together for the past three years. Bishop Smith proposed that it would make more sense to meet in Edinburgh, where they would be better placed to seek the support of persons of influence, and this Hugh agreed to. He slipped out of Moidart in May.

While on the road he took the precaution of adopting new aliases. His ecclesiastical name 'Dian' was far too well known to offer any anonymity, as was the cryptonym 'Sandison' (Sandy's son – i.e., the son of Alexander [MacDonald of Morar]). He now took to styling himself either 'Hugh MacKay' or 'Collome MacKenzie' in both life and correspondence, and on arrival in Edinburgh was introduced as such to all but trusted friends.[17]

Being together for some days gave Hugh and Bishop Smith the opportunity to write what should have been their 'annual' letter to Propaganda. In it they explained that the Government's promise not to pursue anyone on grounds of religion, though apparently sincere, was proving largely ineffectual at the local level. Priests were still being convicted simply for being priests, and such convictions were quite easy to achieve since according to the Act of 1700 the only proof required was that the accused be 'held or repute' to be a priest. Already that spring two missioners had been found guilty in this manner and outlawed, after their enemies had paid a large reward to the military for their arrest.[18]

The penal legislation was in fact now an anachronism at variance with the new religious moderation (and indeed the growing secularism) of the civil authorities. But being still on the statute books it left Catholics as vulnerable as ever. It could be used by the Church's enemies to their own advantage, and they knew it. They realised that, if most law officers were now reluctant to pursue men for their religion, the surest way to bring a priest to court was to accuse him of a *political* crime. In the present climate there was always the chance that the charge would stick, as it had in Hugh's case. But the main thing was to get the case to court. Once there, and having no evidence whatever to bring, they could if necessary change the charge against him to that of his being (reputed) a priest, knowing that the magistrate, even if well disposed, was bound by the existing legislation to find against him and to issue the mandatory penalty of banishment. This was the tactic they were using time and again, frustrating all the Government's promises of lenity.[19]

And who were these enemies? Hugh and his fellow bishops had no doubts as to the answer, as is abundantly clear from their correspondence at this time. Letter after letter points to 'the fanatical preachers' and 'the ill natur'd ministers' of the Kirk as the root of their ills. It was they who were harassing the local landowners and magistrates, and through the synods and the General Assembly continuing to put pressure on the Government and the highest judiciary. There were still bigots to be found among the latter, certainly, who were only too ready to be persuaded. But in most cases, the bishops were convinced, the highest authorities no longer had much relish for or even interest in persecuting Catholics. And the same applied to the landowners, the Justices, and the military: where landlords or officers of the Law harassed priests it was now usually for the sake of peace, being themselves harassed;[20] and where troops sought to make arrests it was either in obedience to direct orders or cynically for the bounty money. The Church's real enemies, and the ones behind almost every persecution, were a diehard element among the Kirk ministers.

These men had actually been given a new opportunity for mischief by the recent government instruction to the county justiciary to collect statistics of Catholics in their areas. The task had been delegated to the parish ministers, and some of them saw it as their chance for further harassment. One Highland minister, whose letter to the county magistrate Hugh had seen personally, had argued that because the Catholics in his parish were too violent to be approached without military assistance he would need an armed force to carry out the task: he would then undertake 'anything' to serve the king, even with blood if necessary. The intentions of men like this were all too obvious.[21]

Towards the end of July Hugh left the capital to visit Traquair House, the seat of Charles, the fifth earl of that name in Upper Tweeddale (plate 7).[22] The old grey-harled, four-storey fortified mansion with its rounded corner turrets lay among the high hills of Peeblesshire, close to where the little Quair Burn flows into the Tweed. It dated in part from the eleventh century and in its time had played host to some two dozen monarchs. For long it had been the only great house in the whole Border Country to hold out for the Old Religion.[23]

Hugh's host had entertained Prince Charles there after the taking of Edinburgh in '45, and had spent nineteen months in the Tower of London for supporting the cause. From the high drawing-room, where Hugh joined him in the evenings, one looked out upon the avenue that led up to the entrance gates of the estate. They had been locked after the prince's departure, and in obedience to a promise of the laird have famously remained locked ever since, awaiting the restoration of the House of Stuart.

Each morning Hugh visited the priest's room at the very top of the house. Here the resident chaplain had his bed, but the room also had an altar in the recess and doubled as a chapel for the household and the little Catholic community in the village. The priest's bookcase had a false back, which when opened revealed a tight, precipitous spiral stair descending to a secret outer door, through which he could make his escape in the event of an unexpected raid. And for his better protection, his white vestments were cut from bed quilt material and could be easily secreted among the rest of his bed linen.[24]

Hugh celebrated Mass daily in the chaplain's room, and afterwards repaired to the terraced gardens at the back of the house to say his Office in the morning summer sun. Whenever possible he would make for the library, the creation of the present laird and his father. He loved the room, with its rows of leather-bound books filling every wall, arranged not by subject but by size, the largest tomes at floor level and up under the ceiling tiny volumes, some little bigger than matchboxes. To make sense of such randomness the earl had devised a simple if idiosyncratic cataloguing system, based on a frieze of frescoes depicting the ancient philosophers, that ran round the perimeter of the room.

During his stay he was introduced to Giovanni Battista Gastaldi, minister in Britain for the republic of Genoa, who was also visiting, and he took the opportunity of explaining to him the accusations being levelled against himself and other churchmen.[25] Signor Gastaldi promised to do all he could for them when in Edinburgh.

When they met again in the capital at the beginning of August he was able to report that he had spoken to all the magistrates there, and that they had assured him 'they had no inclination to trouble any body unless they shoud be oblidged to it by superior orders'. He was about to leave for Inverary, where he promised to speak on Hugh's behalf to the duke of Argyll.

While in Edinburgh Hugh received a letter from Alexander MacDonald of Glenaladale warning him that the troops were even more active in the West than before. 'Glen' had tried his best to glean any information as to their orders regarding Hugh but without success, so that he could not advise if it would be safe to return.[26] Hugh decided to travel at least as far as Drummond, where he arranged to be met by his servant with a horse. By that time he hoped to have firmer news.

Where he went after Drummond is not known, but there is some evidence that he managed to spend at least part of the autumn in his own vicariate.[27] By Christmas, we know, he had returned to the North-East, staying first at Keithmore and then at Scalan in the New Year of 1753.[28] But the constant travelling, the lack of any real home, the price on his head, and the frustration of not being able to 'follow his trade' were beginning to tell upon his health.

In March Hugh's nephew John, his half-brother Allan Ruadh's eldest son, paid a visit to the house of MacDonald of Knock, accompanied by Alexander MacDonell of Barrisdale. Each man was armed with pistol and dirk. Their mission was to recover the sixty guineas and silver watch that Knock had taken from Allan MacDonald in the summer of '46.[29] When Knock refused John struck him over the head with his weapon, and as he ran for his life Alexander chased after him, swearing to shoot him through the heart if he ever breathed a word about their visit.[30] Alexander returned with accomplices in April, and the following month his uncle Archibald, the leader of the notorious Barrisdale Guard, who made their living by offering 'black meal' or protection in and around Knoydart, again attacked Knock with a number of his followers, including Hugh's nephew, John. Knock later gave information to the sheriff of Inverness which led to their arrest. Archibald Barrisdale was imprisoned at Edinburgh Castle and sentenced to death for high treason.[31] But John evaded capture, leaving Knock with a score to settle with him, and – by association – with his family the MacDonalds of Morar. He was a dangerous enemy, being almost certainly at this time in the employ of the Government as a spy in the West Highlands.[32]

The orders for Hugh's arrest remained in force throughout 1753, and once at least that spring the troops thought they had caught their man in Knoydart. But their intelligence had badly let them down. Their captive was a Catholic priest, certainly, but there the likeness ended. Alexander, son of Kinlochmoidart, was twenty years Hugh's junior. Despite the obvious misidentification he was held in Inverness Gaol, the fact that he was a priest being considered sufficient justification, and only released upon payment of a large security.

While Alexander lay in prison Hugh slipped away south. Not only did the capital promise him greater anonymity; perhaps even more urgently, it could offer him better care for his visibly worsening health. He was already a very sick man. By the time the Edinburgh physicians saw him he had deteriorated alarmingly and they diagnosed him dangerously ill.

He lay through the summer in Bishop Smith's house in Blackfriars Wynd, very close to death.[33]

There was no thought of his moving, even in the autumn. On 1 November he and Bishop Smith sent their report to Propaganda, in which they advised that, though now no longer in danger, he was still nowhere near fit to resume his duties.[34] At the same time they reminded the cardinals that Bishop Smith was himself now nearly seventy, and his health growing daily worse, and pled the case again for a third bishop for the Mission.

They also warned that the constant persecution was eroding the discipline of the Mission. Some priests were cracking under the pressure, one had already abandoned his charge, and they themselves as semi-fugitives were ill placed to exercise effective authority. They saw Church discipline as perhaps the greatest casualty of the times, and urged Propaganda to extend to Scotland the regulations issued by Pope Benedict to the English Mission earlier in the year.

That October further raids were made on the homes of priests in Strathavon, Glenlivet and Scalan in the East Highlands. The depute sheriff, who had been pressed to take action by the local Kirk ministers, sent in a detachment of troops with orders to arrest the priests and bring them to the gaol at Banff. For his part the local O/C complied with the order, but with no real heart for it. He actually behaved very civilly towards the priests, tipping them off in advance so that they would not be at home when his men arrived, and only making token cursory searches.[35] An honourable man, he could see that it was a demeaning and quite unnecessary task to deploy large numbers of armed soldiers against men of the cloth, peaceful men who posed no threat to anyone.

Hugh spent the spring of 1754 in Glenlivet, keeping in touch with the West as best he could. The situation in the Hebrides remained extreme. On Uist Alexander Forrester was still under perpetual banishment and technically liable to execution if captured. He was hiding in the mountainous east of the island, surviving in caves. When even this became too dangerous he managed to escape to Ireland, whence he returned to Edinburgh in June, waiting for the troops to be withdrawn from the island.[36]

His young assistant on Uist was less lucky. Alexander MacDonell of the family of Scottas, one of Hugh's protégés at Gaotal, had only returned from ordination in Rome the previous year. He was picked up in the summer and, after being held at Inverness Gaol, transferred to the Edinburgh Tolbooth awaiting trial. He received the now almost routine sentence of banishment, and – almost routinely – ignored it. But he was not to serve the Highlands for long, for the nine-month ordeal destroyed his health and within a year he was dead.

To fill the empty Uist station Hugh chose his nephew John MacDonald, the son of his sister Catherine and Donald MacDonald of Ardnamurchan. John was twenty-six and like Alexander just one year ordained; the two men had in fact been fellow students at Gaotal and Rome. To cover Uist alone at any time would have been a huge responsibility for one so inexperienced. Lying sixty miles out in the sea, its remoteness alone was daunting, and with some 2,500 people to serve it was easily the largest charge in the vicariate. John himself jokingly referred to it as 'Ultima Thule', and he judged it at this time the most dangerous as well as the most laborious station in Scotland.[37]

On Barra too Hugh had been forced to entrust a demanding station to an untried man. Angus MacDonald, son of Angus MacDonald of Dalilea of the solid bone breastplate and a vigorous man himself, had been ordained in Rome one year ahead of John and Alexander. Before John's arrival in Uist he was for some weeks completely alone in the Isles, at the height of the persecution there. Though he managed to avoid arrest the experience entirely broke his health.[38]

Having done all he could for his priests that summer, prudence dictated that Hugh leave the West as soon as possible. In October he returned to the relative safety of the Cabrach, where he again took lodgings with Fr Brockie. He remained at Shenval for seven months, trying to run his vicariate by post.

At the beginning of May 1755 he travelled down to Edinburgh, from where he sent news to Abbate Peter Grant in Rome.[39] He had two 'printices' for the Scots College, he told him. One was a son of Glenaladale and the other his own nephew Allan, which gave the prospect of yet more priests of the name 'MacDonald' in the Highlands. This was hardly ideal at the present time, when 'that name was more obnoxious to the G-m-t [Government] than any other'. Since most of his priests were already of that 'suspected clan' he asked the agent to find some good Irishmen who would be willing to serve in Scotland, and who might be more acceptable to the authorities. Meantime the boys were kitted out with clothes and linens, and ready to travel. But with war looming all available seamen were needed to man military vessels and no merchant ships were sailing.

Hugh was encouraged by Abbate Grant's first impressions of the new cardinal protector recently appointed to the Scottish Mission. Giuseppe Spinelli promised to be far more supportive than his predecessor. He was particularly sympathetic to the shortage of priests in the Highlands and had not only proposed the setting up of a small Highland seminary with three or four students, but had undertaken to finance it and asked for a costing. Hugh estimated that £6 sterling per student per year would meet the need, and offered to supplement this with funds of his own 'with the greatst pleasure', if this meant that more students could be taken on.[40]

For the past five years the alcoholic Neil MacFie had been suspended from his priestly functions,[41] but Hugh had continued to pay his quota, both from a sense of compassion and in order to maintain his goodwill. The man knew too much about his fellow priests to risk making an enemy of him, and in drink he knew no discretion. Hugh was especially concerned that he was known to correspond with MacDonald of Knock, one who had already shown himself quick to give information to the authorities. He was aware too that Knock still had a score to settle with his own family.

In the first week of May he arrived at Shenval, intending to stay only a day or two before continuing west to Glen Garry. But a new development detained him in the Cabrach. Rome had finally agreed to appoint a coadjutor bishop for the Lowlands, and had nominated James Grant the priest of Preshome. But Mr Grant, like his bother John Alexander nearly thirty years before, was diffident to accept the mitre, pleading ill-health and unworthiness, and had so far resisted all attempts of colleagues to persuade him. Now Bishop Smith was calling him to Edinburgh. Hugh thought he might be able to convince him to comply, since Mr Grant had worked under him in Barra and the two men knew each other well. He suggested that he come up to meet him in the Cabrach, and that they could then travel south together.[42] He obviously thought that this was the best way to ensure his reaching the capital, and that the matter was important enough to change his own plans for. James Grant was persuaded. He arrived at Fr Brockie's house on the day after Trinity Sunday.

Later that week the two men set out on the hill road that leads south out of the Cabrach. Three days' easy riding took them via Alford to Balnacraig on Deeside. Thence their road rose into the bare heather hills, until at the summit of Cairn o' Mount it dropped over the edge, and below them lay a green tapestry of fields with the shimmering North Sea beyond. From thereon the terrain was lowland. They forded the South Esk at Brechin, reaching Stobhall in time to celebrate Sunday Mass, and continued south, skirting Loch Leven and the Hill of Beith. They crossed the Forth at the Queensferry, and entered by the West Port of Edinburgh in the second week of June.

It was probably on his arrival that Hugh received Allan MacDonald's letter from Rome asking him to retrieve the sixty guineas stolen by MacDonald of Knock. It was certainly about this time that he contacted Knock on the matter. But in doing so he had to provide a forwarding address, and it seems that he imprudently gave the address of his own lodgings in the capital. This was the very kind of chance that Knock had been waiting for and he at once notified the authorities. A warrant was issued by the lord justice clerk, Charles Erskine of Alva, and on 19 July Hugh was arrested.[43]

He was charged with treasonable offences, including recruiting for the French service. Under examination he answered every question with skill and obvious integrity. He stated that he had come to the capital about a month before, thinking 'he could live more quiet [there] and less subject to any suspicion from the Government', and that he had been lodging in the house of Mr Alexander, a painter. As to the charges, he denied fomenting the rebellion in '45, which indeed he had always considered 'an unseasonable attempt and desperate' (he did not actually state that he opposed it), and also denied any part in anti-government activities since then. He totally rejected the charge of enlisting men for the French service. A packet of sealed letters had been found in his possession, from which his interrogators had discovered his alias 'Colin McKenzie', and this he admitted to using on occasion. When pressed as to his religion and status, he denied nothing but declined to give any positive answer. A written account of his examination was then signed by himself, the lord justice clerk and George Drummond, the lord provost of Edinburgh, and his letters were returned to him resealed.[44]

Since it was clear that there was no hard evidence of political crimes against him the lord justice clerk reduced the charge to that of his being a Catholic priest, and on those grounds committed him to prison. It was a decision fully supported by his senior colleagues in London. Hugh was taken to the Edinburgh Tolbooth, the gaunt old gaol that stood incongruously in the middle of the High Street cheek by jowl with the High Kirk of St Giles (plate 8), and there set among the straw with common criminals.

He immediately appealed to the lord advocate to be released on bail. On 1 August he learned that his petition had been granted, but with three conditions: that he give his bond, under a penalty of £300 sterling, to compear at court whenever called, up to 15 November; that he reside meantime at Duns or Kelso (the choice was his) and remain at all times within four miles of his place of residence; and that he leave the capital within forty-eight hours of his release. He was freed at 10 a.m. the following day, and at 10 a.m. on the 4th, meeting the deadline to the precise minute, he began his journey to Duns.

Though in effect still a prisoner he must have found the country around the little Borders town a freeing landscape. Within his four-mile limit he could walk out east onto the plateau, where all was green and turning yellow under a vast sky of white clouds, with to the south the sunlit Cheviots. But beyond that ridge was England, and this thought was a constant reminder of how far he was from home and from his people.

In his exile he received several letters from Bishop Smith apprising him of developments in Edinburgh.[45] He was cheered to learn that Mr Grant, a writer to the Signet, had seen the 'Liberation' (the document of his release on bail) and thought there was 'nothing in it but the ordinary stile'. It was very possible, the lawyer suggested, that he would not be called at all, and certainly if he had received no 'Requitition' by 15 November he could consider himself free. Some of the clergy were advising him to return to the capital, to be near at hand in the event of his case being called, but he felt that this would be tantamount to inviting a trial, and in any case in breach of the terms of his bail: he thought it better to remain in Duns and have his Edinburgh friends arrange an advocate in readiness.

On 2 November James Grant was consecrated bishop at a secret ceremony in the capital.[46] His elevation changed Hugh's own situation, in that it gave the Mission another bishop and made his own presence not just so vital. His colleagues therefore urged that if his case was heard he should apply for a sentence of banishment, thereby avoiding a pro-tracted and costly trial that would, they were certain, only result in the same verdict. But this Hugh was not prepared to do. If the authorities were going to banish him he was not for making the path easy for them.

On 15 November the case was given a preliminary hearing during which, since he declined banishment, arrangements were made for a full court case on 16 December at the New Session House of Edinburgh, and his petition for extended bail was granted to that date.[47] After the hearing he remained in Edinburgh in order to confer with his advocate, Alexander Lockhart, in the preparation of his case.

Since the charge against him was based upon the Act of 1700 his defence also needed to focus on the Act. And its wording was unambiguous – that if any person was proved or even 'held and repute' to be a priest, and thereafter refused 'to purge himself of popery', this would constitute 'sufficient ground for the Lords of His Majesties Privy Councill to banish him furth of the realme', on pain of death should he ever return 'being still papist'.[48] Hugh appeared to have no defence whatever. Then someone ingeniously suggested that a case might be made on the grounds that he was not in fact a *priest*, but a bishop. It may have seemed a straw to clutch at, but then it also seemed to be the only straw he had.

With the help of his advocate and colleagues versed in canon law and church history he constructed his whole elaborate case around this one point.[49] The witnesses were sure to claim that he was 'reputed a bishop'. His lawyer would then argue that he could not be liable, since the legal maxim '*Favores ampliandi, odia restringenda*' should apply, and the Law must not be strained beyond its exact letter. He would then offer an erudite demonstration of the essential difference between a priest and a bishop, citing texts from Scripture and the writings of the Fathers, as well as precedents within the early, medieval and modern Church of laymen being consecrated bishops. Finally – as it were throwing Protestant practice back at the accusers – he would cite the precedent of 1610 when the Anglican archbishop of Canterbury had deemed it unnecessary to ordain three Scottish Presbyterian ministers to the priesthood before making them bishops.

If confronted with the objection that a bishop is in effect a priest-and-more, the advocate intended to counter that it still should not follow that 'whatever is said of the one must also be understood of the other'. And to prove the point he would offer a simple analogy from the military world: a colonel has all the powers of a captain, plus others, and indeed in almost every case has previously been a captain; yet if an Act of Parliament were to be passed concerning captains, increasing or reducing their pay for example, no-one would consider it as applying to colonels 'if they be not expresly mention'd in the Act'. The present case, he would claim, was exactly comparable.

At their meeting of 16 December the lord justice clerk and commissioners fixed the date of Hugh's trial for 5 January. Since his bail had now expired he presented a written petition to the court, expressing willingness to find new bail and arguing that committal to prison would seriously damage his health. His request was accepted, as was the offer of a Catholic layman, Robert Glendoning of Parton, to stand as cautioner on his behalf.[50]

Over Christmas word came from London that Bishop Challoner firmly supported the stance Hugh was taking, and also advised that any Catholics called as witnesses should in conscience refuse to give evidence against him, whatever the consequences.[51]

The trial began on 5 January.[52] The charge was read and the full penalty called for – banishment from the realm, on pain of death if the accused should ever return. Hugh was then formally offered the chance to take the formula abjuring his faith, which in conscience he declined to do. The case therefore proceeded. One of his lawyers, Thomas Miller, argued that he was entirely innocent of the crimes for which he was charged, and proposed to bring 'many proofs' of his character and 'peaceable disposition', a proposal that was however refused as being irrelevant to the specific charge. The hearing was then adjourned to 9 January.

When the court re-convened the Crown solicitor immediately requested a further adjournment, on the grounds that three material witnesses were absent. Apparently Robert Glendoning (Hugh's cautioner), Thomas Michie a local vintner, and Charles Leslie, a writer, had declined to appear rather than be forced to incriminate Hugh, and none of them could be found. Glendoning had claimed to be house-bound through ill health, and had produced a medical certificate to prove it, but a macer of the court had visited his home and found him out. The lord chief justice ruled that he be fined 100 merks Scots, that all three men be apprehended and imprisoned, and that the case be postponed till 19 January.[53]

After yet another postponement the trial finally went ahead on 2 February. An assize (jury) of fifteen men was appointed, Hugh's declaration was read out, and he was again offered and refused the formula. Seven witnesses were called (none of the three previous absentees among them); the cases of the Crown and defence were heard, and the lord justice clerk then summed up. The returning jury unanimously found it 'proven that the pannel was held and repute to be a Popish bishop'.

It was at this moment that Hugh's advocate, Alexander Lockhart, brought forward the argument that had until now been held in reserve, that since Hugh had not in fact been proven to be a priest he could not be found guilty as charged. Wrong-footed by this novel interpretation, Erskine and his colleagues found themselves in some embarrassment.[54] Uncertain of their ground, they postponed the case yet again while they sought the advice of their senior colleagues in London.

As the weeks passed, with no reply from the South, hopes were raised that Hugh's decision to refuse banishment and defend his case might yet be vindicated. In London Bishop Challoner and Lord Petre had contacted influential friends on his behalf.[55] Legal advice from both England and Scotland suggested that the most senior judges of the realm would not pass sentence on him, and he was even told that a person of influence at court had 'given fair promises' that the whole affair would be dropped.[56]

The date for the hearing was put back four more times in all,[57] inconveniently for Hugh, who had now been forced to appear in court on no less than ten separate occasions. Some of his friends took the delay as an auspicious sign, but more realistic voices were less sanguine of London forgiving a known Jacobite and a MacDonald in the present climate. And their fears proved well founded. In the last week of February their lordships finally gave their decision, that 'as bishops could create priests they must be understood to be comprehended in the act'.

On 1 March Erskine and his four colleagues pronounced upon Hugh the sentence called for by prosecution – perpetual banishment upon pain of death should he ever return.[58] They further decreed that he leave Scotland by 1 May at the latest, allowing him just two months to arrange his affairs and the affairs of his vicariate.

Notes

1. HMD to ?, Moidart, 2.1.1750, Delvine Papers, MS 1306, f. 138, NLS.
2. HMD to Bishop Smith, 7.5.1750, BL, SCA.
3. Ibid. Several boys had been admitted to the Scots College Paris; Glenala-dale's son and heir John had been sent to the Benedictine monastery at Ratisbon.
4. Bishop Smith, report to Propaganda, 13.12.1747, translation of text in Bellesheim A. (1890), vol. IV, appendix XVI.
5. Cf. Lang A. (1897), chap. 3 re his supposed and chap. 4 re his actual whereabouts.
6. Report to duke of Newcastle by 'a loyal subject', MS 98/18, NLS.
7. See p. 131 supra.
8. Report of Capt. Sweetenham, 11.6.1750, including Report of Lieut. Maxwell, Tray in South Morra, in Allardyce J. (ed.) (1896), vol. II, pp. 533ff. A similar promise had also been exacted from MacDonell of Barrisdale in nearby Knoydart, whose estate was also under threat of forfeiture: unlike the Morar estate it was in fact subsequently annexed, in preparation for which a factor was appointed for the Crown in autumn 1751 – cf. Munro R. W. (1964), p. 8.
9. McPherson P. Continuation of J. Thomson's Account of the Mission, Th/10, SCA, also printed in Forbes Leith W. (ed.) (1909), vol. II, p. 350. The appeal to the authorities had been made following the banishment of Fr Robert Innes SJ in March. Fr Innes had been indicted at the Court of Session for allegedly abetting Alexander Bowers to go abroad to study at the Scots College Paris, this being illegal under acts passed in the seventeenth century, see copy of Extract of Inictment, SM 4/11/14, SCA. (The case had been brought by Bowers' Protestant relatives). Fr Innes had been found not guilty, but had still been banished, simply on the grounds of being a Catholic priest.
10. Bishops Smith and HMD to Propaganda, 14.7.1752, BL (in Latin) – '*apud Curiam Londinensem accusatus*'.
11. HMD to Peter Grant, 30.10.1753, BL.
12. Plans were already being discussed for what would later be known as the Elibank Plot, to involve a task force from the West Highlands. The prince and King James had received advice from the West Highlands that a new rising was 'the general say' throughout the area, and that now if ever was the time to 'have one bold stroke for it' – see letters Alasdair MacDonell Glengarry to prince, early 1751, and to James, 15.7.1751, cited in MacDonald N. H. (1979; 1995 edn), p. 120.
13. Cf. Dilworth M., in Forrester D. and Murray D. (eds) (1984), espec. pp. 114 and 121.
14. See p. 55f. supra.
15. HMD to Bishop Smith, 30.3.1752, 6.4.1752, and 5.8.1752, BL.
16. HMD to Bishop Smith, 30.3.1752, BL.
17. See appendix III re Hugh's use of aliases in correspondence.
18. Bishops Smith and HMD to Propaganda, 14.7.1752, BL (in Latin).

19. The present paragraph based on a detailed account in a scroll letter to officials in London, written in Edinburgh, 20.11.1754, SM/3/117/18, SCA. Written in more than one hand, it is probably largely the work of John Gordon.

20. An example was the hearing at Hardhaugh regarding leases to the Catholic Church on the estate of the duchess of Gordon. The duchess and the law officer made a point of very publicly opposing all such leases in court, but privately afterwards advised the priests concerned that their leases would be perfectly safe – William Duthie to George Gordon, 26.8.1753, BL.

21. Bishops Smith and HMD to Propaganda, 14.7.1752, BL (in Latin).

22. HMD to Bishop Smith, 5.8.1752, BL, on which the whole paragraph is based.

23. For an account of Traquair's association with Catholicism see Blundell O. (1907), chaps. 7 and 8.

24. The present chapel was opened shortly after 1829, the year of Catholic emancipation.

25. Mention is made of Signor Gastaldi in three letters from 1757 held in the Traquair House archives. These refer to credit arrangements involving the earl and merchants in Leith and Rotterdam, in which Gastaldi played a part. (Information kindly supplied by Mrs Margaret Fox, archivist). It is therefore very possible that business of a similar kind had brought him to Traquair in 1752.

26. HMD to Bishop Smith, 5.8.1752, BL. HMD usually referred to Glenaladale as 'Glen' in correspondence, this being the equivalent of the name *Fear a'Ghlinne* ['the man of the glen'], by which he was always known in the West Highlands.

27. This may be inferred from the joint letter of Bishops Smith and HMD to Propaganda, 1.11.1755 (in Latin), translation in Bellesheim A. (1890), vol. IV, appendix XVII, which makes it clear that he had not been away from the Highland vicariate for the entire period since their previous letter of 14.7.1752.

28. William Duthie to George Gordon, 23.3.1753, BL.

29. See p. 119 supra.

30. 'Representation' by Allan MacDonald late Tacksman of Knock, March 1753, MS 5127, f. 88, NLS.

31. Barrisdale was finally pardoned after nine years in captivity. 'Spanish' John MacDonell of Scottas was also arrested in June in mistake for Archibald Barrisdale, and held prisoner at Fort William – cf. MacDonell J. (1931; 1993 edn), chap. 9.

32. Cf. Shaw J. S. (1983), p. 165.

33. Bishops Smith and HMD Report to Propaganda, 1.11.1753 (in Latin), translation in Bellesheim A. (1890), vol. IV, appendix XVII.

34. Ibid.

35. The priests were John Tyrie of Achnarrow, Glenlivet; Fr William Scott SJ of Auchriachan, Strathavon; and William Duthie of Scalan; all in the same neighbourhood. The law officer was Depute Sheriff Pringle. Re the tip-off

– William Duthie to George Gordon, 12.10.1753, BL; re the O/C's 'shame [sham] search' in compliance with orders, his gentlemanly conduct, and also the fact that 'all was done and hatched' by the Kirk ministers – Fr Killian Grant OSB to Bishop Smith, 10.11.1753, BL.

36. Alexander Forrester to Propaganda, 15.6.1754, BL (in Latin).

37. John MacDonald to 'Comerades', 23.1.1762, BL. Re the number of Catholics on Uist, see HMD, 'Descriptio Stationum Missionariorum', 1764 (in Latin), printed with translation in MacDonald, R. (1964 J), where the figure is 2,503. Only Strathbogie in the Lowland vicariate was larger.

38. John MacDonald, ibid.

39. HMD to Peter Grant, 26.8.1755, BL.

40. Ibid. Cardinal Spinelli had succeeded Domenico Rivera as cardinal protector of the Scottish Mission in 1752.

41. HMD to Bishop Smith, 7.5.1750, BL. Hugh considered that he should by rights have been suspended long before 1750, but had been saved by the upheaval of the '45 and Hugh's own subsequent absence from the country.

42. HMD to James Grant, 16.5.1755, BL.

43. The present account of the arrest, charges, etc., based on sources cited below, and also *The Scots Magazine*, vol. XVII, July 1755, p. 358; letter to lord justice clerk from Whitehall, 31.7.1755, MS 5078, f. 182, NLS; report of Bishops Smith, Grant and HMD to Propaganda, 20.11.1755 (in Latin), translated in Belleisheim A. (1890), vol. IV, appendix XIV; and George J. Gordon to John Godsman, 13.8.1755, BL.

44. 'Examination of Hew McDonald', 19.7.1755, Processes of the Court of Justiciary, JC 26/156, NAS.

45. HMD to Bishop Smith, 28.10.1755, BL. William Harrison, who had taken no part in the '45, and was supposed to have signed a declaration denying any support for it, was one of very few priests able to travel in relative freedom in the years after Culloden.

46. Strictly speaking canon law required the presence of three bishops at an episcopal ordination. However, in the exceptional circumstances of the Mission Church Rome permitted such ceremonies to be performed in the presence of one bishop and two priests. Hugh was thus not required to break bail and travel to Edinburgh.

47. Session of 15.11.1755, 'Books of Adjournal' (1754–56), JC 3/30, p. 500, NAS; also in 'High Court Minutes', JC 7/30, no pagination, NAS.

48. 'Act for Preventing the Grouth of Popery', 1700, Acta Parliamentorum Gulielmi, *APS*, vol. X, pp. 215ff. As well as 'priests' the act also covered 'Jesuits' and 'trafficking Papists', as well as the laity under some circumstances. But is was as a priest that Hugh was charged.

49. HMD to Bishop Smith, n.d., BL 4/11/19, setting out the proposed argument. His letter begins with the request 'Je vous prie, Mr, d'ecrire cecy immediatement et de me l'apporter'. The body of the letter is in English.

50. 'The Petition of Hugh McDonald Brother to Allan McDonald of Morar', 16.12.1755, Processes of the Court of Justiciary, JC 26/156, NAS; and Bond

given by Robert Glendoning of Parton Esquire, 16.12.1755, written by John Hacket Writer in Edinburgh, Bail Bonds, JC 26/151, NAS.

51. John Gordon to [Bishop Smith], from London, 25.12.1755, BL.
52. Session of 5.1.1756, Books of Adjournal, JC 3/30, pp. 529ff, NAS. The case was also reported in detail in *The Scots Magazine*, vol. XVIII, February 1756, p. 100.
53. Session of 9.1.1756, Books of Adjournal, JC 3/30, NAS, p. 535.
54. According to one of Hugh's colleague priests, they were uncertain as to how to pronounce against him, yet lacked the courage to acquit him – George J. Gordon to Bishop Grant, 1.3.1756, BL.
55. Lord Petre had approached the duke of Norfolk, who in turn made representation to the duke of Argyll 'to see if it [was] not possible to ward of [off] the blow of the tryall' – John Gordon to [Bishop Smith], from London, 25.12.1755, BL.
56. Bishop Smith to Bishop Grant, 2.3.1756, BL.
57. Sessions of 9 February, 16 February, 23 February, 1 March 1756, Books of Adjournal, JC 3/30, pp. 555, 559, 565, and 565ff. respectively, NAS.
58. Session of 1.3.1756, JC 3/30, pp. 565ff, NAS. The five justices were Charles Erskine, William Elliot of Minto, Alexander Fraser of Strichen, William Grant of Prestongrange, and Alexander Boswell of Auchinleck.

Ruling From Afar
(1756–61)

Within days Hugh set out for the North-East. His friends assumed that he was paying a flying visit to Shenval, to uplift what he could of his possessions there and to make arrangements for the rest, before returning to the South and exile.[1] And this may well have been his original intention. But when he reached the Cabrach it was as if he had put Edinburgh and the law far behind him: they seemed like another world. He reflected too that four or five of his priests had defied banishment and survived.[2] Just when he made his own decision to follow suit we do not know. Perhaps he just drifted into it. The 1 May deadline came and went. He was now fugitate, outside the law.

Towards the end of the month he wrote to Peter Grant the Scots agent (prudently omitting his Shenval address), asking Propaganda to use their influence on his behalf, for he believed there might yet be hope of a reduced sentence.[3] From the details he gave of his own plans it is clear that he had now made up his mind to remain as long as possible in Scotland, and not to move unless word came that would force him to do so.

In July he went over to Glen Garry to meet Angus MacGillis and appoint him as his link with the priests of the West.[4] It had become clear that he would not be able to visit the Catholic heartlands of the Western seaboard or the Islands, except on the rarest of occasions in haste and secrecy, and he was resigning himself to 'ruling from afar', perhaps for years to come. It only requires a glance at map 5 to appreciate the practical problems of trying to run a district of such great distances and intractable terrain, actually from outwith its boundaries. Ensuring uniform practice, offering pastoral support, correcting abuses, resolving problems, instilling discipline, keeping abreast of local situations, all these and more could only be done at second-hand or by letter. From now on he was to be bishop by proxy. But at least he was still bishop.

Though British forces had been engaged against the French in North America for the past two years, the summer of 1756 marked the beginning of the war in Europe and a massive swelling of their ranks. The Government needed men, whatever their past record or family history, and several thousand Scottish Catholics enlisted in the years following 1756. Many of them were sent to fight in America and, between those who died and others who stayed on to begin a new life there, few returned.[5] The great majority were from the Highland vicariate. It was a huge loss to the small and struggling Church.

In view of Catholicism's association with the House of Stuart these men were accepted into the army only on condition that they took an oath of allegiance to the Crown and abjured their Catholic faith. Many of the common people who enlisted in the ranks must have treated the religious requirement as an empty formula which they were content to undertake with 'mental reservation' for the sake of a livelihood, reasoning that since they were acting under compulsion it meant nothing. They squared it with their consciences and remained Catholics in their own hearts. Some doubtless drifted away from their faith in the new company they kept, but probably few searching questions were asked of them, either as to their religion or their politics.[6]

For the gentlemen who took a commission the position was rather different. More than an empty formula was required of them. If they hoped for promotion, or to avoid being ostracised by their fellow officers, they had to show themselves genuine Protestants and Hanoverians. For them, entering the army involved a real rejection both of their Catholic faith and their loyalty to the House of Stuart. It was a serious step, turning their back upon their own past, their family and their people, and not one that could be easily retraced.

It is one of the enigmas of the eighteenth-century Scottish Catholic Church that many, even from the most unlikely families, were prepared to take this step. One such was Young Lochgarry, whose father had been perhaps the staunchest of all the MacDonells in following his prince. When he decided to join the army at this time his father cursed him for betraying the Jacobite cause and his faith.[7] Alexander MacDonald, the laird of Kinlochmoidart, also took a commission and apostatised, forgetting his education at the Scots College Paris and his father Donald's execution in the cause of the prince. Several of Hugh's own family took the same route. His two great-nephews, Simon, the heir to the estate, and his brother Colin, both apostatised to take commissions in Highland regiments.[8] Thus the leaders of three families hitherto considered among the most constant and resolute in the west were lost to the faith in the space of a few years.

The one blessing that the war brought to the Catholic Church was the withdrawal of the garrisons from the Highlands for more pressing work elsewhere, allowing priests and people a few years of respite. In the relative peace that followed Hugh alone continued to suffer persecution as a fugitive from the law.[9]

He remained in the North-East through the autumn of 1756, though never for long in one place. From Shenval he moved down out of the hills to Bishop Grant's station at Preshome, where the swell of the land dips into the sea. Later he moved on to Aberdeen and Buchan. In mid-November he arrived at Auchintoul. There the laird pressed him to stay for the Christmas season and minister to the people, and this he agreed to do.[10] Hearing of Fr Brockie's illness at Shenval, he returned there as soon as possible after the New Year. A heavy fall of snow in the Highlands in January and February forced him to abandon plans of visiting Glen Garry, and instead he spent the spring as he had spent the autumn, moving from place to place in the North-East.[11]

For the next six months he followed the same itinerant life, now at Beldorny, now Auchintoul, now Preshome, each time returning to base at Shenval. In every place he used his time serving the people, administering the sacraments, alerting Bishop Smith to problems in this corner of his vicariate and acting on his behalf in resolving them, while always conscious of the delicacy of his own position and the need to avoid encroaching on his colleague's authority.[12]

In October he travelled down to Leith, from where he made the sea and land journey to Paris. To the author's best knowledge no record survives of the visit, which apparently lasted until spring 1758, nor of his reason for going. Canon William Clapperton, who mentioned it in his *Memoirs of Scotch Catholic Priests*, written some 130 years ago, based his account on a reference in a letter of Bishop Smith which he had sight of but which is now unfortunately lost. According to this letter 'Mr Dian wrote from Grisy [the Scots College Paris] to Hamburg [Rome] offering to go that length, if it was thought proper', and received a reply from the Scots agent advising that 'he would not now be welcome, whereas he had been most graciously received had he gone thither straight without touching at Grisy'.[13] Surviving correspondence of the college staff throws no further light on the visit.

The most likely explanation is that Hugh planned to plead his case, both for funding and for support against his sentence, in person, at the Vatican. His stop-over in Paris, though unavoidable, clearly dashed these plans since it made him no longer welcome in the eyes of Propaganda, where the Lercari report was still remembered (and where Niccolò Lercari himself had been secretary from 1743–57). He must have remained at the college for the Christmas–Epiphany season, and then taken the first available ship home. Whatever route he took he was back in the Cabrach by the spring.[14]

Beyond these few inferences, the five months November 1757 to March 1758 must remain a hiatus in our story. But we can say with certainty

that Hugh returned to Scotland poorer than he had left it, and that an
excursion which he had hoped might solve his financial problems merely
left them deeper.

At the beginning of August 1758 he made his first visitation to the West
for almost four years, during which he called at all the stations on the
mainland. He kept his whereabouts as secret as possible, meeting his
priests but not showing himself to anyone else, and was back in the
Cabrach by the beginning of October. But for all his precautions he knew
that sooner or later the authorities would get to hear about the visit, and
that this could well jeopardise his chances of visiting in the future.[15]

Early in November he travelled down to Auchintoul, where a violent
cold in his chest and throat held him up for a month. By then the season
of Advent had begun and he was persuaded to stay on to celebrate the
Christmas feasts there. Then just as he was about to leave in early January
word came that Mr William Reid would not be able to pay his normal
monthly visit for Sunday Mass, so he agreed to remain to cover that also.
'My easie temper was preveal,d upon to continue,' he explained to Bishop
Smith, 'that the peopl might not be dispointed, however I do not repent
of it as I had occation to assist 2 or 3 dying persons who by all appearance
wou,d want [lack] assistance if I had not been near hand, so you see I
am doing all I can for my friends [Bishop Smith's] concerns.'[16]

That 'easie temper' which he recognised in himself made him a man
readily persuaded to do anything that could help others. If it left him
short of that hard edge sometimes required of a bishop it gave him other
qualities perhaps even more necessary – compassion, humility and an
ever-readiness to oblige.

In February he returned to the Cabrach, where he found Fr Brockie
seriously ill. There were already early signs of a killer epidemic developing
in the North-East that spring. He wrote to warn Bishop Smith that three
of the local priests were 'at the point of death', that a number of people
had died without the sacraments, and that more would have done so had
he not been there to assist them. He himself was helping out wherever
he could.[17]

He was 'in great streats' for want of ready money, having received
nothing from the procurator in Edinburgh. He had also seen nothing of
his share of an annual grant that Pope Clement XII had first made to the
Mission twenty years before. According to the Scots agent this had always
been intended for the Lowland and Highland seminaries, but since there
had been no seminary in the Highland vicariate for most of this period,
it had apparently been kept in Edinburgh and used for other purposes.
Hugh calculated that his share now amounted to £100, which he believed
should be made available to him.[18]

He had a need of ready cash at this time, for with a supportive cardinal protector in Rome he was now actively planning to establish his own seminary. Since the closure of Gaotal in 1746 Highland boys intended for the Scots colleges had been receiving their preparatory education at local burgh schools, supplemented with basic spiritual instruction at the hands of a priest. It was an unsatisfactory preparation, and a major drain on the vicariate's resources. Hugh had found himself in the ironic position of actually having to discourage vocations, despite the grave shortage of priests, because he simply could not afford them. He already had more students on his hands than he could cope with.[19] An externally funded seminary of his own was a pressing necessity.

He spent most of the spring at Shenval, where Fr Brockie was now declining fast and clearly had not long to live. He tended him throughout April, and up to his death on 5 May. After officiating at the funeral he remained a further month to attend to the needs of the Cabrach people. For the past ten years he had always been made welcome at Shenval. But something seems to have happened after Fr Brockie's death that soured relationships and made his presence there uncomfortable. There is no record of what occurred, but it may have involved the local tacksmen or perhaps a visiting priest. In any case it hastened his departure that month.[20]

He had two good excuses for leaving. One of his students, Alexander MacDonell of the family of Scottas, had been accepted that spring for the Scots College Rome. Hugh wished to accompany him as far as Aberdeen, where the boy was to meet up with the two Lowland students who were to travel to Rome with him. He also needed to see a city doctor about his own persistent ill health.

Bishop and student set out together in the first week in June. Alexander was almost nineteen, tall and fair haired, and getting to know him on the road Hugh found him 'a douce sensible youth, and fully determin'd to follow his trade'.[21] At Aberdeen they took lodgings with the resident priest, George J. Gordon, Hugh's one-time fellow student and friend who had been ordained with him at Scalan, their quarrel of the mid-1730s long since forgotten.

Hugh's illness was a recurrence of his severe cold from the previous winter, which he had never really thrown off. He had a constant need to cough, but every time he did so he suffered a choking sensation and a searing pain in the side of his head. He had hoped that the sea air would ease the condition and was disappointed to feel no improvement during his stay in Aberdeen. The physician gave him medicines and recommended as much riding as possible to ease his chest.[22]

After three weeks he returned to Banffshire, leaving his young companion well provided with clothes and money for Rome. Since he himself

now intended to visit the West he contacted Bishop Grant, asking him to
come north at once so that the two of them could get together before he
left. When they met at Preshome in August they penned a letter to the
cardinal protector concerning the most pressing needs of the Mission, in
which they particularly highlighted the case for an assistant bishop for
the Highland vicariate. This was the first time that the matter had been
mooted, but Cardinal Spinelli's reply was encouraging: he supported the
request in principle, and suggested that Hugh should make it again the
following year and nominate several possible candidates.[23]

It was five months after Fr Brockie's death before Bishop Smith was able
to find a permanent replacement for him. The man he chose was John
Geddes, newly returned from his ordination in Rome. The twenty-four-
year-old had already revealed an exceptional charism for pastoral work.
His mildness, discretion, energy and practical good sense, and his gift for
being at ease in any company without compromising principle, all suggested he would rise in the Church. He had barely found his feet at
Shenval before Bishop Smith had him earmarked for a move to Scalan.

The seminary was in need of a man of calibre to reverse its declining
fortunes. It had taken years of patient work by the master, William Duthie,
to restore it after its destruction by Government troops in 1746. But all
that he had achieved was now being undone by the present master, the
ageing deacon, William Gray, whom Bishop Smith had reluctantly appointed for lack of any priest. Mr Gray had neither the training nor the
temperament for the task, and in the nine months since his appointment
standards had fallen alarmingly. The teaching was shoddy and uninspired,
discipline was in decline, books were falling apart through misuse, the
house was unclean and the housekeeper threatening to leave.

Hugh was now back at Shenval, and well placed to form an opinion
of Mr Geddes. He was able to confirm all the good reports of his young
host. He supported his proposed move, and believed that he could
persuade him to agree to it. The real problems, he forecast, would be in
persuading the people of the Cabrach to let him go, and finding anyone
to take his place in this remote upland station familiarly known as the
Siberia of the Mission.[24]

Though Hugh had been made to feel welcome and at his ease in John
Geddes' home he intended to leave the Cabrach by Whitsun at the latest.
If possible he wanted to return permanently to the West. Failing that, he
hoped to find a suitable winter base somewhere in the North-East, from
where he could visit his own vicariate every summer.

He left in May, but only got the length of Auchintoul before his journey
was interrupted. He allowed himself to be detained there for two months,
feeling it his duty to stay to discuss with the laird the practice of his faith

that had been neglected for twenty years past. Perhaps in his heart he was in no hurry to leave the comfort of his temporary lodging, where he had stayed so often that it was almost a second home, and to face the rigours of the West. If so, he soon had cause to repent of the delay.

One night when he was away from the house someone entered his bedroom, took the small coffer that he kept there, broke it open, and took the entire contents of £40 sterling. All the evidence pointed to a local man, Sandie Geddes, whom he had engaged as a servant. The old man knew about the chest, and he was seen with a supply of gold in the days following the theft. But recovering the money was another matter, for Geddes was 'a desperat headstrong fellow', and if challenged would certainly have 'run off the Country'.[25] Hugh reluctantly wrote off the £40, though it was all that he possessed and he could ill afford the loss. He was given a bill of promise by the laird, but he could not expect any prompt help from it: such bills were commonly left unpaid for months or even years, and in any case Auchintoul, who had been unable to sell his meal that summer through lack of demand, was himself in great straits at the time.

In their joint report to Cardinal Spinelli that summer the bishops repeated their request for a coadjutor bishop for the Highlands and nominated Hugh's preferred candidates as he had suggested. Hugh also wrote a personal letter to Abbate Peter Grant, summarising the arguments that had been put to the cardinal and asking him to make the same case 'strenuously' to Propaganda. Since his letter gives perhaps the fullest picture of his own situation at this time, it is worth quoting at length:

In ye first place you are to represent clearly and strongly Mr Dians situation for several years by past, and that it was, and still is, impracticable for him to perform the duties of his office in his owne bounds; and tho he goes there some times, as he,s to do very soon, in a privat way, yet as he cannot appear publickly or continue for any considerable time, without eminent danger, the poor people are still depriv'd of the necessary helps of C-tion [Confirmation] &c to his great mortification, as that is much wanted now in every part of that Country. In the 2^d place youl please to remember and insist much on it, that tho Mr Dian had more liberty than he,s ever like to have, yet considering yt he is much spent and exhausted, partly by labour and old age (their being now 35 years since he was a Laborer) but much more by frequent and long seekness, he being continualy troubl,d with pain in his head and weakness in his stomack, he will never be able to bear the stress that most [must] unavoidly attend the office of ane overseer [bishop] in the west, where he must walk on foot over hills and mountains, and take up with the worst accomodation as you know. I do not mean by this that Mr Dian inclines to forsaik that Country; on the contrary he,s fully resolv'd to live among his owne people as much as circumstances will allow and to help them to the outmost of his power conform to his health and strength. Its also to be observ'd that whoever is overseer in the west, must not only perform the duties anext to his station, but likwais act the part of a laborer [priest] and serve the people where ever he is, considering the small number of tradsmen, every on of whom has much more to do than what might be sufficient for two, therfore he wou'd need to be vigorous and healthy.[26]

The question of preferred candidates pretty well answered itself. There were only eight priests in the Highland vicariate, and most of them could be eliminated immediately. Iain Mór MacDonald and Alexander Forrester were ruled out by age and sickness. William Harrison was also too old and infirm, and in addition disqualified 'for want of prudence &c' (he was the 'fantastical Doctor' who had entered Hugh's house in 1739, taking away and burning books that he judged heretical). Æneas MacGillis suffered from a recurrent and dangerous illness, lacked the required education, and came of 'a mean family ... a thing much noticed in the west'. There were certain 'strong objections' against Alexander MacDonald, which Hugh left unspecified, while poor Neil MacFie was 'never to be mention'd'.

In effect this left John and Æneas MacDonald who were, Hugh believed, 'not only the most hopfull to succeed well, but truly the only we cou'd well mention for the purpose'. Both were 'descended of the best families in that Country', a circumstance that would certainly gain them more influence and favour locally. They were equal in terms of experience and in most other respects. Hugh recommended both, but named John MacDonald as his first choice 'as being a man of greater parts and Learning, and exceedingly good nature and temper'. But since he was his own nephew, his sister Catherine's son, he preferred to say no more but 'leave the chose to God almighty and to our freinds at Hamburg'.

From his letter to Bishop Smith that same month we know that he intended to make the appointment his highest priority, if need be neglecting all other matters in order to bring this one to an early and successful conclusion.[27] And from the wording of the letter it is also clear that both men were already as good as certain that John MacDonald would be appointed. Hugh was already making arrangements for bringing him to the mainland and organising a spiritual retreat for him before his consecration.

During September and early October he visited every Highland station in the West, before running into atrocious weather which put any thought of sailing to the Western Isles out of the question. Everywhere he went he made a point of gauging the opinion of priests and people concerning John MacDonald, and found them unanimous in their praise of him.

Though the situation of the Highland Catholics was improved the shortage of priests remained as chronic as ever. In BraeLochaber the sad sight of Iain Mór MacDonald, now barely able even to pray in public, touched Hugh to the heart. He asked Æneas MacGillis and the other priests within striking distance to support the old man, though he knew that they themselves were already stretched to the limit. He intended to go to BraeLochaber himself once the question of his coadjutor was resolved, and cover the station personally for as long as he was able.[28]

For thirty years the Scottish Mission had had no catechism, following the withdrawal of two previous editions on grounds of Jansenist heresy. After the '45 Bishop Smith had prepared a new version, but his draft had encountered fierce opposition at home, and had only finally been approved after close scrutiny in Rome in 1750. Its publication had then met with further delays, and it was only now being made available.[29] The Highland vicariate's consignment, including larger copies for adults and simplified versions for children, was sent in the autumn. The crate was brought by ship up to Strontian, where a wooden pier had been built in the 1720s to serve the great lead mine opened in the hills nearby.[30] From there it was carried overland to Kinlochmoidart. In Hugh's view this route was certainly the best and cheapest, far better than sending it via himself at Shenval, where the distance was so great and the carriage irregular. He believed that the consignment should last many years 'considering how few their were that cou'd make use of them'. His verdict offers a vignette of the kind of problems of communication and literacy that he faced at this time.[31]

On 25 February John MacDonald was nominated coadjutor bishop by the cardinals of Propaganda, and his credentials were sent on to Edinburgh. Hugh wrote to him at Easter time calling him to the mainland but not divulging the reason. He calculated that by the time his letter arrived, and assuming that John set out at once, it would be mid-May at least before he would reach Morar. He therefore sent word to his priests calling them to a meeting there towards the end of the month. There in John's presence he broke the news to them.[32]

In August both men headed east to the Cabrach, where the bishop-elect undertook a month-long retreat under Hugh's guidance. They then rode down to Bishop Grant's station at Preshome in the Enzie, where the consecration was to take place and where their two Lowland colleagues awaited them. In deference to his seniority and at Hugh's request it was agreed that Bishop Smith would act as chief celebrant. On 27 September, as the farmers of the Enzie eagerly awaited the Michaelmas holiday, John MacDonald was consecrated bishop.

Ever since the time of his own consecration Hugh had seen his episcopal role above all as that of helper, a servant of his priests and people, in accordance with a long tradition of the Church in imitation of the Humble

Servant of Mankind. For three decades he had been trying, alone, to act according to that ideal. Now at last, to use his own words, there was to be 'a helper to the helper'.[33]

Notes

1. Bishop Smith to Bishop Grant, 2.3.1756, BL, SCA.
2. There was in fact a (sporadic) tradition of Catholics ignoring or returning from banishment, often with impunity, dating at least from the early seventeenth century – see, e.g., MacInnes A. I. (1989 J), p. 40 re 1618. As MacInnes notes (p. 63), the penal laws were often 'more honoured by their breach than in their observance'.
3. HMD to Peter Grant, 25.5.1756, BL.
4. HMD to Bishop Smith, 27.5.1756, BL. Mr MacGillis had been acting as unofficial procurator for the Highlands for some time, and Hugh asked him to continue in this role and to forward monies to and from Shenval. The vicariate was in dire financial straits, not least because Hugh had received only three of the four annual payments due to him from the Scots College Paris since 1752, when John Gordon (Dorlethers) had taken over as principal from George Innes.
5. Estimate by Abbate Peter Grant, the Scots agent, cited by McPherson P. Continuation of John Thomson's 'Some Account of the Mission, etc.', Th/10, SCA, also printed in Forbes Leith W. (1909), vol. II, p. 360.
6. See further p. 213f. infra. There was in fact a tradition, dating from the late sixteenth century of some Catholics participating in Protestant practice, and even formally embracing the Protestant religion, while privately remaining Catholics. They did so through fear of the law, and in particular (in the case of men of standing) to retain their positions and property. Their action had always been condemned by the Church, though in the early seventeenth century some priests had permitted limited participation in Protestant worship in cases of duress – cf. e.g. Forbes Leith W. (ed.) (1885), p. 279; Hay M. V. (1929), p. 195.
7. Cf. MacDonald N. H. (1979; 1995 edn), p. 123.
8. MacDonald C. (1889; 1996 edn), pp. 188ff.
9. Cf. e.g. John MacDonald to 'Comerades', 23.1.1762, BL, re withdrawal of troops from the Islands in 1756; and William Duthie to Bishop Smith, 6.9.1756, BL, re the easing of the situation in and around Glenlivet. That Hugh remained the one missioner still suffering persecution – McPherson P. op. cit., p. 355.
10. HMD to Bishop Smith, 18.11.1756, BL. The Gordons of Auchintoul were one of the foremost Catholic and Jacobite families in the North-East. Alexander Gordon had held the rank of general in Mar's army in the '15.
11. HMD to Bishop Smith, 4.3.1757, BL; at the beginning of March he was in Preshome, at the end of the month back in the Cabrach with Bishop Grant for the annual blessing of the oils.
12. HMD to Bishop Smith, 18.11.1756, 4.3.1757, and 15.10.1757, BL.

13. Bishop Smith to George J. Gordon, 9.1.1758, quoted in Clapperton W. (c. 1870), transcribed G. Wilson (1901), p. 2137. Clapperton notes that Hugh 'paid a quiet visit to Paris. So quiet that no note of his departure or arrival has been discovered'. The present author has also found no reference to the visit in the Mission correspondence of this date. Hugh had some reason for keeping his whereabouts hidden, of course. On the other hand, is it at all possible that Clapperton misread the date of Bishop Smith's letter, and that it was in fact written on 9.1.1748, when Hugh was certainly in Paris?
14. HMD to George Gordon (Stobhall), 12.3.1759, BL.
15. HMD to Bishop Smith, 13.10.1758, BL.
16. HMD to Bishop Smith, 22.1.1759, BL.
17. HMD to Bishop Smith, 8.3.1759, BL.
18. The matter would not be resolved until 1775, two years after Hugh's death. The original grant of 46 scudi (c. £11 8s. 0d. sterling) p. a. had been made for supporting students, but in the early years had been used for general Mission needs. Cardinal Spinelli had raised the sum to 100 scudi (c. £24 sterling), at the same time insisting that it be used solely for the education of students – see Minutes of Admin. meeting at Scalan, August 1775, in Clapperton W. op. cit., p. 2067. Hugh reckoned that the Highland vicariate was owed half of the sum for each year – 23 scudi (= £5) up to the time of Spinelli and 50 scudi (= £12) thereafter, £100 in total.
19. HMD to Bishop Smith, 22.1.1759, BL.
20. See further p. 162.
21. HMD to Bishop Smith, 14.6.1759, BL. Alexander MacDonell did indeed follow his trade. He was ordained in Rome in 1767, returning to be domestic chaplain at the family home at Scottas from where he also served Knoydart. In 1786 he accompanied the 520 emigrants, mainly from Knoydart and North Morar, who sailed to the New World in the *McDonald*. There he founded the parish of St Raphael in Charlottenburg, in what later became known as Glengarry County, Upper Canada, where he died in 1803.
22. Account based on HMD to Bishop Smith, 14.6.1759 and 1.7.1759, BL, and George J. Gordon to same, 3.7.1759, BL.
23. HMD to Peter Grant, 12.8.1760, BL.
24. HMD to Bishop Smith, March ? 1760, BL 3/146/1.
25. HMD to Bishop Smith, August 1760, BL 3/146/3
26. HMD to Peter Grant, 12.8.1760, BL.
27. HMD to Bishop Smith, August 1760, BL 3/146/3.
28. HMD to Bishop Smith, 26.11.1760, BL.
29. It was finally approved following the personal intervention of Cardinal Spinelli. For an account of the whole affair, see Gordon J. F. S. (1867), pp. 2f.
30. The mine was first opened in 1724 by a partnership led by Sir Alexander Murray, and from 1730 leased to the York Buildings Company. The vein, over 2 miles long, was the largest in Britain at the time. The ore was smelted on the site, using logs brought in by sea. After industrial disputes the mine was closed in 1740, but reopened and worked until the early nineteenth century. See Cameron A. ('North Argyll') (1937–41 J).

31. HMD to Bishop Smith, 26.11.1760, BL. Re the catechisms see also HMD to Bishop Smith, 8.3.1759 and 14.6.1759, BL, and George J. Gordon to same, 3.7.1759, BL.
32. HMD to Bishop Smith, 9.5.1761, BL.
33. Hugh used this expression in his letter to Peter Grant, 12.8.1760, BL.

Letting Go the Reins
(1761–69)

Ideally this should have been the opportunity to divide the vicariate between the two bishops according to a rational plan. But the shortage of priests precluded any such luxury. It was quite impossible to free John MacDonald from his station, and he continued to serve Barra and also support the ageing Alexander Forrester on Uist, at the same time attending to his episcopal duties as best he could from the furthest edge of the vicariate.

For Hugh himself the dangers of living within his district remained, but the need to do so was becoming increasingly urgent. All his priests were overstretched, and none more so than Æneas MacGillis, who, following the death of Iain Mór MacDonald, was now covering Brae-Lochaber and Badenoch as well as his own Glen Garry station, an area some fifty miles from end to end. Moving into Mr MacGillis' station, something he had been planning even before Iain Mór's death, now seemed the best answer to Hugh's own needs: it would bring him within the vicariate, but to a place less dangerous than the West.[1] Glen Garry was far from ideal, nonetheless, being well inland and isolated from the Catholic centres on the coast by some of the most intractable terrain in Scotland, but he was only thinking of it as a temporary home.

Though the main part of the Glengarry estate lay west of the Great Glen it included also an adjunct on the east side across the River Oich. Most of the latter was in the hands of John MacDonell of Leek at this date, but the farm lands of Aberchalder belonged to his younger brother Alexander, who held them in wadset from the clan chief.[2]

In summer 1762 Hugh took possession of a small house on the Aberchalder lands, looking out over the long open corridor that is the Great Glen (map 7). To the front lay the mile-wide valley, its flatness broken by knolls formed of the detritus of the Ice Age, its further side bounded by a somewhat featureless ridge. A mile or so to the west he could glimpse Loch Oich, with the high masses of Meall Dubh and its satellites beyond; while to the east the land fell away into Loch Ness and the hills that enclose it on its north side. Almost past his door ran General Wade's road linking the two forts named after William and Augustus, its paved surface a daily reminder of government, law, and the 'pacification' of his people.[3]

After a couple of months he wrote a hurried letter to Peter Grant, giving him news of the untimely death of Æneas (Angus) MacDonald, Dalilea's son. Broken by the persecution he had suffered on Barra, his death at thirty-six was a further blow to the Highland Church, for it left only three fit priests in the whole vicariate.[4] Hugh begged the Scots agent 'to represent over and over again, our desperat condition' to the cardinals of Propaganda.

His long-term hope lay in his Highland students. He had three boys at this date under the care of John Godsman, the aptly named and saintly priest of Auchinhalrig, who were also following their secular studies at the burgh school at Fochabers.[5] They were the latest of a number whom he had prepared in this way at his own expense since the destruction of Gaotal in 1746.[6] His difficulty was that the Scots College Rome demanded students on its terms, when it had a vacancy rather than when the boys were ready, yet expected them to be of the required standard of education.

He was still hoping to take up Cardinal Spinelli's offer and open an all-through seminary in the Highlands that would allow him to cut out Rome altogether. He was not alone in thinking this the only way of ensuring sufficient Highland priests, and that the colleges abroad were actually harmful as a preparation for the rigours of the Highland Mission.[7] But ironically, it was his very shortage of priests that made this solution impossible. He could not even contemplate setting up a junior seminary, since this would have tied up a priest full-time and there was none to be spared. It was a matter of deep frustration to him that he could not take advantage of the money at his disposal. And yet, he told the Scots agent, the Church was growing against all the odds, and this outweighed every frustration: 'amiddst all these miseries, kind Providence gives us on great comfort, which is, that the number of our Coustomers are rather augmenting, than deminishing, and this satisfaction over ballances all our troubles.'[8]

In spring 1763 Cardinal Spinelli contacted the bishops requesting them to conduct a census of the Mission, to give him facts and figures with which to fight Scotland's corner at Propaganda. Bishop Smith completed the Lowland section within a few weeks, but the distances and shortage of priests in the Highlands made the task there a far more more drawn-out process. It had barely been started, in fact, when word came in May that Spinelli had died. No cardinal protector had been more sympathetic and effective than he, and his death was greeted with dismay by the Scottish bishops.[9] It dominated their annual administrators' meeting in Edinburgh in August, where it was agreed that the two census reports should still be completed for the benefit of his successor.

When the meeting adjourned Hugh headed north in the company of George Hay, the priest of Preshome. Mr Hay was an Edinburgh man and

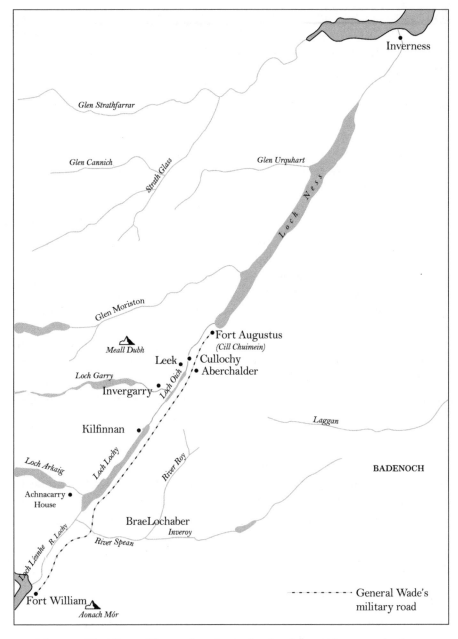

Map 7. The Great Glen and environs (in the eighteenth century): places mentioned in the text

had been a medical student there when the city was taken by the Jacobite army in the '45. His conversion to Catholicism soon afterwards had ruled out any chance of his qualifying, and effectively ended his medical career. He had then entered the Scots College Rome, where he was ordained in 1759, and on his return had immediately been given the important Lowland station of Preshome in the Enzie. It had always been recognised that he was destined to rise in the Church. His education and previous experience, his formidable intelligence, energy and single-mindedness, and his ascetic piety all pointed in the direction of leadership. By 1763 he was already an administrator of the Mission; within six more years he would be consecrated bishop.

While the two men took the land route north Bishop Grant was on the sea, bound for Aberdeen where they were due to meet. Off the Angus coast his ship ran into a fierce summer storm and was forced to creep in close to the shore. She struggled on, rounding the great precipitous rock topped by Dunnottar Castle looming through the flying spume, and at last found grateful shelter in the grey harbour of Stonehaven. There the bishop lay half dead until a chaise was sent from Aberdeen to bring him into town.[10]

Once he had recovered, Hugh and Mr Hay continued their journey to Preshome. Their road led through the Garioch and Strathbogie, skirting the northern edge of the hills, and on to the Enzie. There they parted, Hugh taking the coast road to Inverness, and thence down the Great Glen to Aberchalder.

Soon after he reached home he learned that Cardinal Spinelli had bequeathed a special 'foundation' to finance students at the Scots College Rome, which by his explicit instructions was to be used solely for the benefit of Highland boys. The tradition had always been for Rome to accept Highland and Lowland students in equal numbers, but Spinelli seems to have been persuaded that there was now a case for positive discrimination in favour of the Highland vicariate.[11] The decision promised to benefit Hugh in the long term, but it posed him the immediate problem of finding enough suitable boys and of preparing them up to the required standard.

Later that autumn, however, he learned that Spinelli's successor, Gian-franco Albani, intended witholding the legacy until he received the return from the Highland census. The new man was insisting on an exact and detailed account, including numbers, names and duties of clergy, and resources.[12] He was already proving a far sterner patron than his prede-cessor. He had even persuaded Propaganda to make their normal Mission funding conditional upon receiving the Highland report.

Hugh immediately contacted all his priests, instructing them to visit every dwelling within their stations and compile an exact inventory of the Catholics there with all speed. The mainland priests completed the task and sent in their returns by the early new year. But winter storms in the Minch cut all communication with the Outer Isles up until Easter and delayed the final writing of the report. It was late May 1764 before Hugh brought the lists and report personally to Mr Hay at Preshome, whence they were promptly despatched to Rome.[13]

The two reports provide invaluable information concerning the Mission at this date, though because of the way they were produced the conclusions drawn from them must be tentative.[14] Hugh's insistence on accuracy had ensured that the Highland census was conducted with great care. Its figures were precise. Those of the Lowland, by contrast, were merely approximations rounded to the nearest hundred and perhaps in some cases not much better than guesses. It seems also that different criteria were used, in that the Highland figures included all baptised Catholics, whereas some at least of the Lowland included only communicants. Nonetheless, the aggregates – 13,166 Highland and *c.* 14,550 Lowland – suggest that for the first time since the Reformation Catholics in the Lowlands perhaps now outnumbered those in the Highlands.[15] Even more striking was the imbalance of manpower. The Lowland vicariate was served by twelve secular priests, twelve Jesuits and one Benedictine, an embarrassment of riches when compared to the Highland with its four seculars and three Jesuits.

Bishop Hugh's report also noted that in some of the strongest Catholic areas the clan chiefs and gentlemen were now Protestant. He particularly mentioned Clanranald and 'most of the gentlemen' on South Uist, 'some of the gentry' on Barra, the chief of Chisholm in Strathglass, and Mac-Donald of Keppoch in BraeLochaber. (We may add to these some of the leading members of the Lochgarry, Kinlochmoidart and Morar families who, as we saw, had also recently converted to Protestantism).

At the time of Hugh's consecration all these houses had been Catholic.[16] Their turning from the Church was part of a general drift during the eighteenth century, prompted mainly by the laws forbidding Catholic inheritance, a growing desire on the part of the Highland gentry to integrate with the Edinburgh and London establishments, and (in a few cases) by their taking commissions in the army. It was a trend that was to continue. By the early nineteenth century only one senior aristocrat and a few lairds would remain to the Church.[17] Perhaps it says something of these Highland houses that they had held firm through the hardest times, only to succumb to the lure of opportunity.

Fortunately for the faithful the worst effects of this trend were obviated by the gradual consolidation of the Church itself during the course of the eighteenth century. Put crudely, in the seventeenth and early eighteenth centuries, when the Church had little organisation and few native Highland priests to call on, the leadership and protection of the Catholic chiefs and gentlemen, and the structures of clan society in general, had been crucial in fostering and preserving the faith of the people. But from the mid-eighteenth century onwards, as many clan leaders apostatised and at the same time their power over the people diminished with the loosening of the old clan ties, it was the priests and structures of the Church itself that became ever more important. By the end of the century, thanks to its success in training native priests, its financial prudence, and the relaxation of anti-Catholic laws and attitudes, it would have grown strong enough to serve its people effectively. But during the thirty-or-so years that followed the '45 – the last three decades of Bishop Hugh's episcopate, in fact – it enjoyed neither the resources, the freedom nor the active support of landlords under which it might have thriven. During that time there was little to be done but hang on, keep the nerve, and lose as little as possible.

A further difficulty for the Highland Church at this date was the annexation of several of the Catholic estates by the Crown. Though the Annexing Act had been passed as long ago as 1752, apathy, dilatoriness and dispute among those appointed to implement it, and the dislocation caused by war between 1756 and 1763, had meant that its effects were only now beginning to be felt.[18] Schools, kirks and manses were now being built, rural industries established, and some estates colonised with incomers, all as part of a deliberate policy of 'civilising' the indigenous communities – that is, of watering down their Gaelic and Catholic traditions.[19] At the time it was not known how long the annexations were likely to last, or whether indeed they might be permanent.[20]

Annexation and apostasy together had the effect of opening the door to the Kirk for the first time in areas of the Highlands where hitherto it had always been resisted as a 'foreign' and alien incursion. Ministers and catechists, who in the past had often complained bitterly of obstruction and even intimidation by the Catholic landowners, now found themselves welcomed by men ready to contribute to their churches, manses and salaries. In most cases, Hugh explained to Rome, they had no flocks of their own to serve there, so that 'their whole work was to have a constant look out, to know what's adoing, and to notice every step we take'.[21]

For the most part their presence probably made little difference to the local people, but we know of at least two cases where it led to victimisation. The first occurred in November 1764 on the annexed Kinlochmoidart estate, when at the prompting of the local minister the factor ordered all the tenants to attend the kirk, threatening them with eviction if they did not.[22] Frightened though they were they unanimously refused to obey.

The second incident took place the following spring in BraeLochaber, where the landlord, Angus MacDonald of Keppoch, had recently returned from the war. The Catholic Church had thriven on the estate under the protection of his grandfather and father. But he had apostatised at the time of his marriage and like some in that position turned bitterly against his former faith. He was looking for ways to harass his tenants and at Easter sent a threatening letter to the local priest, Æneas MacGillis, forbidding him to trespass on his land and warning that if he did he would have him arrested.[23]

In neither case was the persecution long-lasting. At Kinlochmoidart the Crown commissioners intervened after representation from the bishops and forced the factor to climb down, and at BraeLochaber the problem resolved itself when Keppoch returned to his military career abroad. Both incidents were nonetheless a reminder that the Catholic common people remained vulnerable to the whim and bigotry of chiefs and bureaucrats. Nor would they be the last, as we shall see.

Once back in the Highlands Hugh wrote to the Scots agent asking Propaganda to send two Irish priests from Rome as soon as possible to ease the clergy shortage.[24] He planned to station them in the Outer Isles. He would have to finance them from his own funds, of course, and the cost of doing so had risen steeply since the '45. Food prices had doubled and he estimated that £20 sterling was now the minimum annual salary necessary for a priest 'to live anywais decent or convenient'. The old lifestyle, living in the homes of the people, continually on the move and with no house of one's own, was no longer either feasible or appropriate. He considered it 'dangerous both for soule and body', for he had seen more than one of his priests destroyed by exposure to wild weather or convivial company.

The crisis worsened in the autumn when he lost the services of William Harrison, who had been serving on the west coast for close to thirty years. In 1763 the shortage of priests had forced Hugh to place him in charge of the whole of North and South Morar and Knoydart, a vast area that would have been beyond a man half his age. Mr Harrison had long been known for his imprudence and had a history of crossing swords with members of his flock,[25] a record that he had maintained in his new station. By the late autumn of 1765 relations had become so acerbic and the burden so great that he simply abandoned his charge. Probably his action merely hastened what ill health would soon have forced upon him. Nor was there anything Hugh could do to prevent it.

In December the Irishman Matthias Wynn was sent to Scotland as one of Propaganda's temporary auxiliaries, and was posted to South Uist. Early the following spring the newly ordained Alexander MacDonald arrived from Rome and was settled in the Barra station, which had latterly lain vacant and which Bishop John MacDonald had been struggling to cover from Uist. The arrival of the two men enabled Hugh to withdraw his coadjutor to take over Mr Harrison's station in Morar and Knoydart.[26]

Bishop John's transfer to the mainland, albeit enforced, was timely. It put him closer to the centre of the vicariate, more accessible himself, and free to travel in all seasons without the hazardous and uncertain obstacle of the Minch. He was now well placed to assume greater responsibility, at a time when Hugh himself was declining and looking to loosen the reins. The older man could begin to place greater authority on his shoulders and let him take the initiative, content himself to rubber stamp his assistant's decisions and to retain control over the purse. For the first year after the move, however, Bishop John had no real home and lived wherever he could, trying to serve his own congregation and at the same time visit every other station on the west coast and the islands.[27]

Bishop Smith was now eighty-two, and like Hugh worn out by years of struggle against the tide of the times. He was failing fast, and on 21 August (1767) he died. A man of piety and generosity of heart, too otherworldly to manage money and too full of charity to save it, he left the Mission's finances in chaos.[28] Since the current procurator appeared unable to unravel the tangle, Bishop Grant took George Hay out of his Preshome station and sent him to Edinburgh to take on the task.

Mr Hay examined the books with meticulous care and discovered numerous debts both at home and abroad. He then drew up a detailed plan for clearing them which he put to the bishops for approval. When Hugh returned home in October from a round of confirmations he found Mr Hay's proposals waiting for him. He wrote back giving his full approval, and also giving the new procurator authority to act on his behalf in regard to the finances of the Highland vicariate.[29]

That same month he finally opened the seminary that he had been planning for some years. It was sited at Glenfinnan with Bishop John as its first rector. It had in fact taken the dynamism of the new coadjutor to turn this long-cherished hope into reality. It was only a beginning, just a 'small family' of boys at this stage, but with every expectation that it would grow.[30] Despite the outlay Hugh believed that it would bring a saving in the long run, for keeping students at Fochabers had been costly, and he had in any case been dissatisfied with the standard of education they had received there.[31] It also solved the problem of a home for his coadjutor.

The young bishop was undertaking the work of three or four men. He had three mainland stations plus the Small Isles to cover, in addition to supervising the students and attending to his duties as bishop.[32] He was also learning at first hand the special problems of the Highlands. Like

Hugh before him he discovered that even a routine matter like ensuring a supply of Communion hosts for his priests could be a major task. He had to send to Edinburgh for the bread-irons for baking and the pyxes for carrying them, and even for the required wheaten flour, for though this could be purchased in Fort William the quality was so poor that he dared not use it for fear it was not genuine.

Hugh was now sixty-eight, and feeling his age. Throughout his correspondence at this time we find him leaning more and more upon his assistant and the Lowland bishops, happy to agree to their proposals, supporting their initiatives but rarely proposing any of his own. This was the case even in his dealings with Mr Hay, to whom he constantly deferred. He was in fact visibly slowing and growing less effective as a bishop. His letter-writing too, which had never been the promptest, was now becoming even more dilatory. When the rector of the Scots College Douai wrote to him requesting students he was kept waiting without word for more than a year until he finally lost patience. And after Bishop Smith's death it was sixteen weeks before Hugh finally got round to writing to his successor – far too late, he admitted, for condolences.[33]

His health was also in decline. The autumn of 1767 was a particularly bad one, with the corn lying wasted in the fields. Throughout it he suffered eruptions on his face, a sure sign that he was badly run down, and the potashes that he ordered to ease them never reached Aberchalder. With the passing years the thought of another Highland winter filled him with dread, and he was now looking for a home closer to the coast where he could spend whatever winters remained to him.[34]

On 8 January 1768 his half-brother Allan Ruadh died in Morar. His had not been a life of great piety or honour, and he had been known more for his drinking than for leadership. But the imprint of a devout upbringing had never quite been erased. For a full year past he had been preparing for death, and when it came he was ready.[35] Hugh had probably never been very close to Allan: in boyhood there had been too many years between them, and for much of their manhood too many miles. Their temperaments, and the roads they had taken in life, could hardly have been more different. He was nonetheless consoled by his brother's holy death, fortified by the rites of the Church. He could not have anticipated the serious consequences that his going would soon have for himself.

The spring of 1768 brought no improvement to his own health. Any kind of travel was now difficult and only served to remind him how cut off he was in Glen Garry. It was no easy matter for his priests to visit him. Only the previous year Alexander MacDonell had been caught in a snowstorm on the pass above the head of Loch Nevis when trying to reach Aberchalder in Holy Week for the blessing of the Oils, and had barely escaped death. Travel and communication were far easier on the west coast, where his coadjutor, by geography as well as age, was perforce now becoming the effective leader of the vicariate.[36]

In April George Hay received a letter from Paris alerting him to the precarious position of the Scots College in Madrid. From its original foundation in 1627 the college had been under the control of the Society of Jesus. The great majority of its students had always been creamed off to join the society, and in 140 years only five had returned to work as secular priests on the Scottish Mission. In 1734 its few students had been transferred to Douai, the college itself being retained merely for the revenue from its estates. It had always been quite the least effective of the Scots colleges abroad.[37]

Most of the Catholic states of Europe were by now deeply opposed to the activities of the Jesuits, and were exerting pressure on Pope Clement XIII to take action against them (pressure that would lead to his successor dissolving the society altogether). France had expelled all Jesuit priests in 1764, and Spain had followed suit three years later. But the implications for the possible loss of the Scots College in Madrid appear not to have occurred to Hugh and his colleagues. Probably they had almost forgotten its existence.

The letter from Paris[38] explained that the English bishops had already sent a petition to the Spanish ambassador in London for the recovery of their own college, and that this had been sympathetically received. They had also sent a representative to Spain, and it was he who had written to Paris advising that the Scots College might yet be saved if the Scottish bishops moved at once: they should first write to the Spanish ambassador, and then send Madrid a 'procuration' signed by themselves and legalised by the ambassador. And in order to convince the Spanish authorities that the college was worth keeping open they would also need to place staff and students in it.[39]

Mr Hay immediately sent Bishop Grant an account of the situation. At the same time he called Alexander Geddes up from Traquair to compose the memorial and procuration, and then sent him north with instructions to present Bishop Grant with the scrolls at Preshome within five days.[40] He also took it upon himself to advise Hugh to travel without delay to Preshome to meet his colleagues, and requested that he instruct his coadjutor to do the same.

Mr Hay's promptness stood in marked contrast to the tardiness of the bishops. After a fortnight Bishop Grant wrote to tell him that there had been no word of Hugh, and no meeting. 'We will be sadly straitened if you come not north,' he wrote; 'I would fain wish that you come; we are all a Set of Invalides ... that can do little or nothing, especiall as to writing lers.'[41] Both men were looking to their younger, dynamic procurator for leadership and action. When Hugh finally arrived he added his signature to the letter and procuration, which were then despatched to London by Mr Hay. There they were handed to the ambassador, who undertook to present them personally to Carlos III in Madrid.[42]

The bishops now had the problem of finding a principal and a few students, to recreate a living college. Since the Lowland vicariate was already providing the rectors at Paris and Douai it was accepted that the Madrid post should be 'paid for' by the Highland vicariate, either by Hugh sending one of his own priests or by his loaning one to Bishop Grant to release a Lowland priest for the task.

Hugh argued that there was no fit Highland candidate,[43] and this was not special pleading: it was literally true, in every sense. Even the young clergy were in a 'totering condition'. James MacDonald at BraeLochaber was 'almost quite gone without hopes of recovery', though not yet thirty; Hugh's nephew Allan was 'the puniest of all men' and was acting as master at Glefinnan because he was unfit to run a station; Alexander MacDonald on Barra, also still in his twenties, was 'always subject to considerable infirmities'; his namesake in Moidart, who had long been thought the most robust of all the priests, was now the victim of frequent bouts of coughing and vomiting and loss of sleep and appetite; Alexander MacDonell at Knoydart, who had been ordained only the previous year, was 'far from being healthy'; and Æneas MacGillis was finally beginning to lose his heroic fight against long illness.[44] There was not one remotely fit for Spain, even if any could have been spared.

It was mainly for this reason that Hugh gave permission for the early ordination of John McKenna on All Souls Day. The Irishman was another of Propaganda's gifts to the Mission. Though he had completed his training at Louvain he was still at the level of deacon when he arrived in Scotland, and Hugh had placed him with Bishop John at Glenfinnan in order to gauge his readiness. When they met in the summer Mr McKenna had pressed to be ordained at once. Hugh had counselled patience and humility, at which – in the coadjutor's words – the young man 'took such a desperate fit of grief that you would think he had lost his senses'.[45] They managed to calm him only with the promise that he would be ordained that autumn. It was a promise that Hugh deemed wise to grant, in view of the chronic shortage of priests and the fear that to offend Rome by dismissing him might well jeopardise similar help in the future. He believed that the Irishman's behaviour had sprung from the 'ignorance and rusticity' of his upbringing rather than from any disqualifying flaw in his nature.

In December Bishop John accompanied Mr McKenna to BraeLochaber, to support James MacDonald over the Christmas season, and then left him there to take over from the ageing priest. The young man was openly and noisily critical of the food and lodging provided for him, and not surprisingly the local people resented the incomer with his blunt tongue and strange *blas*, and called for Mr James's return. Bishop John was glad to be relieved of him, and vowed not to 'receive any of these unfinished pieces hereafter' unless expressly ordered to do so. For Hugh, the arrangement at least solved the crisis in BraeLochaber, and also freed a priest for the post in Madrid.[46]

On his journey west from BraeLochaber Bishop John called at Aberchalder to make arrangements with Hugh for the two of them to attend George Hay's episcopal ordination. He himself would not be free until the octave of the Ascension, which effectively fixed the date for the ceremony at Pentecost. Since it was felt that Mr Hay's present and previous stations, Edinburgh and Preshome, were both too public and 'provocative' as venues, it was decided that the consecration would be held at Scalan.

Hugh arrived there on 6 April, a full six weeks in advance of the date. It was his first sight of his *alma mater* for some years and he found the place changed beyond recognition. The old building that he had lived and learned in had been replaced by a far larger one on the other side of the burn. The new house stood two storeys high, its fresh harled walls sparkling white. It was in fact by far the most impressive Catholic building in the whole of Scotland at this date, and the only one purpose-built to plan.[47] It was nothing in comparison to the finest Protestant schools, of course. But it seemed to symbolise the progress of the Faith in its slow and painful recovery from near-extinction, and Hugh was delighted when he saw it. Yet it was hard for him to resist a tinge of envy when he compared it with Glenfinnan and was reminded of the old inequality between the Lowland and Highland Church, for which there seemed to be no remedy. His people remained the disadvantaged of the disadvantaged.

George Hay was consecrated in the little upstairs chapel, his tall spare figure almost touching the bare rafters of its low ceiling whenever he stood. Hugh left shortly after the ceremony and took a roundabout road home via familiar houses that had often harboured him before – Shenval, Beldorny, Preshome and Aberlour. He arrived at Aberchalder exhausted and quite unfit to visit the West as he had planned. Instead he remained at home, caring for the local people and freeing Mr MacGillis to visit BraeLochaber where many were dying of an epidemic.[48]

His chief anxiety that summer and autumn was for his students at home and abroad. He had the general problem of trying to find and prepare more boys than usual, to meet the increased demands of the new rector at Douai and the quite new demands of Spain. He was also deeply concerned at the conditions at the Scots College Rome and the plight of his boys there. The college had been in steep decline since the sacking of its highly regarded rector, Lorenzo Alticozzi, in 1766. The introduction of a new régime by his successor had badly undermined morale and discipline, and the bishops had already written to Propaganda requesting radical change.[49] Now Hugh learned that Francis MacDonald, one of the most promising students, had actually died in college that June, and that John Rory MacNeil had almost lost his sight there and had been forced to abandon his studies.[50]

At home he was becoming increasingly unhappy with the seminary at Glenfinnan. Its two most senior students, whom he had earmarked for Douai, had returned to their parents and showed no sign of answering his call. He blamed his coadjutor for letting them leave the seminary without any firm assurances. Nor was this his only criticism of Bishop John's management. The exorbitant outlay of £8 6s. sterling per student per year was not, he believed, due to real educational costs but unnecessary spending: 'The Shop in West does not answer my exspectation,' he advised the Lowland bishops, 'for I cou'd keep boys at Fochabers much cheaper than there, the reason is that Mr John house is full of comers and goers every night and what shoud be spent on boys, is spent on straglers this gives me great uneasiness.'[51] He was in fact seriously considering abandoning Glenfinnan and reverting to the arrangement at Fochabers, less than ideal though that was.

We have evidence from elsewhere of Bishop John's largesse, and indeed he seems to have been generous to a fault with the vicariate's money.[52] But in Hugh's letter we also catch a hint of the tension that by now was developing, inevitably perhaps, between the younger man and the older. From his isolation and enforced inactivity at Aberchalder Hugh must have viewed his coadjutor's very different life and his host of visitors at Glenfinnan with some vexation. It was to himself, after all, that the responsibility fell for balancing the books. And though he would not have admitted it to himself, letting go the reins was never painless.

For his part, Bishop John was finding Hugh not always easy to do with, and while he tried to face this with Christian patience his frustration occasionally came out in his letters. So for instance when he wrote to advise John Geddes that Hugh was thinking of retiring to that preist's station at Preshome: 'If he takes that resolution the weight of his old age shall fall upon you, unless you decline it, which I believe he does not expect. As he did not make any mention to me of it, I said nothing to him. There are reasons for & against. Yet I know not whether he would have me mention it to any body, but I think there is no harm in it.'[53]

Though he remained as discreet as he was able, he felt he was being kept uninformed of matters that were properly his concern. Nor was he certain of Hugh's temper. His position had become less than comfortable.

Hugh's Lowland colleagues favoured his moving to Preshome, where the coastal climate would be kinder to his health and they could contact him more easily. And as the winter approached retirement seemed ever more tempting to Hugh himself. He knew that he was declining and could now be of little service where he was. His public days seemed to be drawing to a close. It was time, he told his friends, to attend to the 'care of my poor soule, which ought to be my only affaire now'.[54] But he was not to be granted that consolation.

Notes

1. HMD to Peter Grant, 1.2.1763, BL, SCA.
2. For family details see Scott W. L. (1939–45 J), correcting MacDonald A. and A. (1895–1904) and MacKenzie A. (1881).
3. See e.g. Dorret J. *A General Map of Scotland and the Islands*, 1750; copied from EMS. s. 26a, NLS.
4. HMD to Peter Grant, 1.2.1763, BL.
5. HMD to Peter Grant, 1.2.1763, BL, gives us a glimpse of their secular studies: 'the two oldst are about fourteen years, and are learning Gramer and the ordinary latine authors such as Cornelius Nepos, Cesars Comentaries &c, the youngst is learning the Rudiments and Corderies &c, they begin to make some little theams and versions.' The 'Rudiments' was Thomas Ruddiman's *The Rudiments of the Latin Tongue* (Edinburgh, 1714), the standard book of grammar of the day; the 'Corderies' was a selection of the colloquies of Maturinus Corderius, *Colloquorum Centuria Selecta*, edited with English translation by Clarke (York, 1718).
6. Bishop Grant to Bishop Smith, 6.11.1762, BL, mentioning that this had been the practice 'these many years past'.
7. This was also Bishop Grant's view – Bishop Grant to Peter Grant, 23.8.1762, BL – and indeed the general opinion of Scotland's bishops since the time of Thomas Nicolson.
8. HMD to Peter Grant, 1.2.1763, BL.
9. Thus Bishop Smith wrote of 'the sad loss of our great Fr[d] [friend] Father & Bfactor worthy C. Spin[l], whom we can never forget ... I fear we shall too often have reason to regrate the loss of such a kind & powerful Patron' – Bishop Smith to Peter Grant, 28.5.1763, BL.
10. George Hay to George Gordon (Stobhall), 17.9.1763, BL.
11. William Reid to Bishop Grant, 16.12.1763, BL. Mr Reid believed that Spinelli had been persuaded by Allan MacDonald, Hugh's fellow student from Eilean Bàn, who was still in Rome following his banishment after the '45.
12. Albani sent the instruction via Cardinal Castelli – Cardinal Castelli to HMD, 3.12.1763 (in Latin), BL.
13. HMD to Peter Grant, 22.5.1764, BL.
14. Reports for the Highland and Lowland vicariates, copy, BL 3/161/13, SCA (in Latin). Text and translation of the entire Highland report, and of the Scots agent's summary of the Lowland, in MacDonald R. (ed.) (1964 J).

15. The Lowland aggregate amounted to 15,250 or 15,350, including 700–800 from Corgarff/Braemar, but the latter figure should be deducted since this station was in fact part of the Highland vicariate (the Highland census estimated 900 for the same station). Most of the Lowland figures were probably rounded *up*, since part of the purpose was to highlight the priests' workload; but any such exaggeration would be at least counterbalanced by the exclusion of children (non-communicants).

16. At the beginning of the century Bishop Gordon had reported fourteen senior Scottish aristocratic houses, as well as many lesser lairds, as being Catholic – Gordon J. *Narratio*, 1703 (in Latin), SM 3/3, SCA. When Hugh was ordained in 1725 every Catholic area of the Highlands except Upper Deeside and Glen Garry enjoyed the protection of a Catholic landlord – cf. *Memorial concerning Popery*, 1726, CH 1/5/51, pp. 73ff., NAS.

17. Bishop Kyle's Report of 1822, cited in Johnson C. (1983), p. 43, which includes a discussion of the drift. The one remaining Catholic aristocrat in 1822 was the earl of Traquair.

18. Annexing Act – 25 Geo II c. 41. Re the delay in implementation, see Smith A. M. (1982), chap. 3 *passim*, espec. p. 38. The Catholic estates annexed were Barrisdale on Knoydart, Kinlochmoidart, and Lochgarry.

19. A schoolmaster was appointed on the Barrisdale estate in 1758, financed by the SSPCK, and a stone-built school was opened there in 1763 – see Munro R. W. (1984), pp. 30f. At about the same time a parish school was established at Kinlochmoidart – see Smith A. M. op. cit., p. 35. (The SSPCK also opened a school at Keppoch, Arisaig, on the South Morar estate in 1756 – cf. SSPCK Records, Register of Schools, GD 95/9/1, p. 92, NAS.) Re the colonisation of Barrisdale with incomers, drawn there by the offer of rent-free housing, fishing equipment and bounty money, see Munro. R. W. op. cit., pp. 21f.

20. It is clear that the Church leaders saw the annexations in this light, and had such fears – cf. e.g. 'What was scarc heard formerly is now becomeing ordinary, they not only take away Estates, but Children also from their parents, as has lately happen'd, so still threaten & frighten our people' – Bishop Grant to Peter Grant, 23.8.1762, BL.

21. HMD to Peter Grant, 17.8.1765, BL.

22. Ibid. HMD's reference to a 'new' minister suggests that the estate was Kinlochmoidart rather than Barrisdale.

23. HMD to John Godsman, 8.4.1765, BL. The chief at the time was Ranald, but HMD is apparently referring to his older brother Angus (who had been chief between 1746–52, when he had ceded to Ranald) since he describes him as holding only a small wadset and a few tacks.

24. It had been Propaganda's suggestion to send Irish- and English-speaking priests to the Mission as temporary auxiliaries. When the proposal was discussed at the annual administrators' meeting in August 1766, Bishop John was the only one of the four bishops to support it, believing it was the only realistic plan at the time. Hugh later came round to his coadjutor's view. See Bishop John MacDonald to Peter Grant, 22.8.1766, BL, and HMD to Peter Grant, 17.8.1765, BL.

25. Most famously with the bard Alasdair mac Mhaighstir Alasdair – cf. e.g. MacDonald A. and MacDonald A. (eds) (1924), Introduction.
26. HMD to Peter Grant, 9.8.1766, BL. Alexander MacDonald, son of Mac-Donald of Bornish, was consecrated bishop and vicar apostolic of the Highland district in 1780.
27. Bishop John MacDonald to Peter Grant, 22.8.1766, BL.
28. Bishop John MacDonald to George Hay, 27.10.1767, BL, wrote of Bishop Smith's 'loose way' of managing finances, and his 'facility in taking on debts'. His lack of financial acumen had been the subject of severe criticism as early as 1718, when he had briefly held office as procurator at the Scots College Paris – cf. Halloran B. M. (1997), espec. p. 150.
29. HMD to George Hay, 6.10.1767, BL.
30. HMD to George Hay, 29.10.1767, BL. On his first visit to Glenfinnan Hugh promised a further £200 for the seminary. Bishop John's proposed solution to the financial crisis was that every missioner should take a cut in his quota, rather than eating into the small capital that the Mission had invested in stocks – Bishop John MacDonald to George Hay, 27.10.1767, BL.
31. HMD to Peter Grant, 18.7.1768, BL.
32. HMD to Peter Grant, 10.12.1767, BL.
33. Re George Hay chiding him – cf. HMD to George Hay, 10.10.1769, BL. Re Douai – Robert Gordon (Rector) to Bishop Smith, 20.7.1767, BL, 'For God sake tell Mr Scot [Hugh] to dispatch the matter and not go on in this tedious manner'. Re Bishop Smith's death – HMD to Bishop Grant, 10.12.1767, BL.
34. HMD to George Hay, 29.10.1767, BL.
35. HMD to Bishop Grant, 23.2.1768, BL.
36. Ibid.
37. Cf. Taylor M. (1971), espec. pp. 42ff.
38. John Gordon to George Hay, 27.3.1768, BL. John Gordon was at this time principal of the Scots College Paris. He wrote to Mr Hay, the procurator of the Mission, since revenue was at risk, and also (we may guess) because he believed he could count on prompter action from him than from either Bishop Grant or Hugh.
39. Ibid. The English bishops' representative was Fr Perry. Quite apart from any other consideration the Scots College Madrid was too valuable to lose in that it brought in a revenue of £1,000 sterling per annum.
40. George Hay to Bishop Grant, 7.4.1768, BL. Alexander Geddes was a biblical scholar of national repute, and Mr Hay thought him the man best fitted for the task. The documents were to be composed in French. Mr Geddes was house chaplain at Traquair at this time.
41. Bishop Grant to George Hay, 21.4.1768, BL. Bishop Grant was almost sixty-two, seven years Hugh's junior.
42. Geddes J. *Memoirs of the Translation of the Scotch College from Madrid to Valladolid*, 1780 (Scots Coll. Spain Archives, 54/13), cited in Taylor M. op. cit., pp. 49 and 53.
43. HMD to George Hay, 11.10.1768, BL. He even suggested that Allan

MacDonald might be recalled from Rome for the task. Since Mr Allan was over seventy and had not been on the Mission for more than twenty years this was an incredible proposal. He perhaps saw this himself, since he suggested as an alternative that Mr Allan could be settled at Traquair, thus releasing a Lowland priest. The tone of the letter suggests that the proposal was made seriously, but it would be hard to tell with Hugh; it may have been his way of making a gesture of goodwill that he knew would not be taken up.

44. Bishop John MacDonald to George Hay, 9.11.1768, BL.
45. Ibid.
46. HMD to George Hay, 23.1.1769 and 9.2.1769, BL. John McKenna in fact went on to do excellent work in BraeLochaber until 1773, when he sailed to America as chaplain to Highland emigrants.
47. For a detailed account of the new building, see Dean A. and Taitt M. (1995 J), and Watts J. (1999), pp. 127ff., figs. 2 and 3, and plates 3–6, 7–10.
48. HMD to George Hay, 18.7.1769, BL.
49. Altacozzi had been dismissed by Pope Clement XIII, along with his counterparts at the English and Irish colleges, for welcoming Prince Charles Edward Stuart to Rome and having Te Deums sung for his future coronation after the death of his father James III, in defiance of explicit papal instructions. Re the new régime, loss of morale, etc. – Bishop Grant to Peter Grant, 15.7.1768, BL. This was to be the beginning of thirty-five years of dissent and mismanagement at the college under a succession of disastrous appointments. Alticozzi's immediate successor, Giovanni Corsedoni, had good qualities among the bad, and was lovingly remembered, for example, by Paul McPherson, one of his students at the time. But several of the later principals considered the post something of a sinecure – cf. McMillan J. F., in McCluskey J. (ed.) (2000), pp. 52ff. McMillan calls the Alticozzi era 'a golden age' and 'undoubtedly one of the happiest times in the College's history' (pp. 50 and 52).
50. Re Francis – HMD to Peter Grant, 18.7.68, BL, and to George Hay, 14.8.1769, BL; re John Rory – ibid., HMD to Bishop Grant, 9.9.1769, BL, and to George Hay, 10.11.1769, BL. John Rory was originally to return home, but was transferred to Douai where he recovered his sight and his education.
51. HMD to George Hay, 10.10.1769, BL, and similar sentiments in HMD to Bishop Grant, 24.10.1769, BL.
52. Cf. e.g. Blundell O. (1917), vol. II, p. 111.
53. Bishop John MacDonald to John Geddes, December 1769, BL.
54. HMD to Bishop Grant, 24.10.1769, BL.

Bleak Winter
(1769–72)

For over a year the bishops had received no word from Madrid. It seems that their petition never reached Spain and they, hearing nothing, had allowed the matter to drift.[1] Towards the end of November news came to Bishop Grant that the delay had caused 'great if not insuperable difficulties' for the recovery of the college, and that plans for its amalgamation with the Irish College at Alcalá were already at an advanced stage.[2] Bishop Grant at once alerted his Highland colleagues. The following month Hugh wrote to his coadjutor giving permission for the release of Alexander MacDonell (Scottas) for the post of principal, as required by the Spanish authorities.

Despite ferocious weather Bishop John immediately set out to meet Mr MacDonell in person at Morar. He was doubtful of persuading him, knowing him to be 'very tender of his mother' and reluctant to leave her. She was seriously considering converting to the Catholic faith, plans that would probably come to nothing if she were to remain behind among her Protestant kin. Bishop John was less than happy that Hugh had left the delicate matter to him.

He found things as he had feared: the young priest declined to be moved. Hugh received the news by express post just after Christmas, and found himself in a dilemma. Should he order Mr Alexander to Spain, and risk the consequences in regard to his mother's faith? Should he nominate someone else? Or could Bishop Grant see his way to releasing John Geddes, who was certainly the best candidate, from the Lowland station of Preshome? Conscious of his own indecision and the danger of delay, he assured the Lowland bishops of his willingness 'to part with any Laborer in our bounds for that purppose notwithstanding our streatghs'.[3]

By now, however, they had already decided that they could wait no longer, and had contacted John Geddes advising him to be ready to travel.[4] While Hugh's letter was still in the post Mr Geddes was on his way south. At Edinburgh he was provided with documents designating him rector and granting him authority to act on the Mission's behalf in Spain, as well as a letter to King Carlos III requesting him to revoke the order to unite the Scots and Irish colleges. He continued his journey via London and Paris, travelling incognito and revealing as little as possible even to friends, since it was vital that neither the Jesuits nor the Irish College should know of his coming; some even feared that if his whereabouts became known there might be a kidnap attempt upon his person.[5]

Since the Lowland bishops had provided the principal for Spain Hugh felt honour-bound to offer them one of his priests *quid pro quo*. And again Alexander MacDonell seemed the fittest for the purpose. In March 1770 he wrote to his coadjutor 'to inform M[r] McDonell positivly to make himself ready for going north [i.e. to the North-East], and to bring his mother with him if he pleases, but that whether his mother goe or not, he must certainly goe'.[6] But the message back was that the mother refused to move house, and that her son would not travel without her. Bishop John was for compelling him, but when it came to it Hugh was unwilling to take that step. For all his firm words he was backing down again, and he could only complain somewhat impotently to Bishop Grant, 'It's very hard that he, or we shoud be directed by his mother.'[7] But directed by his mother they were.

Hugh's health had taken another turn for the worse during the winter, with the recurrence of an old illness in which his skin felt so burning hot that he could not sleep. Neither salts nor bleeding brought relief, but Bishop Hay found him a 'smelling ointment' which reduced the fever. His heart was still set on retiring to Preshome, but John Geddes' departure for Spain forced him to postpone the plan again, as had George Hay's consecration the previous year.[8] The bishop suggested that he move to Traquair instead, where he could live in some comfort and act as house chaplain, and where serving the needs of the tiny Catholic community would be by no means arduous. But he felt himself unfit even for such light responsibility, and wanted to enjoy retirement 'at full liberty'.[9]

The following spring Bishop John came up with the proposal of transferring the seminary from Glenfinnan to Buorblach. As Hugh explained to Bishop Hay, the move made long-term economic sense, though he could ill afford the initial outlay:

> I am certainly said to be in greater streats this year for want of money then I have been of a long time, for this reason that M[r] Tiberiop: [Bishop John] with my owne consent is to take a farm in the lower end of North Moror on the sea side a much more convenient situation for a shope than where it is, if this farm was stocked with Cattle and on a right footing it wou'd be a great help for supporting a small family, but as the stocking of it will require at least £50 it will be hard for me to procure such a sum all at once.[10]

As he noted, Buorblach's main attractions were its site on the estuary, which made it far more accessible than Glenfinnan, and the fact that it included a farm. The Lowland seminary at Scalan had its own farm and had always been partly self-supporting, and this he knew was a main reason for its surviving so long.[11] He saw Buorblach as his opportunity for a Scalan in the West.

The five Glenfinnan students – all MacDonalds – transferred to the new site, with Bishop John moving in to continue his role as spiritual director and overseer of finance and discipline.[12] But Buorblach was not destined to become the success that Hugh hoped. Rather it would be one more in a series of short-lived, ailing seminaries, none of which the Highland vicariate could really afford. Despite giving it his blessing he later blamed his coadjutor for 'putting him to difficulty by it', while Bishop John would in time find it a crippling burden to himself and the vicariate.[13]

About Easter Hugh was warned that Colin MacDonald of Boisdale had begun a quite unexpected persecution of the Church in South Uist. Colin's father Alexander had been granted the lease of much of the south end of the island by Clanranald in 1750, including the farm of Boisdale after which the whole tack was named, and in the same year had purchased further land in the neighbourhood from Hugh's own family the MacDonalds of Morar.[14] Colin, who inherited the estate on his father's death in 1768, had been baptised a Catholic but by this date had lapsed. (The tradition is that he turned his back on the Church for ever after the priest Matthias Wynn had ordered him out of Mass for forcing his tenants to work at the harvest on the great Uist feast of St Michael). After succeeding to the estate he had engaged a Protestant schoolmaster to educate his own sons and the children of his tenants.

According to Hugh's account the master was a bigot who abused his powers in the classroom in attempting to turn the local children from their faith.[15] He first had them copy 'blasphemous sentences' (presumably against the Mass among other things), and when this failed to have the desired effect he had meat brought into the school in Lent and 'forced it into their mouth, and whoever did not take it was severely scourged'. When word of his actions reached Matthias Wynn he asked the parents to withdraw the children. Boisdale then forbade Mr Wynn and the ailing Alexander Forrester to exercise their priestly functions, and ordered them off his land. The Irishman, never one to be pushed, replied that he would not forsake his charge without the consent of those who had given it to him. Boisdale's response was to call all his tenants together and invite them to sign a paper solemnly renouncing their religion and promising on oath never to receive a priest again: those who declined the invitation would be put off the land at Whitsun. They refused to a man, and returned home 'to pack up their all and go where God should direct them'.

Bishop John proposed going to Uist that autumn to plead for them in person, and this Hugh agreed to. He did not yet know that Boisdale, realising that 'no tenants' would mean 'no rent', had already recalled the people and given them a year's grace to come into line.

He withdrew the prickly Mr Wynn and gave him his wish of returning to Ireland meantime, hoping that by replacing him with a more prudent man the quarrel might yet be resolved.[16] His fear was that the persecution would spread to other parts of the Catholic Highlands under the control of Protestant landlords. Boisdale's action had already been copied on Muck where Mr Alexander Kennedy had been arrested, held captive and expelled from the island. When he asked the landlord's wife what offence he had committed she had merely answered that she was following Boisdale's lead in dealing with Catholic priests.

Before Bishop John left for the administrators' meeting in July he was sought out by John MacDonald of Glenaladale. 'Glen' was in his late twenties and a widower with no family. He had inherited the estate on reaching the age of majority, when he had also been appointed *tànaiste* or second-in-authority to Clanranald. A man of education and culture, it was said that he could speak, read and write seven languages.[17] When he met Bishop John he put to him a radical proposal to solve the plight of the Uist tenants. His suggestion was nothing less than that they should turn their backs on Boisdale and come with him to the New World.

The social position of Highland tacksmen like Glenaladale had been in decline and growing ambiguity for decades. Their traditional value in war long since gone, and with it much of their usefulness to their chiefs, they had become an expensive luxury. The chiefs themselves had lost much of their former trappings of status and their legislative powers, and were learning to rely ever more heavily on cash to maintain their wonted place in Highland society and secure a niche in the society of Edinburgh and London. The old mutual obligations between them and their tacksmen were no longer compatible with the money economy that they practised.

For some years now their policy had been to raise rents and redeem wadsets wherever possible. Not only were the tacksmen being pressed financially, they were suffering a quite new experience – insecurity as to their future and a realisation that somehow their world was yesterday's world. And they in turn were passing the pressure and insecurity on to their tenants, who had endured a threefold rise in rents in a single generation.[18]

Since the end of the Seven Years' War the opportunities in America had been vigorously publicised by a British Government keen to stock its newly-won colonies with loyal subjects. It had been backing schemes to open up Nova Scotia, and since 1767 had been negotiating the sale of plots of land on St John's Island, the former Ile Saint Jean.

Many of the thousands of Highlanders who had fought in the war had stayed on in America to make a new life there. They still kept in touch with their Highland kinsmen, and their letters home seemed to confirm the Government propaganda. Their reports of land aplenty were an alluring bait to men for whom – by instinct and age-old custom – land was life.[19] By 1770 emigration had become the great topic of discussion throughout the Highlands, and hardly a week went by that summer without another ship putting out into the Atlantic.[20]

America had been on Glenaladale's mind for some months, but in his case there was also a particular personal reason for looking to his future. He had fallen out with his chief's wife, and though the quarrel had been resolved it may well have added to his doubts as to the long-term security of his tack.[21] He had been seriously considering emigration with some of his own tenants, and had actually arranged to visit Edinburgh to purchase a plot on St John's Island some time before his meeting with Bishop John. His offer regarding the Uist tenants had in it an element of self-interest as well as genuine compassion.

Bishop John found his fellow administrators more cautious of the plan than he, particularly since the costs were not known. Rather than give an immediate decision they preferred to seek further advice. They alerted the Scots agent to the persecution and sounded out their colleagues in Rome, Douai and Spain regarding possible financial help for the Uist tenants. Bishop Challoner contacted the London embassies on their behalf and offered to make collections among the English Catholics, for which purpose the bishops undertook to compose a memorial giving details of the people's plight. Meantime Bishop Hay agreed to enquire into the likely costs of emigration.

When the meeting closed Hugh travelled west with his coadjutor, making first for Buorblach. He was less than happy when he saw the new seminary for himself. The building work was still unfinished, and he felt that it was taking up too much of Bishop John's energy and his own money. 'Mr Tiberiop: is continually taken up making houses on his new farm,' he complained to Bishop Hay.[22] He had already paid out £74 sterling, with the prospect of much more to come. Worse still, the boys could not be accommodated until the building was ready, and they had been left idle at home all summer.

Hugh spent the whole of August and September visiting every mainland station in his vicariate. He was determined to retire to the Lowlands for the winter this year – at the third attempt – and he wanted to settle affairs in the West before he did so.[23] On his return to Aberchalder he wrote to Bishop Hay in Edinburgh expressing his intention of coming to lodge with him in Blackfriars Wynd. It would be for the winter only, he explained, because he was hoping to find a home in the West where he could retire permanently. His brother John had a 'tollerable good house' at Gaotal, one end of which was presently set aside as a storeroom, which he was willing to make available to him. It should be quite possible to convert it into a 'good warm Chamber', but the work of rendering it wind- and water-proof could not be undertaken before the spring.

But he had been exhausted by his journey to the West and his friends strongly advised him against any further travel now that the year was drawing in. He decided to yield to their advice and see the winter out at Aberchalder, where he still hoped to be of some small service. 'Tho I am sure [Edinburgh] wou'd be more convenient for me,' he told Bishop Hay, 'yet I have a reluctancie to deprive the poor people about here of any little help I can give them, this is my princi motive as it ought to be.'[24] Even in old age he was still first and foremost the pastor of souls that he had always been. Meantime he asked his colleague to cheer his days with a pound of his favourite Strasbourg snuff, the one luxury he allowed himself.

Bishop Hay's enquiries suggested that the cost of purchasing suitable land in America might run to £2,000 sterling, and he had learned that Glenaladale was looking to the Mission for a loan for the same amount. Neither he nor Bishop Grant could countenance taking a risk on such a scale. Hugh himself was also against the loan. Very reasonably, he argued that he 'had not that regard for Cousine Glenaladale, or any freind in the wourld as to be puting the whole fonds of poor Company in danger'.[25]

Bishop John on the other hand supported the loan, and guessing what Hugh's attitude would be he did not consult him, but instead contacted Bishop Hay direct in the hope of persuading him to change his mind. His action left Hugh hurt and angered: 'Tho Mr Tibriop was with me the most part of the time while on the West Coast, and [I] saw him the day before I left Arisaigg, yet he never spoak a word to me about borowing money from company, and I am surprized he shou'd writ to you of ane affaire of that consequence unknowen to me,' he told Bishop Hay frankly.[26] A month on, he had still heard nothing: 'The project of trans-migration was invented by Tibeop: and Glenaladale and as yet is intirly a secret from me, for it seems they suspect that I wou'd not be for it, as indeed I am not.'[27]

He was being bypassed by his assistant and he could not hide a sense of betrayal. The close working relationship between the two men was falling apart.

Glenaladale was by now in Edinburgh negotiating the deal for land. He learned that the cost might in fact be only a quarter of what he had supposed, and on the strength of this was able to reduce his loan request to £500.[28] The reduction, and the security he offered, convinced Bishop

Hay that he should be supported. One of the attractions of the emigration, as the bishop saw it, was that it would create the embryo of a Catholic colony on St John's Island, where co-religionists could live together, with a chaplain provided to serve their spiritual needs, and where they would soon be joined by others.[29] There was now talk of emigration in most of the Catholic communities of the West, and so alarmed had the landlords become that they were employing 'every condescension to court them to stay'. This could be used to the advantage of the Church, he believed, and also of the tenants themselves.

Glenaladale had managed to secure one of the best plots on St John's Island, 20,000 acres of fertile land for a mere £600 sterling, and he was anxious to know whether the Mission would grant him the loan so that he could clinch the deal before he left Edinburgh. There would still remain the matter of transportation, of course, and he was already thinking in terms of a first-phase emigration for his own tenants, most of whom could afford their own passage, with a second for the Uist families whenever funding could be found for them.

The bishops in fact had hopes of funding from at least two sources. The memorial penned on the advice of Bishop Challoner was now being circulated among wealthy friends in England. And Matthias Wynn had set himself up as an agent on the tenants' behalf in Dublin, and claimed to have promises of money and even land in the west of Ireland.[30] But it soon became clear that, far from unearthing cash, he was likely to dig further into the Mission's scant funds. He had no intention of returning to Scotland, yet he was demanding £50 for his work for the tenants, and looking for a further £100 a year from Propaganda to maintain him in Ireland. 'By these demands,' Hugh told his fellow bishops, 'a body might be tempted to think that his head is turned.' As to the 'miracles' he had promised, there was no sign of them.[31]

Of the two masters required for Spain, one was to come from the Highland vicariate. Perhaps unwisely Hugh left the choice and the decisions on reshuffling the team to his coadjutor. Bishop John had originally decided upon Alexander MacDonald, the priest of Barra, and had brought him over to the mainland to await the call.[32] He was generally considered the best man available, not perhaps 'of the brightest witts', but solid, pious, strong on discipline, and one who could be counted on to champion the Highlands' cause.[33] The bishop intended to accompany his replacement to Barra, and then sail on to South Uist to support the tenants there. The arrangement made sense, and Hugh supported it.

He was therefore 'somthing surprized and not very well pleased' to learn in November that his coadjutor had changed everything.[34] He had sent Alexander MacDonald back to Barra, he himself would not be going to Uist, and – incredibly – he had chosen Hugh's nephew Allan for Spain. Mr Allan had barely coped at Glenfinnan and had never been trusted with a station of his own. How one so sickly would survive the journey, not to mention the demands of the post, who could say? Hugh certainly 'did not incline to have a hand in any bodys death', but having given Bishop John authority in the matter he felt obliged to accept his decision. It was in any case a *fait accompli* by the time he heard of it.[35]

At the beginning of November a messenger arrived at Hugh's door bearing a citation against him from his nephew John, the laird of Morar. Hugh's half-brother Allan Ruadh had ceded the estate to John as early as 1756, retaining only the pendicles of Cross and Scamadale in life-rent until his death in January 1768. But when John succeeded he was inheriting an embarrassed estate. Allan had lived all his life with debts.[36] In 1748 he had been forced to sell the family's lands in South Uist and Benbecula to MacDonald of Boisdale, as we saw. John had tried to have the sale reversed in the courts, but the case had ended in failure and further massive debt. His feuing of Retland and leasing of part of the tack on Eigg in 1763 were attempts to defray these costs. Four years later he had himself been taken to court by Clanranald for a debt of £1,000, which he could only pay off by borrowing from the bank.[37] By 1770, therefore, he was looking at every possible source of income, desperate to recoup whatever and wherever he could, even if need be from members of his own family.

Two years previously he had written to Hugh concerning a bill of promise for £70 sterling granted by his father to MacDonald of Kinlochmoidart in 1745, for which, he claimed, Hugh had acted as cautioner. Hugh had denied any recollection of the supposed transaction at the time, and had since forgotten about it. Now he was being called to pay the debt, with twenty-five years' interest, something he could neither agree to nor afford. But as one still technically under sentence of banishment, he knew that his position would be delicate if the matter were to come to court, and that to refuse payment might well lead to his arrest and imprisonment.[38]

He alerted Bishop Hay, who urged him to leave Aberchalder, where his every move was known, and seek the anonymity of the capital. But his friends in the Highlands believed the charge of horning was a bluff to frighten him into parting with money, that no caption would be served on him, and that he was probably safe where he was. It was now December and he felt that he could not risk a journey to Edinburgh, but he promised to remain watchful.[39]

Winter was setting in, a murderous Highland winter that brought death to men and beasts. In Glen Garry a snowstorm followed by frost over Christmas and New Year left the roads ice-bound, and put paid to any

thought of Hugh leaving the village. On 18 January word came to his
landlord, Alexander MacDonell of Aberchalder, that there was a stranger
in the area, a Lowlander by his dress and speech, enquiring as to where
Hugh lived. He hastily sent word to Hugh, who slipped out of the house
and took refuge with a neighbour. He was barely gone when the man
arrived at the door. He watched him enter, and guessed by the length of
time he spent inside that he was searching the house thoroughly. Finding
no-one at home the man sought out the landlord and left the caption
notice with him, protesting that he was merely the messenger, that he
had now fulfilled his duty and had no personal quarrel with Hugh, but
that the caption must be issued and brought to Edinburgh. This was later
done by Henry Butter, the king's factor of the forfeited estates.

John MacDonald of Morar was himself in the capital when the caption
arrived, trying to sell off his remaining holdings on Eigg, and he took the
opportunity to press the matter of his uncle's 'debt' with his lawyer. Hugh
now knew that it would be taken the whole way in the courts. He himself
could do little but lie low, avoid any public appearances, and await
events.[40]

Boisdale was also in Edinburgh that winter, courting a lady. Before leaving
Uist he had received the thanks of the local presbytery for his 'zeal in
promoting the reformation of religion within their bounds',[41] and when
he returned in April it at once became clear to the bishops that any hope
of a softening on his part had been premature. Whether to impress the
presbytery or his new bride, he resumed the persecution with renewed
vigour, nailing a proclamation on the church door confirming the eviction
of his tenants at Whitsun and threatening to bring in the militia to ensure
that it was carried out.[42]

Hugh's health declined further in the spring. He was suffering no pain,
but he was hardly able to sleep and felt himself extremely dull and sluggish,
one moment shivering and sweating the next. The illness lingered on
through the summer, relieved somewhat by doses of salts.[43] He met Bishops
Hay and Grant at Scalan in June and stayed a week with them, but was
not fit for a formal administrators' meeting. They discussed the desperate
shortage of priests, and Bishop Hay gave him news of developments in
the legal case: he had been negotiating a compromise with the Crown
whereby Hugh would pay a part of the debt, and he was fairly confident
of success.[44]

At the end of July Bishop John visited Hugh at Aberchalder and
generously offered to accommodate him at the seminary at Buorblach,
which was being further extended. Hugh declined for he still had his mind
set on retiring to Edinburgh for the winter. But he was to be disappointed
yet again. Throughout the autumn he waited for fair weather which never

came. 'We had the worse hervest here that ever was seen,' he told Bishop Hay at the end of October, 'which has doon great harm to all the Countries.' By now there was snow in the air and it was too late to consider moving.[45]

He had been ten years in Aberchalder, but now for the first time hints were being dropped by the landlord that he was no longer welcome there. Bishop John read the signs and warned his fellow bishops:

> I would fain get him out of it because they seem to think him too troublesome to them and fond of being quit of him. He is indeed worse to manage than before, for a considerable change of temper is come upon him with every other infirmity ... I have scarce seen any man fail in so short time more than he has done within these two or three years.[46]

His moods were becoming unpredictable, he often needed nursing, and he had become so absent-minded that his coadjutor dared not refer any confidential matter to him, for fear that he might inadvertently divulge it.

Glenaladale's brother Donald had by now arrived on St John's Island with an advance party of a dozen men, to prepare the way for the main emigration scheduled for the spring of 1772. In October Bishop John and Glen himself met with two emissaries from South Uist, from whom they learned that Boisdale was still harassing the tenants at every opportunity, with a malice only inflamed by their refusal to submit. 'They are obliged to avoid meeting him on the high roads,' Bishop John reported, 'as the best appellative he addresses them with is "You devil &c" the blasphemous terms in which he mentions every article of our holy religion to them are intolerable to Christian ears.'[47] Remote from the nearest magistrate and with a monopoly on the trade of the island, he held them in his power. He had reduced most of them to penury, so that only perhaps half could now afford the passage to America. Bishop John calculated that £200 might just about pay for the rest 'by the most frugal method', of which he believed he might raise £60 in the Highlands.

John Glenaladale himself wrote to Bishop Hay in November.[48] The persecution, and its condemnation by responsible opinion in Scotland and England, were causing embarrassment to Clanranald, he reported, who was trying to distance himself from events and protesting that he had no quarrel with Catholics. As to the emigration plan, Glen was beginning to weary of what had become 'a very troublesome job', and wished that the dispute could be settled so that he could be relieved of it. He had already laid out £400 of his own money, and for his pains felt that his motives had come under suspicion 'even from very well meaning persons'.

Bishop Hay on the other hand was determined that the emigration would go ahead. He had personally travelled to London to receive the memorial collection money, knowing that Glenaladale and Bishop John were to visit Uist in March. He was worried that the tenants might be wavering and urged the two men to use all their persuasive powers to hold them to their resolution.[49]

When they reached the island they were shocked by what they saw. 'I found such a change as made me almost repent of going thither,' Bishop John reported; 'No people on earth, not even the Negro slaves excepted, suffer so much oppression and miserie of every kind, as well under Clan [Clanranald], as under Boystle, saving only that the former does not persecute on the score of Rel-n ... I doubt not but that poor Countrey shall one way or other soon become a desart.'[50]

The tenants were now so reduced that not a single family could afford the passage. Some were taking cold feet and only nine families were still definitely committed to sailing. Boisdale had been getting at the men through their wives, warning them of the risks at sea, the uncertainty of life in America, and the finality of the move.[51] But behind the blandishments he was keeping up the persecution and he resented the presence of the two visitors. He dared not oppose Glenaladale, but he had less fear of Bishop John and sent him word 'that he sooner or later would be even with him'.[52]

The disastrous autumn had been followed by a long winter of unremitting frost and snow, and the hunger of the previous year was now full famine. In the West Highlands Bishop John reported men, women and children dying 'for meer want'.[53] Many were afflicted by 'putrid fever' caused by eating rotten food, and even those still on their feet 'carried famine in their aspect'.[54]

For Hugh it was in every sense a bleak winter, as he watched his own health decaying, the old certainties and familiar things of life overtaken, his Church oppressed, and his people threatened with diaspora. He knew of the events in South Uist only at second-hand and had played no part in the decisions there. He was now little more than a dispenser of funds. But this at least he was determined to hold on to, and he wrote to the procurator of the Mission to remind him that no Highland money was to be allocated to anyone without his express instruction: to Bishop John alone he gave authority to draw on the vicariate's funds 'without waiting for his license'.[55]

It was a brief letter from an old man, in which he added a few snippets of news about friends, and it ended with a note about his own condition: 'As for my self I am weak and tender posting on to Eternity, depending much on the help of your good pryrs.'

Close to the end of a life devoted to the salvation of souls, his mind was now fixed upon the one thing that mattered above all, the state of his own immortal soul when he would face his Maker. It is likely that between illness, weariness and disappointment, he wrote very few more letters, and any that he may have written have not survived. These therefore are the very last words from his pen to have come down to us.

Notes

1. John Geddes believed that the petition was intercepted by persons ill disposed to the recovery of the college – Geddes J. *Memoirs of the Translation of the Scotch College from Madrid to Valladolid* (1780), cited in Taylor M. (1971), p. 53.
2. The news had been sent by Fr Perry in Madrid to Bishop Talbot in London, who communicated it to Bishop Grant – cf. Taylor M. op. cit., p. 54.
3. HMD to Bishop Hay, 9.1.1770 and 13.2.1770, BL.
4. Bishop Grant to John Geddes, 10.2.1770 and 13.2.1770, BL, the former intimating and the latter confirming his appointment.
5. Re the documents – Taylor M. op. cit., p. 57; re his journey and fears of kidnap etc., – Geddes J. *Memoirs*, cited in Taylor M., p. 59.
6. HMD to Bishop Hay, 15.3.1770, BL.
7. HMD to Bishop Grant, 16.4.1770, BL.
8. HMD to Bishop Hay, 13.2.1770 and 15.3.1770, BL.
9. HMD to Bishop Hay, 30.4.1770, BL.
10. HMD to Bishop Hay, 15.3.1770, BL.
11. Though by no means wholly so – cf. Watts J. (1999), chap. 14 passim, espec. pp. 151f.
12. Bishop John MacDonald to Bishop Hay, 20.8.1770, BL.
13. See e.g. Austin MacDonald to Bishop Hay, 10.10.1779, BL; and Bishop John MacDonald to same, 30.5.1772 and 10.2.1773, BL; see also p. 212 infra.
14. Confirmation of tack given at Kilbride 30.10.1749, effective from Whitsun 1750, including Boisdale, Smerclate, Kilbride, Eriskay, Linguay, Grogarry, Askernish, Garriehallie, Daliburgh and Kilphedar, with all rights – GD 201/5/1144, Clanranald Papers, NAS. The rental was 1,460 merks (*c.* £81 sterling) p. a. And Extract, Disposition Allan McDonald of Moror to Alexander McDonald of Boysdale, Inverness, 20.11.1750, whereby Boisdale purchased 3 pennylands at Liniclate and Garredhoill on Benbecula and 6 pennylands of 'Macheryminoch' (Machair Meanach) on South Uist, for 1,700 merks (*c.* £94 8s. sterling) – GD 201/5/1015, Clanranald Papers, NAS. Machair Meanach ('Middle Machair land') is close to South Boisdale.
15. HMD to Bishop Grant, 7.6.1770, BL. The present account is based on this letter, with further details from Bishop Hay to John Geddes, 13 and 16.8.1770, BL, and Bishop Hay's *Memorial for the Suffering Catholicks in a violent persecution for religion at present carried on in one of the Western Islands of Scotland* (Edinburgh, 27.11.1771).
16. Bishop John believed that it would have been better if Mr Wynn had not come to the Mission, and that his 'inconsiderate' attitude had 'given occasion to the storm' – Bishop John MacDonald to Bishop Hay, 27.11.1770, BL.

17. Cf. MacDonald R. C. (1843), p. 43. John had been educated at the Benedictine monastery at Ratisbon in Germany.
18. See e.g. Adam M. I. (1919 J), espec. pp. 280ff.; Devine T. M. (1983 J); McLean M. (1991), chap. 1; MacKillop A., chap. 15 of Devine T. M. and Young J. R. (1999).
19. It was estimated that as many as 10,000 Highlanders had fought in the war. Re the schemes and allocation of land, see Toomey K. (1991 Th), pp. 76ff. St John's Island was renamed Prince Rupert Island in 1798.
20. Severe spring storms that year, which killed off nearly all the cattle in some parts of the West, proved the last straw for some Highlanders – cf. Bishop John MacDonald to Charles Cruickshank, 23.4.1772, BL. It was estimated that some fifty emigrant sailings were made from Highland harbours in 1770.
21. Cf. MacKay I. R. (1965 J), pp. 17ff.
22. HMD to Bishop Hay, 11.10.1770, BL.
23. Re his visits – ibid, and Bishop John MacDonald to Bishop Hay, 20.8.1770, BL; re his plans – Bishop Hay to John Geddes, 13–16.8.1770, BL.
24. HMD to Bishop Hay, 24.10.1770, BL.
25. Ibid.
26. HMD to Bishop Hay, 11.10.1770, BL.
27. HMD to Bishop Grant, 14.11.1770, BL.
28. William Harrison to Bishop Hay, 25.9.1770, BL. Mr Harrison was at this time procurator for the Highland vicariate.
29. Bishop Hay to Bishop Grant, 17.11.1770, BL. Glenaladale was willing to repay the loan at 4.5% interest, and MacDonald of Retland had agreed to stand as surety. Bishop Hay had learned that the lord advocate was sympathetic to the needs of Catholic emigrants, unusually for the official of a government still doubtful as to the loyalty of its Highland Catholic people. (Bishop Grant doubted the sincerity of his sympathy). Bishop Hay had also learned that the small French community in the area might be willing to bear part of the cost of a chaplain.
30. Bishop Hay to Peter Grant, 20.10.1770, BL.
31. HMD to Bishop Grant, 6.11.1770, BL; also William Harrison to Bishop Hay, 17.10.1770, BL.
32. Alexander MacDonald had sailed in late September – Bishop John MacDonald to Bishop Hay, 20.8.1770, BL, in which he expected him on 'the first fair wind'.
33. Bishop Hay to John Geddes, 13–16.8.1770, BL, and William Harrison to Bishop Hay, 17.10.1770, BL, though Mr Harrison had some doubts regarding his health in a hot climate.
34. HMD to Bishop Grant, 14.11.1770, BL.
35. Mr Allan set sail from Leith at the beginning of December – Bishop Hay to Peter Grant, 20.12.1770, BL. They arrived in Valladolid in February 1771, several weeks before their Lowland colleagues. The journey and the Spanish climate apparently suited Mr Allan, who settled well to his new work (cf. John Geddes to Bishop Hay, 2.4.1771, BL), where he was to remain for more than five years.

36. In 1759 he was taken to court over a debt dating back to the end of the previous century! – Allan MacDonald to ?, 17.7.1759, Ms 68, f. 136, NLS.

37. He would eventually be forced to sell the rest of his land on Eigg as well as the farm at Meoble to clear his debts. The Eigg land was sold to Clanranald for £1,070 in 1773, the Meoble farm to Ewan Cameron of Fassfern around 1800 – cf. Fraser-Macintosh C. (1888–89 J), p. 67; and MacDonald A. and MacDonald A. (1895–1904), vol. III, pp. 256f.; also pp. 217 and 219f. infra. Re the summons by Clanranald – GD 201/5/1309, Clanranald Papers, NAS.

38. HMD to Bishop Hay, 6.11.1770, BL.

39. Bishop Hay's proposal was made at the suggestion of the Edinburgh lawyer Colquhoun Grant. Hugh asked that Grant be engaged to act as his legal adviser in the event of prosecution.

40. HMD to Bishop Hay, 22.1.1771 and 20.2.1771, BL.

41. Minute of meeting of 28.9.1770, minute book of the presbytery of Uist 1768–1818, CH 2/361/1, p. 11, NAS.

42. John MacDonald of Glenaladale to Bishop Hay, 6.7.1771, BL, and Bishop Hay to John Geddes, 24.6.1771, BL.

43. HMD to Bishop Hay, 14.8.1771, BL.

44. Bishop Hay to John Geddes, 24.6.1771, BL.

45. HMD to Bishop Hay, 27.10.1771, BL.

46. Bishop John MacDonald to Bishop Hay, 29.10.1771, BL.

47. Ibid. The tenants most at risk were those on Boisdale's own 'property lands', i.e., the land at Machair Meanach that he had purchased from Allan Ruadh, rather than on the more extensive land he held in tack from Clanranald. The tenants on the land held in tack were far less persecuted, partly because Boisdale could not act with such freedom on Clanranald's land, but also because he kept his cattle on this part of the estate, and needed the tenants (to tend them) as much as they needed him.

48. John MacDonald of Glenaladale to Bishop Hay, 8.11.1771, BL.

49. Bishop Hay to Bishop Grant, 30.1.1772, BL. He met Bishop Challoner in London on 29 January, and received the *Memorial* money from him.

50. Bishop John MacDonald to Bishop Grant, 3.4.1772, BL.

51. There was indeed a finality about emigration, since the companies deliberately made the return fare far more expensive than the outward passage.

52. Charles Cruickshank to Bishop Hay, 28.2.1772, BL, based on Bishop John's account to him.

53. Ibid.

54. The phrase, used by Pennant concerning the people of Rum, was generally applicable – Pennant T. (1774 and 1776; 1998 edn), p. 277. Re the 'putrid fever' – *Callendar of Home Office Papers 1770–72*, p. 1535, cited in Flinn M. (1977), p. 232.

55. HMD to Charles Cruickshank, 29.2.1772, BL. Re the dispensation to Bishop John – Bishop John MacDonald to same, 9.4.1772, BL.

14

Posting On to Eternity (1772–73)

March brought no break in the weather and the old people were now pronouncing this the worst winter in living memory, worse even than the infamous winter of 1740. No part of the country was harder hit than the inland area of the Highlands where Hugh was living.[1] It was no time for stirring abroad. Hugh must have doubted his own chances of surviving till the spring, for why else would he have called his coadjutor over from Buorblach in such conditions? There were important matters regarding the vicariate that he needed to explain to him, and he also wanted to give him a written 'disposition', handing over the Church's monies to him while he still had time.[2]

When Bishop John reached Aberchalder he found Hugh 'still more feeble and tender than usual' but determined to move to Edinburgh as soon as the roads were clear. He wrote on his behalf to Charles Cruickshank – for Hugh himself could barely hold a pen – begging him to provide a warm room for him, either at Bishop Hay's house in Blackfriars Wynd or at least close by.[3]

Back at Buorblach after Easter, he contacted Mr Cruickshank again on the same subject. 'I wish he may have strenth enough to perform that journey,' he wrote, 'for I believe you never saw any person so much decayed in so short a time without any particular ailment, but the general failing of constitution, which convinces me entirely of the near approach of his end in this life; at least I dont at all think he can get over another winter.'[4]

Hugh would have the best of medical care at Bishop Hay's, but his coadjutor feared that his failing health and uncertain temper would make him 'too troublesome' for the bishop, who could certainly not be expected to care for him alone. It would be essential to employ someone 'of prudence and good temper' to attend him, a manservant preferably, and without regard to the cost.

Bishop John also reported that Hugh had yet to complete the 'disposition'. 'If he ever comes your lenth,' he urged, 'I beg by all means that you and Mr Daul: [Dauley, i.e., Bishop Hay] take care to see it done as soon as possible, for it is the only thing that can prevent trouble.' He foresaw quarrels among the Highland clergy and endless arguments over money if Hugh should die without completing it.

Glenaladale had gone to Glasgow in February to arrange for the hire and fitting of a ship. He was still there in April, delayed by financial problems.[5] While they were waiting Hugh and Bishop John secured James MacDonald as chaplain for the emigrants, and provided him with the essentials for his work. The sacred vessels for the Mass, as well as bread-irons for making Communion hosts, were donated by the Highland vicariate, while the general Mission fund paid for his vestments and for pyxes for carrying the Blessed Sacrament to the remotest parts of his vast new parish.

On 13 April the brig *Alexander* of Greenock arrived in Loch Ailort, where 110 tenants of the Glenaladale estate embarked. Ten days later she crossed the Minch to Uist. Glenaladale himself travelled with her, for he suspected that Boisdale might make an eleventh-hour attempt to keep his tenants, and he wanted to see them safely aboard. One hundred of them had committed themselves, and not one renegued. On 3 May they sailed out into the Atlantic, with fair spring weather and a favourable wind.[6]

They had a good crossing of it, by the standards of the day, with only one passenger lost. They were allowed up on deck by day, a few at a time, where the women cooked their meals on small wood fires set in sandboxes. At night they slept in the blackness of the hold, surrounded by the smell of pinewood and fish-oil lamps and the sounds of restless children and the sick. In June they set foot in the New World.

The bishops' vision of a Catholic community on St John's Island was on the way to fulfilment. But their hope that it would remain in their control as an outpost of the Scottish Mission was not to be realised. Rome was unmoved by their arguments and the pleas of the Scots agent, and decreed that the new colony be placed under the authority of the bishop of Quebec.[7]

In May Hugh contacted Bishop John regarding the administrators' meeting to be held at Scalan in July. They arranged to meet at Aberchalder and continue the journey from there together.[8] But when the time came Hugh's health put all thoughts of his travelling out of the question. He had to be content with his coadjutor representing him, and reporting back on his return journey.

High on the administrators' agenda was the emigration, which was already proving far more expensive than originally thought. The total cost, including fares, freight, clothing, equipment and a year's supply of meal, was likely to run to some £1,500.[9] But Bishop Hay was able to report that following the successful *Memorial* collections the Mission had actually been left with a small surplus, which his colleagues decided should be distributed to their own distressed poor.

It had been a risk, but one that they believed, once embarked upon, they could not have pulled out of. To have done so would have caused the whole scheme to collapse, with disastrous results for Catholic tenants throughout the Highlands, who would have faced widespread persecution had Boisdale won. And now the signs were that their firm nerve, and the tenants' own resolve, might be turning the tide. The position seemed likely to improve, for Clanranald, fearing further emigration from his lands, had intervened personally and was trying to effect an agreement between the two parties.

Shortly after the administrators' meeting closed it was learned that Clanranald's intervention had been successful. Boisdale had given his tenants a solemn promise never to molest them again on grounds of religion, while they for their part had agreed to remain on his land for at least three more years.[10]

In many ways it had been a classic landlord–tenant struggle of the period, on one side the tenants using the threat of leaving the land as their lever, and on the other Boisdale employing the standard tactics of threat, divide-and-rule and appeal to the old clan loyalties. But it had differed from the norm in two crucial respects, firstly that a landlord had sided with tenants against a landlord, and secondly that it had sprung essentially from motives of religion rather than profit.[11]

The tenants had won, but the cost had been great. Some had left their homeland for ever; the rest remained in penury, with famine all around them; Boisdale's concessions had been wrung from him, and might yet be revoked.[12] Glenaladale had crippled himself financially. His worst fears had been realised, and he now saw the sale of his estate as the only solution to his debts.[13] He was about to strike an agreement with his cousin Alexander MacDonald of Borrodale, by which the land would pass to the latter and become a part of the Borrodale estate.[14]

Young Æneas MacGillis arrived newly ordained from Rome in August and was brought at once to Buorblach, to act as master at the seminary and as priest of North Morar. His arrival brought a slight relief to the struggling vicariate. In Glen Garry his uncle and namesake was afflicted with 'the gravel' and could not be expected to remain active for much longer. In Arisaig William Harrison was virtually housebound. He was almost blind, and between chronic rheumatism, stranguary, gravel, defluxion and stomach cramps it was hard to find a sound part of him.[15] He hung on through the autumn, tended whenever possible by the young Buorblach master. On 5 February he died. According to his last request, John MacDonald of Morar agreed to arrange his funeral, and the proceeds from his few possessions were distributed to his fellow missioners and to the poor.[16] A generation of priests, and a generation of Highlanders, was passing on.

In the New Year of 1773 Bishop Hay sent John Geddes news of Hugh's deteriorating heath. 'Honest, worthy Mr Dian is quite failed,' he wrote. Rome had already been warned that he could not be expected to live much longer.[17]

He was going out of the world as he had come into it, in the midst of famine. For some months now he had been lodging in a house belonging to Allan MacDonell of Cullochy, a younger brother of Aberchalder, and just a step from the latter's home where he had recently been made so unwelcome.[18] Since the New Year he had hardly eaten a crust. As Bishop John reported in February, he now never stirred from his room:

> He grows still weaker without complaining of any other ailment; he never rises before four in the after noon, when he sits for some time in a chair with blankets about him and after a coupple of hours goes to bed. he has scarce strenth enough to carry him about his chamber when he rises, and all who see him are of opinion he cannot weather this Season. It is a long time since he has not writ to any body and now can read nothing tho' one should write to him.[19]

He had not been brought low by a particular illness: he was simply, like an old shoe, worn out with age and hard use.

He seemed unable to concentrate, or to rouse himself to any enthusiasm for the world outside. And this was hardly surprising. The news he was receiving was nearly all bad. Mr Harrison's death had only served to deepen the crisis that already existed in his vicariate. Bishop John was resigned to filling the larger stations and leaving the rest vacant. 'It is impossible to serve all unless we had wings ... I am utterly at a loss what to do,' he reported.[20] He knew he should visit Hugh but he was tied to Buorblach, for the seminary's very existence was now in doubt and he dared not leave it. If it went, the priests of the future would be lost with it. Glenaladale was about to quit the country, and others seemed certain to follow his example: many on the Glengarry estate had already signalled their intention to emigrate, and the misery and famine in the West seemed sure to drive away more. And it was the men of spirit and enterprise – the very ones they most wished to keep – who were leaving.

These disappointments filled Hugh's last days. The things that he had devoted his life to – the welfare and future of his Church, and of the Highlands – seemed to be slipping away, beyond his or anyone's control to halt.

His landlord Cullochy tended him as often as possible, as did old Mr Æneas MacGillis, despite his own infirmity. On the afternoon of Friday 12 March they both paid him a visit, and sat a good while at his bedside.[21] The company seemed to rally him, and he was brighter than they had seen him for some weeks. They stayed on into the evening, and Mr Æneas even had thoughts to stay the night. They conversed together, of the

Mission and the emigration and the news in the neighbourhood, the visitors doing most of the talking, and Hugh sitting alert and sometimes putting in a word or two. It was now close to nine o'clock. Hugh was asking about the condition of the cattle at Cullochy. Then almost in the middle of what he was saying he stopped, and rested his head down upon the pillow, and closed his eyes as if overcome with weariness. When the two men bent over him they could see that he was dead.

MacDonell of Cullochy undertook the arrangements for the funeral. He wrote at once to Bishop John giving him the news and the date and details of the interment, but though he had the letter sent by express it arrived too late for him to travel. It was therefore left to Æneas MacGillis to celebrate the Requiem Mass.

Hugh's body was then borne to the graveyard on the flat meadow at Kilfinnan by the shore of Loch Lochy, close to the water's edge. Beside the black trench, dug with difficulty, the piled earth lay upon the snow. He was lowered into the grave, and his soul prayed for. Then the tiny crowd dispersed. The place where they left him was far inland, far from Meoble and his home, far from the bones of his kin who rest on the hill at Kilmory above the western sea.

Notes

1. So, e.g., Bishop Hay to John Geddes, 20.4.1772, BL, particularly mentions Glen Garry and Strathspey.
2. Bishop John MacDonald to Bishop Grant, 3.4.1772, BL, and to Charles Cruickshank, 23.4.1772, BL.
3. Bishop John MacDonald to Charles Cruickshank, 3.4.1772, BL.
4. Bishop John MacDonald to Charles Cruickshank, 23.4.1772, BL.
5. He had been counting on receiving £700 from insurance money on a trading venture undertaken by his brother Donald in the West Indies, but this had fallen through – Bishop John MacDonald to Bishop Hay, 25.8.1772, BL.
6. They also had a doctor on board, Glenaladale's cousin Roderick MacDonald having agreed to travel with them.
7. Re the bishops' hopes of maintaining episcopal authority in St John's Island, see e.g. Bishop Hay to Bishop Grant, 25.11.1771, BL; the Vatican's initial decision was challenged, but confirmed.
8. Bishop John MacDonald to Bishop Hay, 18.5.1772, BL.
9. Bishop Hay to John Geddes, 20.4.1772, BL. The cost for the 11 Uist families, which the Church covered in its entirety, was £256 15s. 9d. – John Mac-Donald of Glenaladale to Donald MacDonald, n.d. (1772), details in Bumstead J. (1978 J), p. 521. It was also agreed that the bishops' involvement in the emigration should not be made public, lest the Church should be seen as abetting a 'disloyal' enterprise.
10. William Harrison to Bishop Hay, 11.8.1772, BL.

11. Toomey argues that Boisdale's frustration at the disruption of work on his estate (and in particular the collection of tangle for kelp) on Catholic feast days, rather than religion itself, was the real motive for the persecution – Toomey K. (1991 Th). But while this was undoubtedly a factor, the contemporary letters of Hugh and Bishop John leave no doubt that religious bigotry was the true underlying cause.

12. Bishop John MacDonald to Bishop Hay, 25.8.1772, BL.

13. Ibid.

14. Ibid. Alexander was known as 'Alasdair an Oir' (Alexander of the Gold) on account of a fortune he had amassed in the West Indies. It is probable that he did not actually purchase the Glenaladale land, but rather that he gave John a loan and took the land as security should he not repay. John, who saw his future now in America, was content that the matter should remain thus. Cf. also, MacDonald C. (1889; 1997 edn), pp. 182f. and p. 200 n.

15. Re Æneas MacGillis Jr – Æneas MacGillis Jr to Bishop Hay, 18.9.1772 and 19.11.1772, BL, and Bishop John MacDonald to same, 25.8.1772, BL. He found the seminary almost without religious books; nor could he get more from the Mission's HQ at Edinburgh, since the latest consignment from Rome had been confiscated and burned by the authorities. Re Æneas MacGillis Sr – Bishop Hay to Peter Grant, 5.11.1772, BL. Re William Harrison – William Harrison to Bishop Hay, 11.8.1772, BL; Mr Harrison begged to be allowed to spend his last days in retirement.

16. Bishop John MacDonald to Bishop Hay, 10.2.1773, BL. John MacDonald of Morar was now having his children educated as Catholics and was himself anxious to return to the practice of his faith.

17. Bishop Hay to John Geddes, 15.1.1773, BL; and Bishops Hay, Grant and John MacDonald to Cardinal Castelli, 10.7.1772 (in Latin), copy BL.

18. At this time the three sons of the family of MacDonell of Leek – John, Alexander and Allan – had possession of the lands of Leek, Aberchalder and Cullochy respectively. 'Cullochy' was the normal eighteenth-century spelling of the name, 'Collachie' the preferred modern spelling.

19. Bishop John MacDonald to Bishop Hay, 10.2.1773, BL.

20. Ibid.

21. Based on Bishop John MacDonald to Bishop Hay, 18.3.1773, BL.

15

Honest Worthy
Mr Dian

Eight months before Hugh's death his fellow bishops wrote to tell the
prefect of Propaganda Fide of his failing health after forty hard years
leading the Highland vicariate. Their letter included an encomium for
their colleague and friend that was as just as it was affectionate; it
translates thus: 'a man most worthy in his work for religion, in his
watchful care, in his concern for the common good; yet a man of humanity
and sweetness of manners, at pains to preserve fraternal harmony in the
affairs of the Mission, ever much loved by all.'[1]

Their words touch on the essence of the man, for it is indeed the
qualities of dedication, the desire for the peace and welfare of his church,
and what he himself called his 'easie temper' that best sum up his life.

His 'easie temper' was a source of both strength and weakness. We
have to concede that it gave to his character an occasional slackness that
at times lessened his effectiveness as a bishop. Thus he was not always a
prompt correspondent; he did not relish confrontation, and was inclined
to temporise and criticise afterwards; in matters that required decision he
perhaps made over-use of the subjunctive. In later life particularly he was
rarely an initiator, preferring to go along with the actions and ideas of
colleagues.

On the other hand, it gave him a willingness to oblige, a genuine desire
to support whatever 'tended to the general good of Company', a generosity
with his time, energy and scant savings, and an unhesitating readiness to
make personal sacrifices for others. Behind it was a deep humility, planted
by nature, nurtured by hard circumstance, and for which Christ – *pauper
servus et humilis* – provided his model. When faced with hardship or
disappointment his most common response was 'there's no help but prayer
and patience'.

Whether the newly created Highland vicariate most needed a leader so
pliant is open to question. In the first real test of his authority, when his
priests were pressing for a course of action he himself judged unwise, he
preferred 'to satisfi them, and to gain their hearts and affections' rather
than impose his will directly. It was probably a mistaken tactic, and it
set the tone for a decade. But it would be unjust to conclude that the

internal problems of his episcopate were wholly self-imposed. When raised to the mitre he was younger than most of his priests; he was plunged into an intractable dispute before he had time to establish himself; and perhaps no approach would have 'worked' with a clergy so hard to please, who moreover knew their scarcity-value and were not averse to playing upon it.

He sought to mould his style of leadership on the *Instructions* laid down by Rome,[2] leading by example, living much as his missionary priests lived, keeping close contact with them and with Propaganda, exercising discretion at all times and charity even in times of blame. The one episcopal power that he failed to use, contrary to the guidelines, was that of dismissal in cases of serious misconduct, but in this he – like Bishop Gordon – felt his hands tied by the severe shortage of priests at his disposal.[3]

And in the long term, his style was vindicated. Time, changes of personnel, and the need to face their enemies together, brought greater harmony to the vicariate in his later years. By the end of his life men like William Harrison and Æneas MacGillis, who had once caused him much trouble, had long since become colleagues and friends, mellowed with age themselves, no doubt, but also won over – one would like to think – by his gentle leadership, patent goodness and willingness to forgive.

Among his contemporaries Hugh was not the tireless dynamo that Bishop Gordon was, not a man of unquestioned authority like Bishop Hay, nor a diplomat able to move in high circles for the sake of his Church like Bishop Geddes. Accomplished, well read and an elegant Latinist, he was nonetheless not a scholar in the mould of Alexander Geddes or Thomas Innes. Nor was he particularly noted as an orator or teacher. And far from being a prolific writer and controversialist like George Hay or Bishop Challoner, nothing of his authorship has survived other than his correspondence.

As we can see from that correspondence, his was a quite narrow world where much of what he dealt with was local and parochial. Most typically it concerned funds, distress and 'great streats'. This does not make him one of the great letter-writers. Nor of course does it prove a narrowness or lack of the broader horizon on his part, but rather that his concerns were properly those of a small, fragile and beleaguered church on the far edge of Europe. His priorities were its unremarkable daily business, visiting the needy, administering the sacraments and caring for souls.

Because he was not a giant above the crowd he was perhaps closer to the ordinary men and women of the Mission than several of his more extraordinary contemporaries. He certainly had an intuitive empathy with his own poor and scattered flock. But if this was in part a matter of personality, it was partly also an effect of the fundamental oneness of the native Catholic Highland community, co-heirs of a shared culture essentially unchanged for a thousand years. He was himself what (at its best) his Highland Church was – devout, loyal, tenacious, suffering and ready to suffer. As such he represents a time and place in the history of Scotland and of the Catholic faith.

His life spanned an era for Scottish Catholicism that opened with the persecutions of William III and ended just before the dawn of Repeal. Furthermore, its main stages mirrored remarkably closely major developments in the fortunes of the Highland Church at the time. His first twenty-five years, his years of boyhood, school and seminary, were a period of notable growth for his Church in the Highlands, of consolidation in its traditional areas and expansion into new territory. His ordination coincided with the beginning of a Protestant counter-offensive in the Highlands, supported by the Crown. During his priestly life, and more particularly during his forty years as a bishop, the successes of the Church's enemies, its own self-inflicted wounds and the long-term political, economic and religious effects of the '45, together ensured that growth ceased.

The census of 1764 revealed an overall reduction in the number of Highland Catholics since the beginning of the century, a contraction made the starker when set against the substantial growth in the Lowlands. And for Hugh the stakes were of the highest – the survival and restoration of the true Faith, on which, in the confessional thinking of the day, hung the salvation or loss of immortal souls. He was only too painfully aware of the weight of responsibility placed upon his shoulders. From the first he had felt his episcopal office 'a burden which even angels might fear to bear',[4] and it must have been a great sorrow to him that in his time, for reasons almost wholly beyond his control, the early momentum had not been maintained and the Church had struggled in the doldrums.

Hugh nonetheless deserves the prominent place he holds in the history of the Penal Church in Scotland, and the affection still accorded to him by Highland Catholics. He would merit a special place of honour simply for having been the *first* Highland bishop, of course. But beyond this, his episcopate was, and remains, unique in several ways. He was consecrated at the age of thirty-two, and his term of office spanned forty-one years and five months. No-one in the post-Reformation Scottish Catholic Church has ever received the mitre so young, or served so long.[5] He is the only true 'heather' bishop the Church has had – one, that is, who received his entire training in the primitive conditions of Penal Scotland. He is one of only three to have suffered imprisonment, and the only one ever to have been banished from his native land.[6]

Inevitably he lived his life, and certainly his whole episcopate, in almost constant tension with society at large. His Jacobitism, which he recognised as 'a thing inseperable from his very nature', set him at odds with Government and Crown, and in the '45 put him outside the law. But further, it imposed a tension on his role as bishop, between what he saw as his moral duty to stand up on behalf of his Jacobite flock and the cause of right, and his Church's injunction to bishops of the Mission countries not to intervene in domestic politics.

His religion also put him outside the law. The practice of it remained technically punishable by banishment – and in the second instance by death – throughout his lifetime. The most explicit law to this effect had been passed just one year after his birth, and would not be repealed until twenty years after his death.[7] Though rarely invoked it remained an ever-present threat, always available in times of real or imagined national crisis. As a priest he was a particular target of the legislation, and as a bishop doubly so. He spent his whole priestly life under hazard of arrest, and its last two decades in the shadow of banishment. Nor was it only through the law that he suffered. Because of the times his episcopate, which in another time or place would have carried dignity, respect and applause, brought him only danger, malice and obloquy.

More generally, it could be said that he lived his whole life in tension, very much at one with his immediate world but deeply at odds with the dominant national culture. To a degree that very few in Scotland today could appreciate, he found almost all the prevailing *mores* of national life profoundly opposed to his own. In every matter that he cherished most dearly – his faith, language, society of kin and clan, the royal house he followed, his whole vision of polity and right – he was implacably at odds with the world he was forced to live in.

Such tensions were with him at all times, but they came together in sharpest focus in the '45 and its aftermath. I have called the '45 his climacteric, the pivotal chapter in his life. It is true that he had suffered setbacks before it, but he was young then and there remained much to hope for. After it, his story was little but disappointment: for the House of Stuart – the death of James, the disappearance of Charles Edward from the political arena, and the evaporation of a dream; for Highland society – annexation, the outlawing of its dress and music, the dissolution of a way of life; for Hugh himself – exile in France, banishment, advancing age and declining health; for his people – hardship, famine, the beginning of diaspora.

After Culloden he watched society moving ever further in directions he could not support. He now represented the old ways, and in his latter years must have been acutely aware that he was already one of yesterday's men. It was only after his death that Scotland would see an upturn in its economic fortunes, and his Church begin to glimpse the light of freedom ahead.[8] It was his misfortune that he did not live to see these things. But he would in any case have placed his hopes of social prosperity and religious freedom in the restoration of the Stuart line, rather than in a softening of the House of Hanover.

If he looked back at the end of his life and viewed it in isolation and by the standards of the world, he might have been tempted to conclude that failure had at least matched achievement. He had established the structures of the Highland Church, certainly, and bought it forward in a number of ways, not least in the training of priests to serve it. But, for the most part, his unglamorous task had been to hold the line. Yet we may reflect how much greater the Church's losses might have been, and how much less its achievements, without his leadership. But in any case, he did not view his life in isolation or by the world's standards. He saw it in the far wider, slower and more lasting context of providential history, in which he was one in a long line of men and women, one stone (by no means a keystone or a cornerstone) in an edifice. A devout, God-fearing man, he had accepted office as priest and bishop in obedience to what he saw as God's will, whatever the painful task or the likelihood of 'success', and he had undertaken it in the same obedience. It was his Magnificat.

The hopes that he had expressed at the start of his episcopate, that the Catholic Church in the Highlands would build and grow under his care,[9] had only to an extent been realised, and at the end of it as much seemed lost as gained. But the ground had been prepared under his stewardship, and quite soon after it new shoots of growth would begin to appear in other, unexpected places and circumstances, in a world he did not live to see.

Notes

1. Bishops Hay, Grant and John MacDonald to Cardinal Castelli, 10.7.1772 (in Latin), copy BL.
2. See Propaganda's instructions to vicars-apostolic of the Mission territories, *Instruttione per il supe [Superiore] d'una Missione*, 1680 (handwritten, in sixteen sections) (in Italian), SM 2/21/12 (1) to (6) (in reverse order to that of the text), SCA.
3. Bishop Gordon also preferred to solve this kind of problem internally, as when he arranged to move John Tyrie to the West following his involvement in sexual scandal in the North-East. Quite apart from the problem of lack of priests, it was natural that both men preferred to avoid action that would need to be reported and justified to Rome. Even when Hugh withdrew Neil MacFie's faculties he continued his quota, and may well not have sent an

official report of his action. Francis MacDonell was the one case judged serious enough to require official dismissal.

4. HMD report to Propaganda, 18.3.1732 (in Latin), BL.
5. Others consecrated at a young age include Angus MacDonald (Diocese of Argyll and the Isles, aged 33, 1878); Hugh's nephew John MacDonald (Highland vicariate, aged 34, 1761); and Alexander Smith (Western district, aged 34, 1847). In terms of length of service, George Hay lived for 42 years 5 months after his consecration, but resigned his office some five years before his death in 1811; in more recent times Cardinal Gray retired in 1985, eight years before his death, after serving 35 years 8 months as bishop.
6. One other bishop, James Kyle, received his training at Aquhorties, Aberdeenshire, in the early nineteenth century, but this in the far different and more advantageous conditions that the Church enjoyed after the passing of the Scottish Catholic Relief Act. Bishop Nicolson was imprisoned in 1694 and very briefly again in 1716. Bishop Gordon was held in custody for a short time at the beginning of 1729. James Grant was imprisoned after Culloden, but this while still a priest.
7. Cf. p. 216 infra.
8. Re the economy, see Flinn M. (1977), p. 229: '[the years 1760–81] cover a crucial period in Scottish economic growth, dividing in 1773. Before that year Scotland suffered from shortage of capital and from balance of payments trouble. After, economic growth was sufficiently assured to continue despite the American troubles of non-importation and war. It is in this period that we see a decisive upwards movement in wealth.' Re the granting of freedom of worship to Catholics, cf. p. 216 infra.
9. HMD report to Propaganda, 18.3.1732 (in Latin), BL.

The World
He Did Not Live to See

On Hugh's death Bishop John automatically succeeded as vicar apostolic for the Highland district. Almost his first act in charge was to close the seminary at Buorblach. It was a heartbreaking decision, forced upon him by the exorbitant running costs and the need to move the master Æneas MacGillis, elsewhere due to the shortage of priests.[1]

Several of the Buorblach students were transferred to the Lowland seminary at Scalan to complete their courses, but the arrangement was less than ideal. The Highland and Lowland boys never really mixed, soon forming two separate groups always at odds, often quarrelling, sometimes even fighting.[2] Their inability to live together was one of the main reasons advanced by the Lowland bishops against developing Scalan as a national seminary. A second reason was the unwelcome prospect of a high-risk partnership: in their view Bishops Hugh and John had squandered money on Glenfinnan and Buorblach, and they were unwilling to be associated with what might turn out another costly failure.[3]

With Hugh's death Bishop John had lost his 'chief support' and he now found himself in severe financial straits.[4] In the autumn his problems deepened when the court finally ruled against Hugh in the case brought by his nephew John of Morar, and much of what remained of his legacy had to be surrendered.[5]

Between poverty, stress and overwork John MacDonald's first year in office stretched him to the limit and severely damaged his health. Those who knew him well said he was now but a shadow of his former self.[6]

On St John's Island the emigrants were struggling to survive. The shock of their first Canadian winter, the need to clear the forests before they could begin sowing, and the poor yield they achieved, had left them on the brink of starvation.[7] In the summer of 1773 Glenaladale disposed of his estate and set out to join them. He arrived in Boston in October, where he bought stocks of grain to get them through the winter and give them something to sow in the spring.[8] Gradually their despair gave way to a belief that they could thrive: the second sowing was more successful than the first, and each sowing thereafter promised to be easier than the last.[9]

The tenants who had elected to remain on Uist were also enjoying better days. Boisdale had held to his promise not to harass them on account of their religion. On the surface at least he seemed well disposed to the Church, and was even receiving the local priests into his home.[10] Materially too they were now past the worst, for after three disastrous years the harvest of 1773 was a good one.

But it would take more than one good harvest to bring full recovery. Throughout the West the people's confidence in harvests and landlords had been shaken, and many were packing up and leaving. Just months after Hugh's death his old landlords Aberchalder and Cullochy set out for New York with their brother Leek and 400 Highlanders in the *Pearl*, one of many ships to sail that summer. Samuel Johnson, who toured the Highlands and Isles that same year, commented on the 'epidemick desire for wandering which spreads its contagion from valley to valley'. His companion James Boswell also noted the ominous change that had come over the people in the space of two years: where before they would have been distracted with grief at the sight of relatives departing, now there was 'not a tear shed' and they seemed resigned to the fact that they would soon follow.[11]

So alarmed were the landlords that they actually tried to secure a Government order for the forcible repatriation of emigrants.[12] They proposed that they be brought home in the British troop ships that were already plying the Atlantic, ferrying soldiers in preparation for the war with the American colonies that now seemed inevitable.

The formal declaration of hostilities in 1775 put an end to emigration to the New World meantime. And this in turn affected the position of the Highland tenants. In the first place it encouraged the landlords to return to their former repressive measures. In the second, it diverted the stream of emigrants elsewhere, in particular to the urban Lowlands. Bishop Hay watched the Highland poor flooding into Edinburgh, their families at their heels, where 'they applied themselves to day labour, carrying chairs [sedan chairs], or any other way by which they could earn a mouthful of bread'.[13] He believed that more than four hundred Highland Catholics had fled to the city, with scarce a word of English between them, enough to merit his opening a Gaelic chapel for them in the Old Town.

The Government needed every Highlander it could find for the American War, Catholics not excepted. The issue of Catholics serving in the army had been raised in Parliament before. In 1770 General Burgoyne had spoken warmly of the bravery of those who had fought under him in the Seven Years War, and the incongruity of their having to pretend to be Protestants in order to enlist. They used to slip off to Mass whenever possible, he told the house, and since they were not in uniform he had turned a blind eye.[14]

Now as hundreds of Catholic Highlanders were once more enlisting for the American War the question of their standing in society again became an issue between the Church and the authorities. In summer 1778 a meeting of bishops and leading Catholic laity was held in Edinburgh to consider what demands they should make for a relaxation of the existing laws. It was agreed that a draft bill be prepared and presented to the secretary of state, based on the recent English and Irish relief bills. It was further proposed, and agreed enthusiastically by Bishop John and the Highland gentlemen present, that the Church should offer to raise a regiment of a thousand men to support the war effort. In the negotiations with government officials that followed, Bishop Hay pointed out that to make such a regiment possible those sections of the 1700 Act that concerned Mass attendance and the oath would need to be repealed.[15]

There now seemed every chance that the Catholics of Scotland would see an end of the penal laws in the very near future. The negotiations were most cordial. Attitudes within the Edinburgh and London establishments had mellowed. The bishops were able to advise Propaganda that the position of the Church had 'never been more hopeful', that the faithful already enjoyed greater freedom than ever before, and that the generosity of king and government promised more to come.[16] But there were interested parties in Edinburgh and elsewhere intent on sabotaging the process. Working on public opinion behind the scenes and appealing to the mob's baser instincts they incited riots in Glasgow and Edinburgh that winter, and succeeded in frightening the government into shelving plans for new legislation, and setting back the emancipation of the Catholic Church in Scotland indefinitely.[17]

The willingness of Highland Catholics to enlist in an army lately so hated, and the enthusiasm for forming a Catholic regiment, were indicative of a more general change of attitude to government and law that had overtaken the Highlands in a few short years. When William Gilpin toured the area in 1776 he noted that 'the whole system of manners' was now radically changed. 'You may travel through any part,' he wrote, 'and rarely hear of an atrocious deed. Contention among the chiefs is subsided; and theft and rapine among the inferior orders are at an end. There are very few instances in the annals of human nature of a country so suddenly reclaimed.' [18]

With the demise of the old ways devotion to the Jacobite cause was also waning. After his victory at Culloden the duke of Cumberland had warned, with particular reference to the Highlands, that Jacobitism was 'so rooted in the nation's mind that this generation must be pretty well wore out, before this country will be quiet.'[19] His words had been prophetic. Now by the late 1770s the Culloden generation – Hugh's generation – was wearing out, and with it Jacobitism was dying as a serious force.

In the spring of 1779 an epidemic broke out in Knoydart. Bishop John hastened there, ignoring the risk, in order to be among his people. Inevitably he contracted the fever, and within days he was dead. With him died the last real champion of the Jacobite cause among the Catholic bishops of Scotland. His successor Alexander MacDonald had been only a boy in '45, while in the Lowlands Bishop Hay and his newly appointed coadjutor John Geddes, whatever their private views, both understood the benefits of working with government.

Significantly, in their joint pastoral letter of January 1780, the first issued after John's death, the three bishops called on the Catholics of Scotland to join their fellow Christians in offering prayers for the nation on a national fast-day appointed by the Kirk. Their letter enjoined all Catholics to pray for the Royal Family, civil magistrates and rulers of the realm, and to live in peace under their authority.[20] This, the first public assertion of Scottish Catholicism's acceptance of the *de facto* Royal House and Government, may be seen – symbolically and perhaps in reality – as the moment of *peripeteia* in its relationship with the régime and in its slow re-emergence from the underground.[21]

In Lent 1786 Bishop Geddes travelled on foot from his home in Edinburgh to visit the Catholics of Glasgow. At the time he was their nearest priest. Until very recently there had been virtually no Catholics in the Clyde Valley, and the number was still tiny. But it was beginning to grow. 'Of Lowlanders, Highlanders and Irish I am persuaded there are in Glasgow, Greenock and Paisley near to two hundred Catholics,' he told Bishop Hay, adding that his visit had convinced him of the need for a resident priest to serve there.[22]

As well as referring to the presence of Highlanders on Clydeside his letter was the first reference by a leader of the Church to a new phenomenon, the presence of the immigrant Irish. At this date they were but a handful, the immigration still a mere trickle. But it was soon to become a flood, easily swamping its Highland counterpart, that in time would utterly change the demography of Catholic Scotland, swelling it tenfold and relocating its epicentre in the west central Lowlands.

It had now become clear that the riots of 1778–79 had been no more than a hiccough, postponing but not cancelling the inevitable repeal of the penal laws. The Catholics of England and Ireland already enjoyed a degree of freedom, and those of Scotland seemed certain to follow. In confidence of imminent change the bishops had already begun a programme of church

building. The unobtrusive little chapel of St Peter had been opened in
Aberdeen in the very year of Hugh's death, the first since Culloden and
a sign that the times were beginning to change. Four years later a chapel
had been erected in Moidart.[23] In the 1780s at least five churches were
opened in the North-East, all small, most thatched, none provocative, and
in the last two years of the decade the church of St Gregory was completed
at Preshome (plate 9). Unlike the others this last was designed quite openly
as a church, the first such since the Reformation, and more than any it
symbolised the new confidence and the anticipation of a change in the
law.[24]

In 1793 the Scottish Catholic Relief Act was finally passed, relieving
Catholics (as its title suggests) of most of the penalties of the penal laws.
It did not offer them full emancipation: they would have to wait a further
thirty-six years for that, and meantime were required to take an oath
affirming their allegiance to the Crown and denying the claims of any
pretender as well as the temporal claims of the papacy.[25] But they were
now free to worship as they pleased. The bishops at once sent a personal
letter to the pope informing him of the great news, rare good news for
a church still reeling in many parts of Europe from the shock waves of
the French Revolution.

They themselves took the oath and instructed that the faithful do
likewise. The injunction was generally obeyed, though it was resisted in
the enclaves of remnant Jacobitism in the West, where many believed that
the Relief Act was merely a snare to bring them into military service.[26]

And indeed in part it was. The Government needed its Highland
Catholics again, this time against the French, and the new legislation
cleared the way for conscience-free enlistment and the formation of a
Catholic regiment. Within a year the 'Glengarry Fencibles' was established,
many officers transferring into it from existing Highland regiments. They
were to be used against the erstwhile protectors of their Stuart king.

In face of the common enemy across the Channel the *raprochement* at
home continued. In the century's final year the British Government saw
no contradiction in aiding Henry, cardinal of the Catholic Church and
younger brother of Charles Edward Stuart whom they had once declared
outlaw, granting him an annual life-pension of £4,000.[27] In the same year
they made a substantial gift to the Scottish Mission for new seminaries
for the training of its future priests – priests who, six years before, would
technically have been living under pain of banishment or death.

In government circles, and to some extent in public opinion, there was
now a degree of acceptance of the small and patently harmless Catholic
community, and the riots of the late 1770s were almost forgotten. The
irony was not lost on the bishops. 'O how wonderful are the workings
of Divine Providence!' they enthused to Rome, 'Twenty years ago they

were burning our homes and chapels; now they are helping us to build chapels and colleges!' [28]

Though Hugh's nephew John was still living at this date he had given up the lairdship of Morar, having ceded the estate to his son Simon at the time of the latter's marriage in 1784. Shortly after Simon succeeded the family had left their old home at Cross. Simon himself had moved into the newly-built Traigh House, while John had taken possession of Bunacaimb, the house at the southern edge of the Morar estate that Hugh had been living in at the time of the Rising, and which is still standing today. Simon predeceased his father in the first year of the new century. Soon afterwards the estate was further reduced when John cancelled the tack of Meoble and sold Hugh's boyhood home to Ewan Cameron of Fassfern. [29]

Simon left three sons: James, who died of wounds received at Corunna in the Peninsular War; Simon Og, accidentally killed in Moidart; and John, who died insane at Cross. Each inherited the estate in turn and all died without issue. With John's death the direct line of the MacDonalds of Morar ceased and the estate passed into other hands. [30]

By the turn of the century the West Highlands were gradually being opened up to the outside world. Proposals had recently been published to extend the sparse network of military roads built after the '15 and the '45 that were already in existence in Hugh's lifetime. [31] Among others, new carriageways were planned to the west coast, one linking Loch Nevis with the existing Wade road in the Great Glen, [32] a second to run from Aberchalder to Kinlochhourn, [33] and a third running from Fort William to Keppoch in Arisaig. Construction of this last began as the new century opened, and by 1808 was far advanced. [34]

At about the same time work began on the most ambitious scheme of all to open up communications in the Highlands. It was in the year of Hugh's death that the celebrated engineer James Watt had first prepared designs to create a navigable waterway from the Atlantic to the North Sea by cutting a canal, or rather a series of canals, joining the lochs of the Great Glen. Its purpose was to provide an alternative to the difficult sea route round the North of Scotland, and it promised to revolutionise transport and travel in the area.

But it had taken thirty years for the plan to become reality. In 1803 Thomas Telford finally began construction, with two teams working inland from the west and east ends. The canal was officially opened in 1822, bringing large sea-going vessels daily up past Aberchalder and Cullochy, Hugh's old homes. [35]

The design involved several major works of engineering that altered the landscape. Among them was the construction of the Laggan Locks at the eastern end of Loch Lochy, which raised its water level by more than ten metres, drowning several acres of low meadowland on its north bank.[36] The old cemetery of Kilfinnan which stood upon the meadow was submerged, and Hugh's grave was lost for ever.

A new graveyard was later opened higher up the hill, enclosed by a rectangular wall and with a small mausoleum within it. It is still in use today, a place of peace, silent but for the soft soughing of the trees and the ceaseless murmur of the burn close by. In 1900 the people of Glen Garry erected a granite Celtic cross here (plate 10), to commemorate Bishop Hugh and two fondly remembered local priests.[37]

It seems an apt irony that Hugh's grave was submerged and obliterated by Lowland industrial technology and the mercantile impulse of the new age. And fitting that the men and women of the West have preserved his memory in Highland stone, in association with humble priests who, like him, had devoted their lives to serving a poor, remote, unheard-of people. This surely is how he would have wished to be remembered.

Notes

1. Bishop John MacDonald to Bishop Hay, 20.4.1773 and 4.5.1773, BL. Bishop John tried to bring in a lay master from the Lowlands, but the only one available had a wife and family, and since engaging him would only have exacerbated the financial problem the plan had to be abandoned. The seminary was closed at the beginning of May.
2. John Paterson (the Scalan master) to William Reid, 14.10.1778, BL.
3. Cf. Bishop Grant to Bishop Hay, 1.4.1775, BL. Despite the problems, and although Bishop John was later able to reopen Buorblach, Scalan continued to take some Highland boys throughout the time that John Paterson was master (he died in post in 1783).
4. Bishop John MacDonald to Bishop Hay, 20.4.1773, BL. He suggested to Bishop Hay that to use the residue of Hugh's life pension from the French Government would more than cover his present debts – 'If what is due of <u>Marolle</u> could be depended upon, it would be much more than sufficient to answer.' Bishop Hay must have made enquiries in Paris for he received word back in December that the 'Marolle Rent' now stood at 3,210 livres (*c.* £133 15s. 0d.) – Robert Gordon (in Paris) to Bishop Hay, 2.12.1773, BL.
5. Bishop John MacDonald to Bishop Hay, 5.10.1773, BL.
6. John MacDonald of Morar to Bishop Hay, 30.11.1773, BL.
7. James MacDonald (the emigrants' chaplain) to Bishop Grant, 9.6.1773, BL. They had been led to expect an eighteen-fold yield, but achieved only a two-fold.
8. John MacDonald of Glenaladale to Bishop Hay, 16.10.1773, BL. In Boston Glenaladale learned that a ship-load of supplies that he had sent out the previous year had never arrived.
9. Bishop John MacDonald to Bishop Hay, 25.10.1774, BL. But the new

community ran into problems later. In time all but six families left and settled elsewhere in Canada, mainly because Glenaladale refused them freehold of the land. Glen himself remarried and had five children by his second wife. He remained active in developing the local community, and was even offered the governorship of the island, which he refused since acceptance would have required his taking an oath against his religion – cf. MacDonald A. F. (1964 J), pp. 26ff.

10. Alexander MacDonell (priest on South Uist) to Bishop Hay, 25.9.1774, BL.
11. Johnson S. (1775; 1925 edn) p. 132; Boswell J. (1785; 1955 edn), p. 193. Re the voyage of the *Pearl* and the subsequent history of the emigrants, see McLean M. (1991), pp. 84ff., and Hunter J. (1994), chap. 4.
12. Cf. MacKillop A., chap. 15 of Devine T. M. and Young J. R. (1999), p. 249.
13. Bishop Hay to John Gordon, 14.5.1777, BL, in which he also analysed the effects of the American War upon emigration from the Highlands.
14. Cf. Gordon J. F. S. (1867), p. 143.
15. Ibid., pp. 153 and 157.
16. Report of Bishops Grant, Hay and John MacDonald to Propaganda, 1778 (in Latin), transl. in Blundell O. (1909 and 1917), vol. II, p. 112.
17. Cf. Donovan R. K. (1979 J), passim.
18. Gilpin W. (1789), p. 209.
19. Duke of Cumberland to duke of Newcastle, 30.4.1746, Newcastle Papers, in Warrand D. (1930), vol. V, p. 71.
20. Bishops Hay, Geddes and Alexander MacDonald, Pastoral Letter, January 1780, quoted *in extenso* in Gordon J. F. S. op. cit., pp. 178f. The national fast day proclaimed by the Kirk was 3 February 1780.
21. Cf. Anson P. F. (1970), p. 150. Anson's book is entitled *Underground Catholicism in Scotland 1622–1878*.
22. Bishop Geddes to Bishop Hay, 30.11.1786, BL.
23. Re St Peter's Aberdeen – McWilliam A. (1979), pp. 1f. The chapel at Tynet in the Enzie dates from 1755, but it was adapted from an agricultural building. Re Moidart – Bishop John MacDonald to Propaganda, July 1778, quoted in Blundell O. op. cit., p. 142.
24. Churches opened in the North-East in the 1780s: Shenval, 1780; Kempcairn, 1785; Tombae, 1786; Huntly, 1787; Tomintoul, 1788 – see Johnson C. (1983), p. 153. St Gregory's Preshome was begun in 1788 (the date above its door) and completed two years later.
25. 'An Act Requiring a certain Form of Oath of Abjuration, and Declaration, from His Majesty's Subjects, professing the Roman Catholick Religion, in that part of Great Britain called Scotland', 3.6.1793, 33 Geo III, cap. 44.
26. Bishop Alexander MacDonald to Reginald MacDonell (the priest of Morar), 28.8.1794, OL, urging that he impress upon his people not to resist. Their belief that the Act was a snare he called an 'absurd notion'.
27. Cf. Gordon J. F. S. op. cit., p. 422.
28. Bishops' Report to Propaganda, 16.8.1799, Propaganda Archives Scozia (in Italian), quoted in Bellesheim A. (1890), vol. IV, p. 262.
29. Cf. Fraser Mackintosh C. (1888–9 J) p. 67, and MacMillan S. (1971),

pp. 181ff. Meoble had up to that time been held in tack by Ronald Mac-Donald of Armadale.

30. MacDonald C. (1889; 1997 edn), p. 193. John died at Cross in 1832. The estate passed briefly to a relative in Benbecula, after which it was sold.

31. The only 'marching' road in the West in the latter years of Hugh's life was that from Fort Augustus to Bernera Barracks, 43 miles in length, that ran via Glen Moriston, Loch Cluanie, Glen Shiel and Ratagan at the head of Loch Duich – see Thomas Bowen, *The Road from Stirling by Crieff, to Fort Augustus and Bernero* [sic], surveyed 1775, publ. 23.1.1776. A lesser route, known as The King's Road, linked the same two termini via Kinloch Hourn and Glen Garry – cf. Marcus Armstrong, *A New Map of Scotland or North Britain*, 1782.

32. The Loch Nevis road was to run to Achnacarry via Loch Arkaig and Glen Dessary, with a second road from Achnacarry to join the Wade road close to Loch Lochy – Brown G. *Plan of the Intended Road from Loch Nevish Head to Loch Lochy below Achnacorry*, 1796, RHP 11608, NAS; and after the completion of the road – Fulton H. *Plan, etc.*, 1803, RHP 11666, NAS.

33. Cuming W. *Intended Road Aberchalder and Laggan to Loch Hourn Head*, 1803, RHP 11624, NAS.

34. Brown G. *Plan of Intended Road Fort William to Loch na Gaul* [Loch nan Ceall], 1796, RHP 11606, NAS. Robertson J. (1808), p. 291, described this road as built in 'masterly style' and better than any previous West Highland road. It 'paved the way' for today's 'Road to the Isles'.

35. It was not finally completed for another quarter-century. For a highly detailed account, see *Caledonian Canal in the Highlands of Scotland: Reports presented to Both Houses of Parliament*, BC CCL/1, NAS.

36. The construction work extended the loch by some 250 metres in length, and by 300 in breadth at that end. For an early, large-scale map, drawn shortly after the final completion of the canal, see 'Plan of Caledonian Canal, Loch Lochy to Aberchalder', 1844, RHP 1618, NAS. The original cemetery lay close to the mouth of the Kilfinnan Burn.

37. The cemetery may be reached by taking the single-track road off the A 82 at the head of Loch Oich, as far as Kilfinnan farm, and then walking through the farmyard. The two priests commemorated were Fr John Lamont (died January 1820) and Fr Donald Walker (died 27 October 1838). Included on the inscription is the verse 'Remember your prelates who have spoken the word of God to you: whose faith follow' (Hebrews 13.7).

Genealogy of the MacDonalds of Morar and Related Families

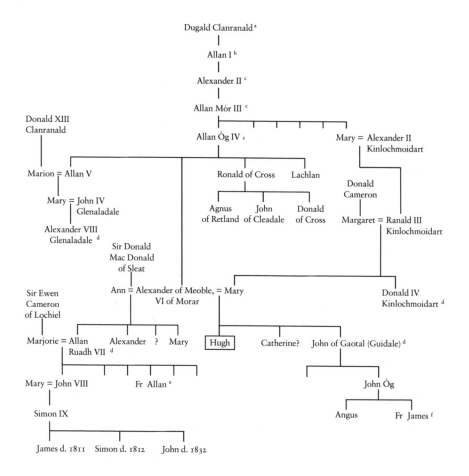

Notes

  a d. 1520
  b Sixteenth century
  c Seventeenth century
  d Alexander Glenaladale and Donald Kinlochmoidart both out in '45, ditto Allan Ruadh and John of Gaotal (Guidale)
  e Fr Allan, Hugh's nephew who went as Master to Valladolid, December 1770.
  f Fr James, Hugh's great-nephew who went with emigrants as Chaplain, spring 1772.

Aliases used in the text

Amsterdam	Paris
Birlie	Jesuit
Mr Cant	The pope
Mr Dauley	George Hay (Bishop of Daulia)
Mr Debree	Lewis Innes
Dian	Hugh MacDonald (Bishop of Diana)
Mr Fife	Bishop James Gordon
Grisy	The Scots College Paris
Hamburg	Rome
Laborer	Priest of the Mission
Mr McAlister	Hugh MacDonald (*mac Alasdair*)
Mr McKay	Hugh MacDonald
Mr McKenzie	Hugh MacDonald
Mr Melville	Thomas Innes
Merchants	Cardinals of Propaganda Fide
Misinop	Alexander Smith (Bishop of Mosynopolis)
Nicopol	James Gordon (Bishop of Nicopolis)
Old Town	Rome
Padrons	Cardinals of Propaganda Fide
Pensioner	Protestant Minister (receiver of King's Bounty)
Physician	Bishop
Prentice	Student for the priesthood
Prussia	Scotland
Mr Rivers	Domenico Rivera (Cardinal Protector)
Mr Robison	Bishop Alexander Smith
Mr Sandison	Hugh MacDonald (Sandy's [Alexander's] son)
Mr Scott	Hugh MacDonald
Shop	Seminary (or school)
Sinit	James Grant (Bishop of Sinitis)
Mr Short	Bishop Alexander Smith
Mr Smellum	Bishop Alexander Smith
Tiberiop	John MacDonald (Bishop of Tiberiopolis)

Note: see appendix III regarding Hugh MacDonald's use of aliases for himself.

Hugh MacDonald's Use of Aliases in Reference to Himself

Like his colleague priests and bishops of the Scottish Mission Hugh MacDonald often used aliases in reference to himself. Since there was always the danger of letters being intercepted it was prudent to use an alias signature to disguise the identity of the sender, while reference to oneself by an alias in the third person in the text of the letter also made identification more difficult. Hugh's use of aliases in correspondence is in effect an index of the standing of the Catholic Church in Scotland at any given time, and of his own standing also.

Before the '45 he hardly ever used an alias signature. Thereafter he always used one when writing to Scotland from exile in Paris (1747–9), after his illegal return under an assumed name (1750–55), and for about twelve years after his banishment (1756–68). These were times of particular danger for him. From the latter date until the end of his life he no longer felt the need to conceal his identity by this means.

Similarly, up to c. 1766 he habitually referred to himself in the third person, but thereafter increasingly used the first person. By this date it was obvious that the authorities had no intention of enforcing his banishment, and he in any case was now of less importance in their eyes, having effectively ceded leadership of the Highland vicariate to his coadjutor.

By now, also, as memories of the '45 receded and the Catholic Church began to distance itself from a Jacobite cause whose threat was in any case diminishing, government attitudes to the Church had begun to soften.

On the other hand, he apparently continued to *receive* mail under his various aliases up to the end of his life, though it is questionable how effective they were. In a letter of 22.1.1771 he advised Bishop Hay to 'avoid ye name Scot which is very much knowen', a warning that suggests he still believed that some attempt at disguise was prudent even at this date.

References to himself in the text of letters

1730 to 1742	Usually McAlister or Sandison, 3rd person
1744 to 1766	Usually Mr Dian, 3rd person *
1766 to 1772	Mr Dian, but increasingly 1st person

* Also Mr Scot, Mr Sandison in 1760.

Hugh MacDonald's signature of letters

1730 to 1737	Hu: McDonald	In Scotland
1738	Hu: Sandison	
1739 to 1741	Hu: McDonald	
1742	Hu: McDonald, Hu: Sandison	
1744	Hu: McDonald	
1747 to 1749	Hu: Sandison *	In Paris
1750	HS	In Scotland
1752	Hu: McKay	
1753	Collome McKenzie	
1755	HMD, Col: McKenzie, H: McDonald **	
1756	no name/address, Dian, HD	Under sentence of banishment
1757 to 1767	HD	
1768 to 1772	Hu: McDonald or HD	

* Also 'Hu: McDonald' in a letter from Paris to Rome which ran no risk of interception by the British authorities.

** His use of 'Hu: McDonald' is in a letter to Bishop Smith from Duns, whence he had been sent by the Court; there was thus no reason to hide his identity in this case. In the text of the same letter he also uses the first person.

A Note on Hugh MacDonald's Written English

From the brief excerpts from Hugh MacDonald's correspondence quoted *verbatim et litteratim* in the text it will have been apparent that his written English, and in particular his spelling, differs somewhat from that in use today. There are several reasons for this that we can identify.

In the first place, at the time of his education the spelling of English still included archaisms, and had not been fully standardised. This is reflected in his letters, where we find numerous old spellings, 'selvis', 'agoe', 'moneth', 'gott', 'allmost', 'saime', 'murther', 'ane', 'wrot', etc.; old graphical or punctuation forms such as 'oy'ʳ' (other), 'youl', 'convinc,d', 'pres'd' (pressed), and 'I,le' (Isle); and a lack of standardisation whereby a word may be spelled variously, as in the address 'Blackfriars Wynd', which at different times appears as 'Wynd', 'Wynt', 'Wyend' and 'Weynd', or the spelling of Scotland's capital as 'Edenbrugh', 'Edenbrough', 'Edinburg', or even 'Eduniburgh'.

Secondly, his written English often reflects his West Highland accent, as in such words as 'imprissonment', 'seek' (sick) or 'shouldiers' (soldiers). He spells the French capital 'Parish' as he pronounces it, and the West Highland loch 'Nevish'. Similarly, his colleague is 'Bishop Smeeth', and for the same reason – though most surprisingly for a man trained for the priesthood – 'Blackfriars' is once written as 'Black-Firayers'. In one letter he three times spells 'bill' in the normal way, and then absentmindedly writes it 'pill', more as he pronounces it.

Upon occasion his English spelling is directly prompted by his Gaelic thought process. Thus his rendering of 'MacNeil' as 'McNill' more accurately follows the Gaelic sound (with its short vowel for the genitive of 'Nial'). Or again, his phrase 'two year past' is in fact a direct parallel to the Gaelic use of the singular in such cases. Most striking of all, he once writes 'command, if he be your pleasure', apparently thinking in his own language, which has no neuter, and translating the phrase *'ma s'e do thoil e'* word-for-word.

Lastly, his English bears clear marks of his classical education. He commonly uses Latinate constructions, particularly in his marshalling of ideas through subordinate clauses and phrases ('... your Brother, being now preest, shoud goe home as soon as possible, the necessity being extreemly pressing ...'). Upon occasion his spellings too betray a greater familiarity with Latin than English – words such as 'exspect', 'transmitt' and 'exemple' spring to mind (though what should we make of 'solem' or 'abrobation' from a Latin scholar?) And like his fellow clergy he is not averse to inserting Latin phrases wholesale into his text where he feels they best express his meaning.

He lived at a critical time in the development of modern standard English. Colleagues born only one generation after his own, like the Edinburgh-educated George Hay or even his own nephew Bishop John MacDonald, used a style and orthography very close to our own. And in fact, through corresponding with them his own spelling became noticeably more 'correct' over time. Thus 'Paris' eventually came to replace 'Parish', 'freind' became 'friend', 'contrey' 'country', 'journy' 'journey', etc., and forms such as 'oy'r' and 'wt' were abandoned.

Modernity did not rub off on him entirely, however, and he successfully resisted many of its standardisations to the end. Indeed there are signs in his last letters that in old age he was reverting, to some extent at least, to the older spellings. By this date errors were also more common in his correspondence, some corrected, others unnoticed. He had become very absent-minded, as we learned from Bishop John, and perhaps his reversion to the older forms was the sign of a tired and forgetful man who remembered best the things he had learned earliest, in the days of his youth.

An Enigma Regarding Hugh MacDonald's Half-brother Allan Ruadh

About the year 1737 the Church of Scotland produced an internal report entitled *A State of Popery in Scotland containing an Hint of the Reasons of it's continuance there, Places where, and proposing some Remedies for removing these Evils* (CH 1/5/119, NAS; n.d., but from internal evidence c. 1737). The document included a detailed breakdown by area ('A more particular but Breiff Condescendence of the State of Popery within the bounds of the several Synods of Scotland' etc.). This latter, which appears based on accurate local information, includes a reference to 'Allan McDonald of Moror', Hugh's half-brother Allan Ruadh, who was the laird of Morar at this date, naming him as a main supporter of the Catholic tenants of Eigg and Canna. But the interesting point is that it describes him as 'an Apostate', i.e., a Protestant who has turned Catholic. Can this in fact have been the case? Is the report accurate in this particular, as it seems to be in others?

We are used to thinking of the MacDonalds of Morar as a staunchly Catholic family, but this was not always so. We know from the report of Prefect-Apostolic William Ballentine to Propaganda (transl. in Anderson W. J., 1957 J, p. 110) that Allan Ruadh's great-great-grandfather Allan (III of Morar) was a Protestant, and that he had his heir Allan Òg (IV) raised in his own faith, though his younger children were brought up Catholics. Nonetheless, Allan Òg's son Allan (V) was certainly a Catholic (see below), as presumably was his own son Alexander of Meoble, Allan Ruadh's father.

How then could Allan Ruadh have been a Protestant? And if so, how did he convert to Catholicism? If the Kirk's report of 1737 is accurate, there would seem to be two possibilities: either he was raised a Protestant before converting, or he was raised a Catholic, turned Protestant at some stage and later reconverted.

The second, which at first sight seems most unlikely, would make some sense if he embraced Protestantism, even outwardly, at the time of inheriting the estate, in order to safeguard his right of inheritance under the 1700 act. The other possibility, that he was actually raised a Protestant, might be explained in that his mother was Protestant, and as the daughter of MacDonald of Sleat, the acknowledged Chief of Clan Donald, must have wielded considerable influence in family decisions. Might she have prevailed on her husband, Alexander of Meoble, to have Allan the heir raised in her faith?

Another Church of Scotland document from 1703 may be of relevance to the question of Allan Ruadh's upbringing, though the information it offers is no more than negative evidence. In 1704 a general instruction was issued to all the Synods of Scotland to compile lists of Catholics within their bounds. The Synod of Argyll produced its lists in anticipation of this instruction, and included them in a written report entitled *Representation of the Most Deplorable State of Severall Paroches in the Highlands Both in the Western Isles and Continent Within the Bounds of the Synod of Argyle in Which Places the Reformation Never Obtained, 1703* (later printed in *Miscellany of the Maitland Club*, vol. III, part II (1843), pp. 41ff.). The lists were the joint work of several ministers and again appear well informed and thorough within their scope. They did not attempt to name every Catholic, confining themselves almost entirely to males and generally to prominent families, including also in some cases their households. The list for Morar is headed by 'Allan McDonald vic Coul' (i.e., *mhic Dhùghaill*), the laird of the day. It makes reference to Ronald of Cross his brother, but surprisingly omits his other brother, Alexander of Meoble, the father of Allan Ruadh. Why the omission? It is hard to believe that the compiler of the list did not know of Alexander, or thought him not important enough to merit mention (he names others less prominent). Alexander was at this date married some six years to his second wife, Mary, of the staunchly Catholic Kinlochmoidart family. Being a female she gets no mention in the list. But why not he? Is it at all possible that he had actually embraced Protestantism himself at the time of his first marriage to the daughter of MacDonald of Sleat, or had at least played down his Catholicism, and that even in 1703 he was still not recognised widely as a Catholic? This would certainly explain his heir Allan Ruadh possibly being at first raised Protestant, and later, under the influence of the second family, converting to Catholicism.

If so, what of Hugh, the oldest son by Alexander's second marriage? Was his father a crypto-Catholic at best during Hugh's young childhood? Was it from his mother that he took his Catholic faith, or at least his piety? The evidence upon which such considerations are based is tenuous indeed. To my best knowledge, neither contemporary documentation nor local tradition throws further light on the matter.

Bibliography of Sources
Referred to in the Text

Primary sources

MANUSCRIPT

Scottish Catholic Archives (SCA)
Blairs Letters   BL
       BL/2 (1695–1732)
       BL/3 (1733–1788)
Oban Letters   OL
Scottish Mission Papers   SM
       SM/2 (1604–1694)
       SM/3 (1695–1732)
       SM/4 (1733–1788)
Thompson, J. 'Some Account of the State of Religion in Scotland', etc. (1787), Th/10

National Archives of Scotland (NAS)
Campbell of Stonefield Papers	(GD 14)
Clanranald Papers	(GD 201)
Court of Justiciary Records	(JC)
Episcopal Church Records	(CH 12)
Forfeited Estates	(E)
General Assembly Papers	(CH 1/2)
Mitchell Papers (copy; orig in Brit. Mus.)	(RH 2)
Private Records	(GD 1)
Report and Survey, Thomas Telford	(BR/CCL/1)
Royal Bounty Commission Papers	(CH 1/5)
Royal Proclamations	(RH 14)
Society of Antiquaries Collection	(GD 103)
SSPCK Records	(GD 95)
Synod and Presbytery Papers	(CH 2)
Acts of Parliament of Scotland	(APS)
Maps	(RHP)

National Library of Scotland
Cameron, Alexander, Argument to Lochiel	(MS 20310)
Delvine Papers	(MS 1306)
MacDonald of Knock, Representation from	(MS 5127)

MacDonald, Hugh, re Arrest of (MS 5078)
Memorials and Representations, Church of Scotland (MS 3430, 3431)
Various (MS 68)
    (MS 98)
    (MS 205)
    (MS 3044)
    (MS 3128)
    (MS 3736)

Traquair House Archives
Correspondence, 1757

PRINTED

Contemporary works

Belsches A. *An Account of the Society in Scotland for Propagating Christian Knowledge from its commencement in 1709* (Edinburgh, 1774).
Boswell J. *Journal of a Tour to the Hebrides With Samuel Johnson* (1785; London, 1955 edn).
Burt E. *Letters From a Gentleman in the North of Scotland* (London, 1754; Edinburgh, 1998 edn).
Ciamberlani X. *Relation sur l'Etat des Missions du Pole Arctique* (Brussels, 1865).
Gilpin W. *Observations, Relative Chiefly to Picturesque Beauty, Made in the Year 1776, On several Parts of Great Britain; particularly the High-lands of Scotland* (London, 1789).
Hay Bishop G. *Memorial for the Suffering Catholicks in a violent persecution for religion at present carried on in one of the Western Isles of Scotland* (Edinburgh, 1771).
Johnson S. *Journey to the Western Islands* (London, 1775; London, 1925 edn).
MacDonald R. C. *Sketches of Highlanders* (St John, 1843).
Martin M. *A Description of the Western Islands of Scotland Circa 1695* (London, 1703; Stirling, 1934 edn).
Pennant T. *Tour in Scotland and Voyage to the Hebrides 1772* (London, 1774 and 1776; Edinburgh, 1998 edn).
Robertson J. *General View of the Agriculture in the County of Inverness* (London, 1808).
The Scots Magazine, vol. ix, 1747, appendix; vol. xvii, July 1755; vol. xviii, February 1756; vol. xxviii, April 1766.
Sinclair J. *General view of the Agriculture of the Northern Counties and Islands of Scotland* (London, 1795).

Manuscript, subsequently published

Allardyce J. (ed.) *Historical Papers Relating to the Jacobite Period 1699–1750*, 2 vols (Aberdeen, 1895–6).
Blaikie W. B. (ed.) *Origins of the 'Forty-five* (Edinburgh, 1916).
Carmichael A. (ed.) *Carmina Gadelica, Ortha nan Gaidheal*, 6 vols (Edinburgh, 1900–71).

Callendar of Home Office Papers, 1770–72 (London, 1881).

Culloden Papers 1625–1748 (London, 1815).

Frogier Lieut. G. F. de K., in *Journal d'Histoire Diplomatique* (Paris, 1959).

MacDonald J. 'A true and real state of Prince Charles Stuart's miraculous escape after the batle of Cullodden', *Blackwood's Magazine*, October 1873.

Forbes R. (ed. Paton H.) *The Lyon in Mourning*, 3 vols (Edinburgh, 1895; Edinburgh, 1975 edn).

Forbes Leith W. (ed.) *Narratives of Scottish Catholics Under Mary Stuart and James VI* (Edinburgh, 1885).

Forbes Leith W. (ed.) *Memoirs of Scottish Catholics During the XVIIth and XVIIIth Centuries,* 2 vols (London, 1909).

Fraser Mackintosh C. *Antiquarian Notes* (2nd. series, Inverness, 1897).

Giblin C. (ed.) *Irish Franciscan Mission to Scotland 1619–1646: Documents from Roman Archives* (Dublin, 1964).

Lockhart G. *Lockhart Papers,* 2 vols (London, 1817).

MacDonell J. *Spanish John, being a narrative of the early life of Col. John MacDonell of Scottos, written by himself* (Edinburgh, 1931).

MacKay M. (ed.) *The Rev. Dr. John Walker's Report on the Hebrides* (Edinburgh, 1980).

MacPhail J. R. N. (ed.) *Highland Papers* (Edinburgh, 1920), vol. III.

MacRay W. D. (ed.) *The Correspondence of Colonel Nathaniel Hooke* (Oxford, 1870).

Masson D. (ed.) *Register of the Privy Council of Scotland* (Edinburgh, 1889).

Miscellany of the Maitland Club (Edinburgh, 1843), vol. III, part ii.

Murray J. of Broughton (ed. Bell R. F.) *Memorials of John Murray of Broughton* (Edinburgh, 1898).

Records of the Scots Colleges at Douai, Rome, Madrid, Valladolid and Ratisbon (Aberdeen, 1906).

Report on the Laing Manuscripts Preserved in the University of Edinburgh (London, 1925).

Robertson J. L. (ed. and transl.) 'Log of the Dutillet', *TGSI*, vol. xxvi, 1904–07).

Tayler H. (ed.) *Jacobite Epilogue* (London, 1941).

Tayler H. (ed.) *A Jacobite Miscellany* (Oxford, 1948).

Terry C. S. (ed.) *Albermarle Papers,* 2 vols (Aberdeen, 1902).

Warrand D. (ed.) *More Culloden Papers,* 5 vols (Inverness, 1927–30).

Secondary sources

BOOKS

Anson P. F. *Underground Catholicism in Scotland 1622–1878* (Montrose, 1970).

Bellesheim A. (transl. Hunter Blair D. O.) *History of the Catholic Church of Scotland,* 4 vols (Edinburgh and London, 1890).

Bil A. *The Shieling 1600–1840* (Edinburgh, 1990).

Black R. *Mac Mhaighstir Alasdair: The Ardnamurchan Years* (Coll, 1986).

Blaikie W. B. *Itinerary of Prince Charles Edward Stuart* (Edinburgh, 1897; 1975 edn).

Blundell O. *Ancient Catholic Homes of Scotland* (London, 1907).

Blundell O. *The Catholic Highlands of Scotland*, 2 vols (Edinburgh and London, 1909 and 1917).

Blundell O. *Kilcumein and Fort Augustus* (Fort Augustus, 1914).

Brown W. E. et al. *The Scots College Rome* (London and Edinburgh, 1930).

Browne J. *History of the Highlands and the Highland Clans*, 3 vols (Glasgow, 1835).

Burton E. H. *The Life and Times of Bishop Challoner*, 2 vols (London, 1909).

Cullen L. M. and Smout T. C. (eds) *Comparative Aspects of Scottish and Irish Economic and Social History 1600–1900* (Edinburgh, 1977).

Darragh J. *The Catholic Hierarchy of Scotland* (Glasgow, 1986).

Devine T. M. *Clanship to Crofters' War: The Social Transformation of the Scottish Highlands* (Manchester, 1994).

Devine T. M. *The Scottish Nation 1700–2000* (Harmondsworth, 1999).

Devine T. M. and Young J. R. (eds) *Eighteenth Century Scotland: New Perspectives* (East Linton, 1999).

Dickson W. K. (ed.) *The Jacobite Attempt of 1719* (Edinburgh, 1895).

Dilworth M. 'Roman Catholic Worship', in Forrester D. and Murray D. (1984).

Dodgshon R. A. 'Pretense of blude and place of their duelling: the nature of Highland clans 1500–1745; in Houston R. A. and Whyte I. D. (eds) *Scottish Society 1500–1800* (Cambridge, 1989).

Dodgshon R. A. *From Chiefs to Landlords* (Edinburgh, 1998).

Dressler C. *Eigg – The Story of an Island* (Edinburgh, 1998).

Drummond-Norie W. *The Life and Adventures of Prince Charles Edward Stuart*, 4 vols (London, 1903–04).

Dunbar J. T. *History of Highland Dress* (Edinburgh, 1962).

Dwelly E. *The Illustrated Gaelic–English Dictionary* (1901–11; Glasgow, 1973 edn).

Fenton A. *Scottish Country Life* (Edinburgh, 1976).

Fenton A. and Walker B. *The Rural Architecture of Scotland* (Edinburgh, 1981).

Ferguson W. *Scotland 1689 to the Present* (Edinburgh, 1968).

Flinn M. (ed.) *Scottish Population History from the Seventeenth Century to the 1930s* (Cambridge, 1977).

Forrester D. and Murray D. *Studies in the History of Worship in Scotland* (Edinburgh, 1984).

Fuller R. C. *Alexander Geddes 1737–1802, A Pioneer of Biblical Criticism* (Sheffield, 1984).

Galbraith P. *Blessed Morar (Morair Bheannaichte)* (Bracora, 1989).

Gibson J. S. *Ships of the '45* (London, 1967).

Gibson J. S. *Playing the Scottish Card: The Franco-Jacobite Invasion of 1708* (Edinburgh, 1988).

Gordon J. F. S. *Journal and Appendix to Scotichronicon and Monasticon* (Glasgow, 1867).

Grant I. F. *Highland Folkways* (London, 1961; 1995 edn).

Grant J. *History of the Burgh Schools of Scotland* (London and Glasgow, 1876).

Gray A. *Circle of Light – The Catholic Church in Orkney Since 1560* (Edinburgh, 2000).

Haldane A. R. B. *The Drove Roads of Scotland* (1952; London, 1973 edn).

Halloran B. M. *The Scots College Paris 1603–1792* (Edinburgh, 1997).

Hanley J. E. *Scottish Farming in the Eighteenth Century* (London, 1953).

Hay M. V. *The Blairs Papers (1603–1660)* (London and Edinburgh, 1929).

Houston R. A. and Whyte I. D. (eds) *Scottish Society 1500–1800* (Cambridge, 1989).

Hunter J. *A Dance Called America* (Edinburgh, 1994).

Jewell B. F. *The Legislation Relating to Scotland After the Forty-Five* (Ann Arbor, 1996).

Johnson C. *Developments in the Roman Catholic Church in Scotland 1789–1829* (Edinburgh, 1983).

Lang A. *Pickle the Spy* (London, 1897).

Lang A. *The Companions of Pickle* (London, 1898).

Livingstone A., Aikman C. W. H. and Hart B. S. (eds) *Muster Roll of Prince Charles Edward's Army* (Aberdeen, 1984).

McCluskey R. (ed.) *The Scots College Rome 1600–2000* (Edinburgh, 2000).

MacDonald C. *Moidart, or Among the Clanranalds* (1889; Edinburgh, 1997 edn).

MacDonald A. and MacDonald A. *The Clan Donald*, 3 vols (Inverness, 1895, 1900, and 1904).

MacDonald A. and MacDonald A. (eds) *The Poems of Alexander MacDonald* (Inverness, 1924).

MacDonald N. H. *The Clan Ranald of Knoydart and Glengarry* (Edinburgh, 1979; 1995 edn).

MacDonell J. *The MacDonells of Keppoch and Gargavach* (Glasgow, 1931).

MacGregor A. Murray (transl.) *A Royalist Family, Irish and French (1689–1789) and Prince Charles Edward* (Edinburgh, 1904).

MacKay D. *Scotland Farewell* (Edinburgh, 1980).

MacKay M. (ed.) *The Rev. Dr. John Walker's Report on the Hebrides* (Edinburgh, 1980).

MacKenzie A. *History of the MacDonalds and Lords of the Isles* (Inverness, 1881).

MacLean A. *A MacDonald for the Prince – The Story of Neil MacEachen* (Stornoway, 1982; rev. edn 1990).

MacLean D. *The Counter-Reformation in Scotland 1560–1930* (London, 1931).

McLean M. *The People of Glengarry* (Toronto, 1991).

MacMillan S. *Bygone Lochaber* (Glasgow, 1971).

McWilliam A. *St Peter's Church Aberdeen* (Aberdeen, 1979).

Moran P. F. *Memoirs of the Most Rev. Oliver Plunket, compiled from original documents* (Dublin, 1861).

Munro R. W. *Taming the Rough Bounds – Knoydart 1745–1784* (Coll, 1984).

Purcell M. *The Story of the Vincentians* (Dublin, 1973).

Ross W. C. A. *The Royal High School* (Edinburgh and London, 1934; new edn, 1949).

Salmond J. B. *Wade in Scotland* (Edinburgh, 1934).

Scotland J. *The History of Scottish Education*, 2 vols (London, 1969).

Scott H. (ed.) *Fasti Ecclesiae Scoticanae*, 7 vols (Edinburgh, 1915–28).

Seton B. G. and Arnot J. G. (eds) *Prisoners of the Forty-Five*, 3 vols (Edinburgh, 1928).

Shaw J. S. *The Management of Scottish Society 1707–1764* (Edinburgh, 1983).

Sher R. B. *Church and University in the Scottish Enlightenment – The Moderate Literati of Edinburgh* (Edinburgh, 1985).

Smith A. M. *Jacobite Estates of the Forty-Five* (Edinburgh, 1982).

Tayler A. and H. *1715: The Story of the Rising* (London and Edinburgh, 1936).

Taylor M. *The Scots College in Spain* (Valladolid, 1971).

Taylor W. *The Military Roads of Scotland* (1976; Colonsay, 1996 edn).

Ure J. *A Bird on the Wing* (London, 1992).

Watts J. *Scalan: The Forbidden College, 1716–1799* (East Linton, 1999).

Whyte I. D. *Agriculture and Society in Seventeenth Century Scotland* (Edinburgh, 1979).

Whyte I. D. *Scotland Before the Industrial Revolution – An Economic and Social History* (London and New York, 1995).

Withers C. W. J. *Gaelic in Scotland 1698–1981* (Edinburgh, 1984).

JOURNAL ARTICLES

Adam M. I. 'The Highland Emigration of 1770', *Scot. Hist. Rev.*, vol. xvi, 1919.

Anderson W. J. 'Thomas Innes on Catholicism in Scotland 1560–1653', *IR*, vol. vii, no. 2, autumn 1956.

Anderson W. J. 'Prefect Ballentine's Report, *circa* 1660', part 2, *IR*, vol. viii, no. 2, autumn 1957.

Anderson W. J. 'Abbé Paul Macpherson's History of the Scots College Rome', *IR*, vol. xii, 1961.

Anderson W. J. 'The College of the Lowland District of Scotland at Scalan and Aquhorties, Registers and Documents', *IR*, vol. xiv, no. 2, autumn 1963.

Anderson W. J. 'Father Gallus Robertson's Edition of the New Testament, 1792', *IR*, vol. xvii, no. 1, spring 1966.

Anderson W. J. 'Catholic Family Worship on Deeside in 1691', *IR*, vol. xviii, no. 2, autumn 1967.

Blundell O. 'Bishop James Gordon and the Highlands of Scotland', *Dublin Rev.*, vol. cxlix, July-October 1916.

Bumstead J. 'The Highland Emigration to the Isle of St John and the Scottish Catholic Church, 1769–1774', *Dalhousie Rev.*, no. 58, 1978.

Cameron A. ('North Argyll') 'A Page From the Past: The Lead Mines at Stontian', *TGSI*, vol. xxxviii, 1937–41.

Cameron W. 'Clan Cameron and their Chiefs: Presbyterians and Jacobites', *TGSI*, vol. xlvii, 1971–2.

Cherry A. 'The Library of St Mary's College, Blairs, Aberdeen', *The Bibliotheck*, vol. 12, no. 3, 1984.

Darragh J. 'The Catholic Population of Scotland Since the Year 1680', *IR*, vol. iv, no. 1, spring 1953.

Dean A. and Taitt M. 'Scalan Reconstructed: Architectural and Documentary Evidence', *IR*, vol. lxvi, no. 1, spring 1995.

Devine T. M. 'Highland Migration to Lowland Scotland 1760–1860', *Scot. Hist. Rev.*, vol. lxii, no. 174, October 1983.

Donovan R. K. 'Voices of Distrust: The Expression of Anti-Catholic Feeling in Scotland, 1778–1781', *IR*, vol. xxx, 1979.

Doran W. 'Bishop Thomas Nicolson, First Vicar-Apostolic 1695–1718', *IR*, vol. xxxix, no. 2, autumn 1988.

Fenton A. 'Early and Traditional Cultivating Implements in Scotland', *Proceedings Soc. Antiquaries Scot.*, vol. xcvi, 1962–3.

Ferguson W. 'The Problems of the Established Church in the West Highlands and Islands in the Eighteenth Century', *RSCHS*, vol. xvii, 1969.

Forbes F. and Anderson W. J. 'Clergy Lists of the Highland district 1732–1828', *IR*, vol. xvii, no. 2, autumn 1966.

Fraser Mackintosh C. 'The MacDonalds of Morar, Styled "Mac Dhughail"', *TGSI*, vol. xv, 1888–89.

Giblin C. 'St. Oliver Plunkett, Francis MacDonell OFM and the Mission to the Hebrides', *Collectanea Hibernica*, no. 17, 1974–75.

Halloran B. M. 'Jesuits in 18th-Century Scotland', *IR*, vol. lii, no. 1, spring 2001.

Hay M. 'Too Little and Too Late', *IR*, vol. vi, no. 1, spring 1955.

Johnson C. 'Secular Clergy of the Lowland District, 1732–1829', *IR*, vol. xxxiv, 1983.

MacDonald A. F. 'Captain John MacDonald, Glenalladale', *Canad. Cath. Hist. Assoc. Report*, vol. 31, 1964.

MacDonald R. 'The Highland District in 1764', *IR*, vol. xv, no. 2, autumn 1964.

MacCulloch D. B. 'Where Was the Jacobite Standard Raised at Glenfinnan in 1745?', *The '45 Assoc.*, 1963.

McGoldrick W. 'The Scots College Madrid', *IR*, vol. iv, no. 2, autumn 1953.

McHugh M. 'The Religious Condition of the Highlands and Islands in the Mid-Eighteenth Century', *IR*, vol. xxxv, no. 1, spring 1984.

MacInnes A. I. 'Catholic Recusancy and the Penal Laws, 1603–1707', *RSCHS*, vol. 23, 1987–89.

Mackenzie A. 'A Short Memoir of the Mission of Strathglass', *Catholic Directory*, 1846.

MacLean D. 'Catholicism in the Highlands and Isles 1560–1680', *IR*, vol. iii, 1952.

McMillan J. F. 'Scottish Catholics and the Jansenist Controversy: The Case Re-opened', *IR*, vol. xxxi, no. 1, spring 1981.

McMillan J. F. 'Thomas Innes and the Bull *Unigenitus*', *IR*, vol. xxxiii, 1982.

McMillan J. F. 'The Root of All Evil? Money and the Scottish Catholic Mission in the Eighteenth Century', *Studs. in Church Hist.*, vol. 24. 1987.

McMillan J. F. 'Jansenists and Anti-Jansenists in Eighteenth Century Scotland: The *Unigenitus* Quarrels of the Scottish Catholic mission, 1732–46', *IR*, vol. xxxix, no. 1, spring 1988.

McRoberts D. 'The Rosary in Scotland', *IR*, vol. xxiii, no. 1, spring 1972.

MacWilliam A. 'A Highland Mission: Strathglass 1671–1777', *IR*, vol. xxiv, 1973.

Roberts A. 'Gregor MacGregor (1681–1740) and the Highland Problem in the Scottish Catholic Mission', *IR*, vol. xxxix, no. 2, autumn 1988.

Roberts A. 'Catholic Kintail: A Marginal Community', *TGSI*, vol. lviii, 1993–4.

Roberts A. 'Highland Catholicism at the Margin: Skye, Lewis and Ardnamurchan', *West H. and I. Hist. Soc.*, 1994.

Scott W. L. 'The MacDonalds of Leek, Collachie and Aberchalder', *Canad. Cath. Hist. Assoc. Report*, 1939–45.

Stewart J. A. (Jr) 'The Clan Ranald and Catholic Missionary Successes 1715–1745', *IR*, vol. xlv, no. 1, spring 1994.

Szechi D. 'Defending the True Faith: Kirk, State and Catholic Missioners in Scotland, 1653–1755', *Cath. Hist. Rev.*, July 1996.

Thornber I. 'On This Spot', *Scots Mag.*, August 1988.

Wilby N. MacD. 'The "Encreasce of Popery" in the Highlands 1714–1747', *IR*, vol. xvii, no. 1, spring 1966.

Wynne T. 'The Conversion of Alexander Cameron', *IR*, vol. xlv, no. 2, autumn 1994.

UNPUBLISHED ACCOUNTS

Clapperton W. *Memoirs of Scotch Missionary Priests* (MS *c.* 1870; rev. and transcribed Wilson G., Elgin, 1901).

Roberts A. *West Highland Priests of the Scots College Rome* (Morar, 2000).

Wynne T. *The Life and Times of Alexander Cameron SJ 1701–1746* (Roy Bridge, forthcoming).

THESES

Dorrian G. *Hugh MacDonald (1699–1773) – The First Vicar-Apostolic of the Highland District in His Religious and Social Context* (M.Phil., Strathclyde Univ., 1990).

Toomey K. *Emigration From the Scottish Catholic Bounds 1770–1810* (Ph.D., Univ. of Edinburgh, 1991).

VERBAL COMMUNICATIONS

Alasdair MacDonald, Port na Dòbhrain.
Allan MacDonald, Arisaig.
Peter MacDonald, Bunacaimb.
Tearlach MacFarlane, Glenfinnan.
Archie MacLellan, Morar.

Index